GOD

THE MOST UNPLEASANT CHARACTER IN ALL FICTION

OTHER BOOKS BY DAN BARKER

Godless: How an Evangelical Preacher Became One of America's Leading Atheists (Foreword by Richard Dawkins)

The Good Atheist: Living a Purpose-Filled Life Without God (Foreword by Julia Sweeney)

Just Pretend: A Freethought Book for Children

Life Driven Purpose: How an Atheist Finds Meaning (Foreword by Daniel C. Dennett)

Losing Faith in Faith: From Preacher to Atheist

Maybe Right, Maybe Wrong: A Guide for Young Thinkers

Maybe Yes, Maybe No: A Guide for Young Skeptics

GOD

THE MOST UNPLEASANT CHARACTER IN ALL FICTION

By
Dan Barker

Foreword by
Richard Dawkins

STERLING
New York

STERLING
New York

An Imprint of Sterling Publishing
1166 Avenue of the Americas
New York, NY 10036

ISBN 978-1-4549-1832-5

Distributed in Canada by Sterling Publishing
c/o Canadian Manda Group, 664 Annette Street
Toronto, Ontario, Canada M6S 2C8
Distributed in the United Kingdom by GMC Distribution Services
Castle Place, 166 High Street, Lewes, East Sussex, England BN7 1XU
Distributed in Australia by Capricorn Link (Australia) Pty. Ltd.
P.O. Box 704, Windsor, NSW 2756, Australia

A complete list of credits appears on page 304.

For information about custom editions, special sales, and premium and corporate purchases,
please contact Sterling Special Sales at 800-805-5489 or specialsales@sterlingpublishing.com.

Manufactured in the United States of America

4 6 8 10 9 7 5 3

www.sterlingpublishing.com

Dedicated to the memory of
Patricia Ruth Barker,
who was infinitely nicer than God.

CONTENTS

PART II.
Dawkins Was Too Kind

FOREWORD

NEXT TIME YOU FIND YOURSELF IN A HOTEL, LOOK IN THE BEDSIDE DRAWER. You know what you'll find—it's so predictable, you need scarcely bother to check. Yes, it's the "Gideon Bible." According to the Gideons' own website, they have distributed nearly two billion bibles, free of charge around the world, since their founding in 1908. They claim to hand out bibles at a rate of two every second. Using a minimal estimate of the cost of production and distribution of a typical hardback book, the 81 million Gideon Bibles distributed in 2013 must have cost about $300 million, or about $1,000 for each of the 300,000 members of The Gideons International. Tax-deductible, no doubt, but still we have here a very considerable outlay in cash and dedication. Why do they do it?

They do it, in their own words, "to make it possible for others to learn about the love of God by giving them access to his word." Yet, if that really is their aim, I can't help wondering how many of these loyal Gideons have actually read the bible. Even a cursory look at the bible should be enough to convince a reasonable person that it's the very last document you should thrust in front of someone if you want to convince them of the love of God. If you happen to be a member of the Gideons, I challenge you to read Dan Barker's book and then ask yourself why you don't instantly resign. Indeed, I can't help wondering whether a good many of those 300,000 Gideon subscribers are actually undercover atheists who have calculated that the best possible way to turn people against Abrahamic religion would be to expose them to the bible. Fortunately, from the point of view of the Gideons' stated aim, I suspect that very few of their bibles are ever actually opened.

Dan Barker's book had its origin, as his Introduction explains, in a single sentence of my own *The God Delusion:* the opening sentence of Chapter 2. It says that the God of the Old Testament is "arguably the most unpleasant character in all fiction" and goes on to list nineteen character-traits which, if they were all combined in a single fictional villain, would strain the reader's credulity to the point of ridicule. Certifiable psychopaths apart, no real human individual is quite so irredeemably nasty as to combine all of the following: "jealous and proud of it; a petty, unjust, unforgiving control-freak; a vindictive, bloodthirsty ethnic cleanser; a misogynistic, homophobic, racist, infanticidal, genocidal, filicidal, pestilential, megalomaniacal, sadomasochistic, capriciously malevolent bully."

The sentence has been controversial. I suspect that it is single-handedly responsible for *The God Delusion*'s reputation for "stridency," for the rest of the book is far from strident. This is the sentence that led the British Chief Rabbi to accuse me of anti-Semitism—an accusation he graciously withdrew on further reflection. Apparently he had focused on the phrase "God of the Old Testament" and took it to mean "as opposed to the God of the New Testament." He took this to mean the Jewish God as opposed to the Christian God, a comparison which revived cultural memories of pogroms and persecutions. Of course that was not my intention. Indeed I gave reasons, elsewhere in *The God Delusion*, for regarding the God of the New Testament as almost equally bad. There's little in the Old Testament to match the horror of St. Paul's version of the ancient principle of the scapegoat: the Creator of the Universe and Inventor of the Laws of Physics couldn't think of a better way to forgive our sins (especially the sin of Adam, who never existed and therefore never sinned) than to have himself hideously tortured and executed in human form as vicarious punishment. As Paul's Epistle to the Hebrews (9:22) puts it, "without the shedding of blood there is no forgiveness." To be fair, Paul's authorship of this epistle is disputable, but it is fully in the spirit of his often-expressed doctrine of atonement.

From the day I wrote it, I always knew that every one of my list of nineteen nasty attributes could be fully substantiated in the bible, but I didn't know quite how richly and thoroughly every one of them could be documented. It occurred to me that it would be an amusing exercise to make a picture with nineteen hyperlinks, each clicking through to a verse, or set of verses, from the bible. I soon realised that my biblical knowledge was inadequate to the task of assembling all the verses, and indeed that they were numerous enough to fill a book. A book! Now, there was an idea. Not a book that I could write. But I knew just the man who could. Dan Barker, of course. Fortunately he jumped at the idea, and this volume is the splendid result.

Dan knows his bible inside out. He's preached from it, thrust it in the face of countless victims of the doorstepping young pastor he once was. He has now seen the light in a big way, and I know nobody better qualified to assemble this remarkable anthology of sheer, unadulterated nastiness.

What will the apologists say in response? "The bible was never meant to be taken literally." Wasn't it? Did the generations upon generations of scribes faithfully reproducing the story of Adam and Eve and the talking snake not take it literally? Really? Were the pious generations of churchgoers, through the Dark and Middle Ages, "theologically" sophisticated to realise it was all a metaphor? Really? When the peasants mustered to defy Richard II and sang "When Adam delved and Evé span / Who was then the gentleman?" did they mutter apophatically under their breath that, of course, it was never meant to be taken literally? Don't be so ridiculous. Even today, more than forty percent of Americans think the world began exactly in the way Genesis describes, less than ten thousand years ago. The pretence by "sophisticated theologians" that the typical Christian in the pew doesn't take the bible literally is nothing short of dishonest.

*　*　*

But anyway, if not literally, how else might our apologists wish to interpret the Bible? As a set of moral tales? A handy guide to what's right and wrong? What? Moral tales? You cannot be serious! Read this book.

Is it, perhaps, unfair of Dan and me to pick and choose illustrations of the unpleasant characteristics of God? Couldn't an apologist come up with a similar list of virtues, backed up by an even larger list of supporting verses? Couldn't the apologist compile a counter to my damning litany? "The God of the Old Testament is . . . magnanimous, generous, encouraging, forgiving, charitable, loving, friendly, good-humoured, supportive of women, of homosexuals, of children, freedom-loving, open-minded, broad-minded, non-violent." Go on. Try and find those nice verses. Do your best. You think you'll succeed? Want a bet?

We have all become acculturated to the idea that criticising religion is somehow not done, it's bad taste, you just don't do it. The result is that even mild criticism sounds a lot stronger than it really is. My Chapter 2, first sentence, is not mild. But it is nothing less than the truth, truth about both the letter and the spirit of the bible. The evidence? Read on.

Richard Dawkins

Introduction

One of the most valued objects in my office is a signed copy of *The God Delusion*—not the published book, but the informally bound manuscript that Richard Dawkins sent to his publisher. Annie Laurie and I were at a Humanist conference in Reykjavik in 2006 when Richard told us he had an extra copy and offered it to us. I have observed visitors breaking the tenth commandment while ogling that treasure on my bookshelf.

We knew it would be an important work, and reading it before it hit the bookshelves was like getting a sneak preview of a movie. What we did not anticipate was that it would become such a blockbuster outside of the scientific and freethought communities. Many people have told me that *The God Delusion* changed their lives.

The book is a passionate defense of reason; but since it challenges precious beliefs, some believers have projected their anger back onto the author, calling Dawkins strident and contentious. When a doctor attacks disease, we praise the aggressiveness; but when Dawkins confronts sectarian savagery, he is accused of malpractice. That is unfair. There is precious little in *The God Delusion* that might be deemed strident.

However, the first sentence in Chapter 2 has especially raised hackles:

> *The God of the Old Testament is arguably the most unpleasant character in all fiction: jealous and proud of it; a petty, unjust, unforgiving control freak; a vindictive, bloodthirsty ethnic cleanser; a misogynistic, homophobic, racist, infanticidal, filicidal, pestilential, megalomaniacal, sadomasochistic, capriciously malevolent bully.*

Needless to say, that renowned sentence has been highly controversial. In order to answer his critics, Richard asked me to help him gather biblical citations. His original plan was a Keynote spider diagram. The body of the spider would be the beginning of the sentence and each of the nineteen legs would be labeled one of the theistic attributes. Clicking on "ethnic cleanser," for example, would bring up "You shall drive out all the inhabitants of the land from before you . . . for I have given you the land to possess" (NUMBERS 33:52–53), followed by more Old Testament verses. As I was sending the compilations, it became clear that the lengthy lists would overwhelm a simple slide. He then had the idea that this wealth of documentation would make a good book (pun intended), with each spider leg becoming a whole chapter. You hold the result in your hands.

The bible should be allowed to speak for itself. It is, after all, a purported message between the creator and his creatures—you and me—and should be accessible to all of us, not just to experts. It can be simply opened and read. I am not a professional bible scholar; I was just an ordained minister with a degree in religion from an evangelical university, who preached from every book of the bible as a pastor, missionary, and evangelist for nineteen years. I took two years of biblical Greek and learned something about Hebrew literary styles. I know my way around concordances, lexicons, bible dictionaries, and commentaries, and have consulted academics more knowledgeable than myself while preparing for the more than 120 public debates I have done as an atheist since leaving the ministry in 1984. But I'm not claiming to be a great authority. You don't have to be an expert to notice that the experts disagree. Just like you don't need a Ph.D. in Literature to appreciate the classics, neither should you be prohibited from simply opening the so-called "Good Book" to see what it actually says.

That is the purpose of this book. If you have never read the bible, you might like to know what is in it. If you are a believer, you should be happy to see us promoting bible reading. As a former clergyman, let me offer some counsel: don't take the word of your pastor, rabbi, or priest. My hope is that you will do what Richard Dawkins has done and simply read the bible for yourself.

God: The Most Unpleasant Character in All Fiction contains verses from all thirty-nine books of the Old Testament. Instead of simply handing you a laundry list, I decided to start each chapter with one or two biblical stories illustrating the particular aspect of God's character in Richard's impressive list. I sometimes add personal remarks, but you can ignore those and draw your own conclusions.

Beyond the nineteen spider legs, a second part rounds out this book. Chapters 20 through 27 expand on Richard's list, and Chapter 28 extends it into the New Testament.

You will notice that I don't capitalize "bible." That is a personal preference. The newspaper *Freethought Today*, published by the Freedom From Religion Foundation, has used this convention for decades. It is not disrespectful; it is un-respectful. Most writers capitalize the word, but I only do it when it appears in an actual book title, such as the *New American Bible*. That is exactly how we handle "dictionary," "thesaurus," and "lexicon." We don't capitalize the adjective "biblical," which we would do if it were referring to a proper noun, like "Victorian." I think "The Holy Bible" is a cultural construct without a direct referent. Because there are so many different bibles in various languages, translations, canons, and arrangements, we cannot pretend we are talking about one particular book.

There are dozens of English translations. I chose the *New Revised Standard Version* (NRSV) for the narrative sections of this book. In my reading, this seems to be the version most often used by scholars. Unless indicated otherwise, all biblical quotations are from the NRSV. For the list sections, I use a variety of translations. The *King James Version* (KJV) is sometimes useful for its familiarity and poetic language, but is not always the most accurate. Biblical translations vary widely and sometimes contradict each other, which is a curious state of affairs for the allegedly most important book to humanity written by a caring and powerful creator. In my book *Godless* I show, for example, how the evangelical New International Version (NIV), while often very good, sometimes distorts and obscures the meaning of the text, making problem passages disappear. You are welcome to compare my choices with your favorite version, but be aware of the occasional uncertainties and ambiguities. If you are not a translator (and even translators disagree), the best you can do is compare the passage in different English versions.

Reading the bible can be laborious, especially during long passages. I have tried to make the task easier by boldfacing the relevant words in each verse. If you are in a hurry, simply scan for the boldface and come back later for the context.

I have avoided footnotes, and there is little reference in the text to scholars and authors—such as Annie Laurie Gaylor's fine work on bible sexism, Hector Avalos's excellent scholarship on biblical violence, or Steve Wells's comprehensive skeptical commentary—but you will see them in the Bibliography. I have tried to let the bible speak for itself.

I have to say a few words in anticipation of the inevitable criticisms a book like this will ignite.

At the National Prayer Breakfast on February 6, 2015, in Washington, D.C., President Barack Obama said "No God condones terror." He claimed the Islamic State is "warping" religion: "As people of faith, we are summoned to push back against those who try to distort our religion—any religion—for their own nihilistic ends." But in the bible, Obama's own deity actually uses the word "terror" to describe his intentions: "a **terror** from God fell upon the cities," "I will send my **terror** in front of you," "I will bring **terror** on you," "all the great **terror** which Moses shewed in the sight of all Israel" (KJV), "hide in the dust from the **terror** of the Lord," "the **terrors** of God are arrayed against me," "I was in **terror** of calamity from God," "they shall be in great **terror**, for God is with the company of the righteous," and "I will make them an object of **terror** and of plunder" (Genesis 35:5, Exodus 23:27, Leviticus 26:16, Deuteronomy 34:12, Isaiah 2:10, Job 31:23, Psalms 14:5, Ezekiel 23:46).

That is what strident looks like. Despite these unambiguous theistic threats, many believers profess that their Lord is a god of love and peace. While they acknowledge there is violence in the Old Testament, they claim their God cannot be blamed for the terrorism committed in his name. Talking about faith-based violence in the Middle East, Obama said on September 10, 2014: "No religion condones the killing of innocents." However, as you read the chapters ahead, you will see that Obama is wrong: the God of the Old Testament not only condoned but commanded and committed the killing of innocents. Those who disagree with this fact because they are squeamish or in denial must first confront the plain meaning of the text before invoking personal theology to try to whitewash what the words actually say.

Some believers argue that the "wicked" people God exterminated were deserving of their punishment. God's genocide was a just genocide, they preach, because the sinful Canaanites brought it on themselves. However, the only reason they think the Canaanites were more corrupt than other cultures is because the bible says they were. Archaeologists have not discovered that any of the Canaanite populations were any worse or better than other groups in that time of history. As we will see, the Israelites (so the bible says) practiced God-ordained infanticide, genocide, kidnapping, slavery, and rape. They killed thousands of animals in religious rituals. They treated their wives and daughters as disposable property. They proudly executed interracial couples, homosexuals, heretics, nonbelievers, and the disobedient. As you read the following chapters, you will notice that the words "evil" and "wicked" did not mean in the bible what we take them to mean today: they merely meant worshipping another god. Simply having the wrong religion made you a bad person, regardless of your actions. The Israelites barbarized the "evil" Canaanites like warring people have dehumanized their enemies throughout history.

"But you're taking it out of context," we often hear. Many biblical inerrantists tell me that if I would situate those harsh Old Testament passages within a broader picture, I would see that God is overall truly good, like a loving but stern parent. They think "The Bible" is an intact and coherent book, a unitary "Word of God" that explains itself harmoniously no matter which author you are reading. A verse or two might seem shockingly immoral close up but, stepping back, we can see God's grander plan and know that although he is uncompromising in his holiness, he is actually a wise, wonderful, merciful, forgiving Father.

Really? Under what possible context is genocide or rape justifiable?

When I ask those believers to give me the context of a troublesome passage, they often produce a verse from another part of the bible—sometimes written centuries later in another language and country, with a different agenda—such as "Whoever does not love does not know God, for God is love" (1 JOHN 4:8, written in Greek around the year 100 C.E.). Rather than seeing this rebuttal verse as contradictory and anachronistic, they pretend that it explains and justifies the crime against humanity they are trying to excuse. I have presented more than fifteen hundred horrific passages in this book, often describing the context and the Hebrew words, but if a believer can find one or two selections by another author claiming "God is not like that," somehow I am the one taking it out of context.

Yes, context is crucial. I am often taken out of context by theistic debaters, and we are speaking the same language in the same culture. If something is truly out of context, I would like to know how. But I think what believers most often mean by "context" is not the broader meaning of a verse as understood by the writers and readers of that time, as the words were used and allusions were grasped in their language and culture, considering the passages before and after the verse as well as the overall purpose of the book within which it resides; I think what they really mean by context is "my theology." (I have written elsewhere that theology is really me-ology.) Their lives are devoted to their God, and they naturally rush to his defense. They want me to see God the way they do, so that I might accept his atrocities as a small part of a greater holy and righteous plan.

Does the bible seem troublesome? Then simply say "context," and presto: evil becomes good.

It is not hard to find contrasting verses, but how can a handful of sycophantic praises mitigate hundreds of cruel commands and bloodcurdling barbarities? Actions speak louder than words. If Yahweh behaves like a thug, his reputation can't be redeemed by one of his minions simply parroting "God is love."

The word "love" occurs in the Old Testament about 400 times, but most of those are top-down: God telling his people that he loves them, or commanding them to love him. Love is almost always connected with obedience and ownership in the bible. It is a possessive one-way dynamic, like a master demanding total devotion from his slaves or a husband requiring his wife to be submissive and adoring. God's love is exclusive: he cherishes his chosen people only. God's love is conditional: he cares only for those who keep his commandments. Very rarely do we see any Israelites declaring that they love God. The psalmist (usually identified as the genocidal King David) twice said he loved God (PSALM 18:1, 116:1), and the author of 1 Kings tells us that King Solomon "loved the Lord" by burning a thousand animals on an altar (1 KINGS 3:3–4). Solomon also loved 700 wives and 300 concubines, and his love for God did not stop him from worshipping idols and ultimately tearing the kingdom apart. It is clear those people did not "love" their god in any normal human understanding of the word.

The first time the word "love" appears in the bible is when God told Abraham to burn the son that he loved:

> He said, "Take your son, your only son Isaac, whom you love, and go to the land of Moriah, and offer him there as a burnt offering." (GENESIS 22:2)

In the Old Testament, "love" is truly an alien word. In context, love for God almost always meant cowering commitment, self-denial, and sacrifice, not a freely chosen joyful adoration. As we will see, God requires his lovers to *fear* him, which turns adoration into a compulsive disorder.

"You are taking it too literally," we sometimes hear from sophisticated believers. I am often told by wise Christians who know how to handle subtlety that I am still reading the bible like a fundamentalist, taking it at face value instead of grasping the allegory and underlying meaning suggested by the literary form. When God told his people to exterminate "every man, woman, and child," he didn't actually mean they should murder innocent babies. That was a figure of speech, they insist, like "lock, stock, and barrel." They offer no evidence for such a claim, but confidently know that since their loving God could not have been malicious, the text must not mean what it actually says. When Psalm 137:9 says believers should be happy to dash babies against the rocks, we have to understand that the Psalms are songs. Like all poets, the psalmist utilized irony, exaggeration, and figures of speech. It's a metaphor! How can I be so dense not to see this?

Suppose a man proclaims to his wife: "I love you so much, my darling, that if you ever look at another man, I will burn your eyes out with a hot poker." When she objects in horror, he smiles and replies, "Calm down. It's a poem. Don't take it literally. The important thing is the message of love underlying my artistic choice of words."

The husband may have been joking, but it's a bad joke. Anyone who talks like that is a dangerous person, or at least crudely insensitive. If I were that woman, I would start running toward the closest shelter.

Yes, there is metaphor in the bible. When Jesus is called the "Lamb of God," we don't start looking for a pair of wool shears. But where do we draw the line? How do those highly sophisticated believers decide what is fact and what is fiction?

I think we should read the bible like any other writings, just like millions of normal people have done throughout the centuries without the aid of scholars by their side explaining what it *really* means. Most believers, trusting that God is capable of making his message clearly and easily known to all humankind, have simply read the bible for what it appears to say to the reasonable reader. We should always start with the face value. It is the face value, after all, that gives metaphor its punch. We should stick with the face value unless it is impossible to do otherwise, or unless there is a stated or understood reason to interpret it figuratively. Obvious irony, hyperbole, and poetic license are good reasons to interpret a text less literally. But we should not simply unsheathe the sword of allegory whenever we read passages that make us uncomfortable. Is there something in the bible you don't like? Well, simply say "metaphor," and the problem goes away!

True believers should not want this to happen. They should insist that metaphor be invoked as sparingly as possible. Otherwise, anything goes. Yes, the Prodigal Son is a parable, and Adam and Eve may be symbolic archetypes, but why stop there? If we can draw the line where we choose, what other characters might we deem to be allegorical exaggerations? What is to stop me from saying that Yahweh himself is just one huge figure of speech?

I need to head off any "gotcha" readers who think that since Dawkins and I are criticizing "God," we must be agreeing that he exists. I hear this all the time. But the title of this book is *God: The Most Unpleasant Character in All Fiction*. The word "fiction" is right on the cover. As you read the following pages where I write "God said this" or "God did that," don't imagine I am treating an invented character as a real person. It would be excruciatingly tedious to keep qualifying "God, a fictional character," or "God, the deity depicted in the Hebrew stories," or say "Yahweh (the god described in the literary account) allegedly performed an (unlikely) action." If you agree with me that the Big Bad Wolf was a bad guy, then you know how to handle literary (not literalist) criticism.

The Big Bad Wolf blew down some flimsy cartoon houses. The God of the Old Testament destroyed whole civilizations. He drowned the entire population of the planet. He is not the only bad egg in literature, but he is the *most* unpleasant character in all fiction. Richard is careful to say this is "arguable," but how could we argue otherwise?

Can you think of a fictional villain who was worse? Shakespeare's Richard III, Macbeth, King Lear, Claudius, and Iago were treacherous and mad, but their deeds involved a handful of victims. They were monsters of human dimensions, not biblical proportions. Dracula's craving was a mere drop in the bucket compared to the oceans of blood demanded by Yahweh (see Chapter 7). Simon Legree from *Uncle Tom's Cabin* is a pale copy of the slave-master of the Old Testament (see Chapter 27). Dr. No from the James Bond series, Sauron from *The Lord of the Rings*, The Joker from *Batman*, Mr. Hyde of *Dr. Jekyll and Mr. Hyde*, Cruella de Vil from *The Hundred and One Dalmatians*, Mrs. Coulter from *His Dark Materials*, Hannibal Lecter in *The Silence of the Lambs*, the Wicked Witch of the East in *The Wizard of Oz*, Voldemort from the Harry Potter books, Captain Hook from *Peter Pan*— these are all comical caricatures of evil compared with the swaggering scoundrel of scripture.

What about Satan? Most bible believers think the Devil is the personification of evil, but what were his actual deeds? Count them. You can show the number of his victims on your fingers. Satan, in the bible, murdered only ten people. And even this was accomplished only with the direct authority and approval of God (see Chapter 18). Poor Satan gets all the blame and none of the respect he desires. Is it any wonder that the legal term for unpredictable, uncontrollable, and destructive events is not "act of Satan," but "act of God"?

Richard Dawkins was not the first to chastise the God of the Old Testament. He reminds us that Thomas Jefferson came to an almost identical conclusion about the "terrific character" of the Jewish god. ("Terrific" used to mean "terrifying" or "terrible.") Talking about Jesus, Jefferson wrote:

> *His object was the reformation of some articles in the religion of the Jews, as taught by Moses. That sect had presented for the object of their worship, a being of terrific character, cruel, vindictive, capricious and unjust.* (Letter to William Short, August 4, 1820)

A couple of decades earlier, Thomas Paine had written:

> *Whenever we read the obscene stories, the voluptuous debaucheries, the cruel and torturous executions, the unrelenting vindictiveness, with which more than half the bible is filled, it would be more consistent that we call it the word of a demon rather than the word of God. It is a history of wickedness, that has served to corrupt and brutalize mankind; and, for my part, I sincerely detest it, as I detest everything that is cruel.* (The Age of Reason, Part I, 1794)

In the nineteenth century, the great orator Robert G. Ingersoll remarked, "If a man would follow, today, the teachings of the Old Testament, he would be a criminal. If a man would follow strictly the teachings of the New, he would be insane" (*Interviews on Rev. Talmage*, Interview 3, 1882). Elizabeth Cady Stanton, working for women's equality, said: "The Bible and the Church have been the greatest stumbling block in the way of women's emancipation" (*The Woman's Bible*, 1895, 1896).

Mark Twain wrote about the biblical god:

> *The fear that if Adam and Eve ate of the fruit of the Tree of Knowledge they would "be as gods" so fired his jealousy that his reason was affected, and he could not treat those poor creatures either fairly or charitably, or even refrain from dealing cruelly and criminally with their blameless posterity. . . . [H]e has almost bankrupted his native ingenuities in inventing pains and miseries and humiliations and heartbreaks wherewith to embitter the brief lives of Adam's descendants.* (Letters From The Earth, Letter VI, 1910).

Ruth Hurmence Green, a Missouri grandmother and author of *The Born Again Skeptic's Guide to the Bible*, said:

> *I had been taught that the bible was a good book. . . . Instead, I found a record of such superstitious silliness and ignorance, such moral obscenities,*

such ghastly atrocities that I had never even imagined. I found the bible's personalities, God's favorites, and even God himself to be utter reprobates. In this book, where I had expected to find simple guidelines, every kind of behavior that was repugnant to me was glorified and rewarded, even perpetrated and commanded by God himself. . . . There wasn't one page of this book that didn't offend me in some way. In fact, after a session of reading it, I always wanted to go and take a bath in grandma's lye soap. (From the film A Second Look at Religion, *1980, produced by the Freedom From Religion Foundation)*

The year after *The God Delusion* was published, Christopher Hitchens came out with his bestseller *God Is Not Great.* (The title was actually *"god is Not Great."* He capitalized "Bible" but not "god.") Like Dawkins, Hitchens had actually read the Old Testament for himself and independently arrived at similar conclusions:

The Bible may, indeed does, contain a warrant for trafficking in humans, for ethnic cleansing, for slavery, for bride-price, and for indiscriminate massacre, but we are not bound by any of it because it was put together by crude, uncultured human mammals.

Violent, irrational, intolerant, allied to racism and tribalism and bigotry, invested in ignorance and hostile to free inquiry, contemptuous of women and coercive toward children: organized religion ought to have a great deal on its conscience.

Hitchens was careful to state that "organized religion" should have a great deal on its conscience. He recognized, as Dawkins does, that in spite of their terrific holy books, most individual believers are nicer than god. They have risen above the brutality of the bible. This book illustrates what we have risen above.

PART I

Dawkins Was Right

RICHARD DAWKINS IS A FOOL. IF YOU BELIEVE THE BIBLE, he is abominably corrupt and has never done any good.

> *Fools say in their hearts, "There is no God." They are corrupt, they do abominable deeds; there is no one who does good. The Lord looks down from heaven on humankind to see if there are any who are wise, who seek after God. They have all gone astray, they are all alike perverse; there is no one who does good, no, not one. (PSALM 14:1–3)*

Is that true? How do we know what is true? Where does knowledge come from?

> *The fear of the Lord is the beginning of knowledge; fools despise wisdom and instruction. (PROVERBS 1:7)*

> *For the Lord gives wisdom; from his mouth come knowledge and understanding. (PROVERBS 2:7)*

The reason the ancient Israelites thought they possessed the source of all knowledge is because it says so in a book that they wrote. As a scientist, Dawkins knows that knowledge comes not from authority, but from observation.

Jealous and Proud of It

> *"A jealous and avenging God is the Lord,*
> *the Lord is avenging and wrathful."*
> —NAHUM 1:2

Richard Dawkins could not have found a better way to begin his list.

If we were forced to reduce the entire Old Testament to a single word, what would it be? It would not be "love." There is not enough love there to fill a communion cup. It would not be "law." Most biblical edicts are dictatorial commands with a divine purpose aimed at something other than the common good.

The one word that sums up the scenario between Genesis and Malachi is "jealousy." Almost every page, every story, every act, every psalm, every prophecy, every command, every threat in those 39 ancient books points back to the possessiveness of one particular god who wanted to own and control his chosen lover by demanding total devotion. "Love me! I am better than the others! Don't look at them—look at me!"

You shall acknowledge no God but me, no Savior except me. (HOSEA 13:4)

That's the Old Testament in a nutshell. Jealousy.

The whole point of the Ten Commandments was jealousy.

If you want some great entertainment, watch the 1956 movie *The Ten Commandments*, directed by Cecil B. DeMille. It's not a great movie, but it is indeed entertaining. Based on the book of Exodus, it tells the story of Moses confronting the hard-hearted Pharaoh with plagues, leading the Israelites out of Egypt guided by a pillar of fire, and ushering them through the miraculously parting waters of the Red Sea, all shown with state-of-the-art Hollywood special effects from the Cold War era. It is hilarious. The overly dramatized scene on Mount Sinai where the super-basso voice of the jealous God booms the Ten Commandments and carves them out with the lightning "swoosh!" of his finger is cartoonish. What makes the movie especially funny is the feeling that while Yul Brynner seemed to be hamming it up as Pharaoh, Charlton Heston was taking his role as Moses very seriously.

It was indeed serious business. Literally. As in business. To promote the film, the devoutly Christian Cecil B. DeMille teamed up with the granite industry to produce hundreds of tombstone-like Ten Commandments markers that now pepper the American landscape. The theistic Fraternal Order of Eagles produced and distributed them. (Free publicity for DeMille.) Those movie props, including meaningless "Canaanite" lettering at the top, continued to be erected decades after the film was released. Protestant versions can be seen on state capitol grounds in Austin, Denver, Phoenix, Jefferson City, and Oklahoma City (recently declared unconstitutional, thanks to the ACLU), as well as on city property in Fargo, North Dakota, and within a city park in La Crosse, Wisconsin. Catholic versions (which omit the commandment about "graven images") can be seen on a public high school and junior high school near Pittsburgh. Yul Brynner himself came to Milwaukee to dedicate one of those decalogues at the municipal building that was later removed after the Freedom From Religion Foundation complained.

They almost always use the King James "Thou shalt not" version that appears in the movie, with these words at the top:

the Ten Commandments
I AM the LORD thy God.
Thou shalt have no other gods before me.

The God of the Old Testament craved attention. To impress his people with a dramatic display of deity, he unveiled his divine decrees in a spectacular Command Performance. The 19th chapter of Exodus describes the setting:

> Then the Lord said to Moses, "I am going to come to you in a dense cloud, in order that the people may hear when I speak with you and so trust you ever after." (Exodus 19:9)

The crowd control was tighter than a rock concert. No one could approach God, on penalty of death.

> You shall set limits for the people all around, saying, "Be careful not to go up the mountain or to touch the edge of it. Any who touch the mountain shall

be put to death. No hand shall touch them, but they shall be stoned or
shot with arrows; whether animal or human being, they shall not live."
When the trumpet sounds a long blast, they may go up on the mountain.
(Exodus 19:12–13)

How do you not touch the edge of a mountain? The only way is if it looks like a cartoon peak rising almost perpendicular from flat ground. In any event, some bouncers (angels?) were positioned to pummel and shoot anyone who got too close. A side musician (Gabriel?) was stationed to blast trumpet fanfares at the opening and finale of the show.

On the day of the epic event, the curtain opened with a breathtaking Shock and Awe light and music show:

On the morning of the third day there was thunder and lightning, as well as
a thick cloud on the mountain, and a blast of a trumpet so loud that all the
people who were in the camp trembled. Moses brought the people out of the
camp to meet God. They took their stand at the foot of the mountain. Now
Mount Sinai was wrapped in smoke, because the Lord had descended upon it
in fire; the smoke went up like the smoke of a kiln, while the whole mountain
shook violently. As the blast of the trumpet grew louder and louder, Moses
would speak and God would answer him in thunder. (Exodus 19:16–19)

It was like standing at the edge of an erupting volcano.

Hidden behind a cloud of smoke—pay no attention to the man behind the curtain—God kept warning Moses to keep the crowd at a distance:

Go down and warn the people not to break through to the Lord to look;
otherwise many of them will perish. Even the priests who approach the
Lord must consecrate themselves or the Lord will break out against them.
(Exodus 19:21–22)

I don't know about you, but an erupting volcano is not something I am tempted to run toward. If I were writing the story, God would say "Block the exits!"

The scene is set. The trembling audience is assembled before the great stage. What are the first words they hear?

Then God spoke all these words: I am the Lord your God, who brought you
out of the land of Egypt, out of the house of slavery; you shall have no other
gods before me. (Exodus 20:1–3)

That's the First Commandment: "You shall have no other gods before me." Me, just me. Pay no attention to those other gods. His Second Commandment fortifies the First:

> You shall not make for yourself an idol, whether in the form of anything that is in heaven above, or that is on the earth beneath, or that is in the water under the earth. You shall not bow down to them or worship them; for **I the Lord your God am a jealous God**, punishing children for the iniquity of parents, to the third and the fourth generation of those who reject me, but showing steadfast love to the thousandth generation of those who love me and keep my commandments. (Exodus 20:4–6)

And there we see it. God proudly announces: "I am a jealous God!"

Later I'll address the cruel injustice of punishing children for their parents' crimes—and they aren't even crimes—but notice that the Big Ten is all about "Me, Me, Me!" The first four commandments have nothing to do with how we treat other people. They are a loyalty pact demanded by a controlling commander.

God's cringing grandstanding on Sinai seems nervous. When reading the Old Testament, I often feel like yelling: "If you are afraid of not being loved, then stop frightening your lover." True respect is earned, not demanded. A confident lover would never be jealous.

Jealousy is insecurity. It is the fear that someone you love will not love you back, a dread that they will choose someone else. It is possessive and controlling, based on an assumed right of ownership. Strong jealousy arises from a desperate need to be validated by the devotion of another, even if (or especially if) that "love" is forced. It is shaky vanity. It is the terror of losing the property that bolsters your sense of self-worth.

Jealousy is rooted in biology. We instinctively choose a mate primarily because of our "selfish genes" that evolved to be copied into future generations. In many primitive cultures, this translated into patriarchy, sexist control of access to females, harems, polygamy (for males only), submissive wives, ordinances permitting wives to be beaten and constrained, and females legally treated as property (see Chapter 9). Notice that the Ten Commandments are sexist. They are directed at males, ending with the prohibition of coveting what your neighbor owns, which includes his wife: "You shall not covet your neighbor's house; you shall not covet your neighbor's wife, or male or female slave, or ox, or donkey, or anything that belongs to your neighbor" (Exodus 20:17). Why don't the Commandments prohibit a woman from coveting her neighbor's husband? It's because wives were property, husbands were not.

It is obvious that the Old Testament writers were projecting their biological feelings of sexual insecurity onto their culturally derived deity, a male god. "For jealousy arouses a husband's fury, and he shows no restraint when he takes revenge" (Proverbs 6:34). God's chosen sweetheart, Israel, is often characterized as a wife or lover gone astray: "And the children of Israel did evil in the sight of the Lord . . . they went a whoring after other gods, and bowed themselves unto them" (Judges 2:11,17 KJV). "But you trusted in your beauty, and played the whore" (Ezekiel 16:15). As we will see later, in the eyes of the macho deity, "evil" and "wickedness" are rarely denunciations of harmful actions; they are most often synonyms for "jilting God." If she doesn't love me, she must be a bad woman.

In case there is any doubt that God was proud of his jealousy, look at the name he calls himself in the actual Ten Commandments in Exodus 34, the ones engraved on stone:

> For you shall worship no other god, because the Lord, **whose name is Jealous**, is a jealous God. You shall not make a covenant with the inhabitants of the land, for when they prostitute themselves to their gods and sacrifice to their gods, someone among them will invite you, and you will eat of the sacrifice. (Exodus 34:14–15)

Notice the word "prostitute." That's like calling a wife or girlfriend a "slut" because she talks to another man. "I will judge you as women who commit adultery and shed blood are judged, and bring blood upon you in wrath and jealousy" (Ezekiel 16:38), bellows the nervous, abusive husband who admits his very name is Jealous.

"God" is just a generic label, not a name. Any god can use it. Calling a god "God" is like calling a person "Person." Why don't we call the Israelite god by his real name, the actual name he proudly chose for himself? Let's call the God of the Old Testament "The Lord Jealous."

The Lord Jealous clearly has issues with sexual insecurity and self-respect, not to mention anger management.

Destructive jealousy

Deuteronomy 6:15 "The Lord your God, who is present with you, is **a jealous God**. The anger of the Lord your God would be kindled against you and he would destroy you from the face of the earth."

Burning jealousy

Deuteronomy 4:24 "For the Lord thy God is a consuming fire, even a **jealous God**." KJV

Unforgiving jealousy

JOSHUA 24:19 "And Joshua said unto the people, Ye cannot serve the Lord: for he is an holy God; he is a **jealous God**; he will not forgive your transgressions nor your sins." KJV

Vengeful jealousy

NAHUM 1:2 "**God is jealous**, and the Lord revengeth; the Lord revengeth, and is furious; the Lord will take vengeance on his adversaries, and he reserveth wrath for his enemies." KJV

Cursing jealousy

DEUTERONOMY 29:20 "The Lord will not spare him, but then the anger of the Lord and his **jealousy** shall smoke against that man, and all the curses that are written in this book shall lie upon him, and the Lord shall blot out his name from under heaven." KJV

Global jealousy

ZECHARIAH 1:14–15 "Thus saith the Lord of hosts; **I am jealous** for Jerusalem and for Zion with a great **jealousy**. And I am very sore displeased with the heathen [NRSV: "nations"] that are at ease: for I was but a little displeased, and they helped forward the affliction." KJV

Wrathful jealousy

ZECHARIAH 8:2 "Thus saith the Lord of hosts; I was **jealous** for Zion with great **jealousy**, and I was **jealous** for her with great fury." KJV (*Notice that he considers Zion a female.*)

Hot, insulting jealousy

EZEKIEL 36:5–7 "Therefore thus saith the Lord God; Surely in the **fire of my jealousy** have I spoken against the residue of the heathen, and against all Idumea, which have appointed my land into their possession with the joy of all their heart, with despiteful minds, to cast it out for a prey. Prophesy therefore concerning the land of Israel, and say unto the mountains, and to the hills, to the rivers, and to the valleys, Thus saith the Lord God; Behold, I have spoken **in my jealousy** and in my fury, because ye have borne the shame of the heathen: Therefore thus saith the Lord God; I have lifted up mine hand, Surely the heathen that are about you, they shall bear their shame." KJV

Seismic jealousy

EZEKIEL 38:19 "For in my **jealousy** and in the fire of my wrath have I spoken, Surely in that day there shall be a great shaking in the land of Israel." KJV

Holy jealousy

EZEKIEL 39:25 "Therefore thus saith the Lord God; Now will I bring again the captivity of Jacob, and have mercy upon the whole house of Israel, and will be **jealous for my holy name**." KJV

Provoked jealousy

PSALM 78:58 "For they provoked him to anger with their high places, and **moved him to jealousy** with their graven images." KJV

Long-lasting jealousy

PSALM 79:5–6 "How long, Lord? wilt thou be angry for ever? shall thy **jealousy burn like fire**? Pour out thy wrath upon the heathen [NRSV: "nations"] that have not known thee, and upon the kingdoms that have not called upon thy name." KJV

Spurning jealousy

DEUTERONOMY 32:19–21 "The Lord saw it, and was **jealous**; he spurned his sons and daughters. He said: I will hide my face from them, I will see what their end will be; for they are a perverse generation, children in whom there is no faithfulness. They made me **jealous** with what is no god, provoked me with their idols. So I will make them jealous with what is no people, provoke them with a foolish nation." NRSV

Furious jealousy

EZEKIEL 5:13 "My anger shall spend itself, and I will vent my fury on them and satisfy myself; and they shall know that I, the Lord, have spoken in my **jealousy**, when I spend my fury on them." NRSV

Consuming jealousy

NUMBERS 25:10–11 "And the Lord spake unto Moses, saying, Phinehas, the son of Eleazar, the son of Aaron the priest, hath turned my wrath away from the children of Israel, while he was zealous for my sake among them, that I consumed not the children of Israel in my **jealousy**." KJV

Smoking jealousy

DEUTERONOMY 29:20 "The Lord will not spare him, but then the anger of the Lord and his **jealousy** shall smoke against that man, and all the curses that are written in this book shall lie upon him, and the Lord shall blot out his name from under heaven." KJV

Stranger jealousy

DEUTERONOMY 32:16 "They provoked him to **jealousy** with strange gods, with abominations provoked they him to anger." KJV

Stirred-up jealousy

ISAIAH 42:13 "The Lord shall go forth as a mighty man, he shall **stir up jealousy** like a man of war: he shall cry, yea, roar; he shall prevail against his enemies." KJV

Idol jealousy

I KINGS 14:22–23 "And Judah did evil in the sight of the Lord, and they provoked him to **jealousy** with their sins which they had committed, above all that their fathers had done. For they also built them high places, and images, and groves, on every high hill, and under every green tree." KJV

Image of jealousy

EZEKIEL 8:1–4 "And it came to pass . . . that the hand of the Lord God fell there upon me. Then I beheld, and lo a likeness as the appearance of fire: from the appearance of his loins even downward, fire; and from his loins even upward, as the appearance of brightness, as the colour of amber. And he put forth the form of an hand, and took me by a lock of mine head; and the spirit lifted me up between the earth and the heaven, and brought me in the visions of God to Jerusalem, to the door of the inner gate that looketh toward the north; where was the seat of the **image of jealousy**, which provoketh to **jealousy**. And, behold, the glory of the God of Israel was there, according to the vision that I saw in the plain." KJV

Generational jealousy

DEUTERONOMY 5:9 "Thou shalt not bow down thyself unto them, nor serve them: for I the Lord thy God am a **jealous God**, visiting the iniquity of the fathers upon the children unto the third and fourth generation of them that hate me." KJV

If God tells us his name is Jealous, why do some call him Jehovah? It turns out that "Jehovah" does not appear in the original bible. It is a fake name. You will find it in the King James Version and New World Translation (of the Jehovah's Witnesses, of course), but not in the NRSV or the NIV, for example. "Jehovah" is a cobbled construction, a Latinized guess from a Hebrew ambiguity.

Modern Jews have many names for God, but the proper name of God for the early Israelites was "YHWH," the tetragrammaton (four-letter word), which was not supposed to be pronounced. Like Voldemort in the Harry Potter books, he was the original "he who must not be named." The word "YHWH" may have meant "he who creates," or "he who is," but since Hebrew is written with no vowels, the pronunciation was lost long ago. Modern Jews sometimes render it Yahweh or Yehowah, which is a guess for the vowels. When the Hebrew scriptures are being read aloud, the forbidden YHWH is replaced with Adonai ("Lord"). Some readers, seeing the vowels "a-o-a" in Adonai, simply inserted them into YHWH to create a fake word: Yahowah or Yehowah. In Latin, YHWH became JHVH, which turned into Jehovah. This would be like calling an HSBC bank a "Hasobac," or a BMW a "Bamowa."

In many English translations, YHWH is rendered LORD in all capital letters, to distinguish it from Adonai, which is shown as leading-cap "Lord." When YHWH appears together with Adonai (or any other name, such as "Elohim"), it is usually translated "LORD God." In GENESIS 2:4 in the NRSV, for example, we see "In the day that the LORD God ['YHWH Elohim'] made the earth and the heavens."

Many of the famous "Baruch Adonai" ("Blessed be the Lord") readings in Jewish temples are not technically accurate. "Adonai" is often replacing YHWH, as in Psalm 144:1 ("Praise be to the LORD"). Since they need a substitute name, and since "Adonai" is not a name but a title, and since God told us his actual name is "Jealous," I think they should say "Baruch Qannā"—"Blessed be Jealous."

And shouldn't Jehovah's Witnesses be called Jealous's Witnesses?

2

Petty

"I am against your pillows!"
—Ezekiel 13:20, KJV

The first four commandments the Lord Jealous decreed from Mount Sinai have nothing to do with ethics or morality. The first one says "Look at me only," and the next one continues "Don't make images of any other god." The third commandment is "You shall not make wrongful use of the name of the Lord your God" (KJV: "Thou shalt not take the name of the Lord thy God in vain."). Scholars do not agree about what "wrongful use" or "in vain" means when applied to a name, but we can take it as: "Don't say anything bad or untrue about me." Or "Don't say 'God damn it!'" Or perhaps "If you swear a vow in my name, you better keep it." Or maybe it's a trademark law, like barring a baker from making "God's™ Cookies."

The fourth commandment prohibits work on the Sabbath day, because "in six days the Lord made heaven and earth, the sea, and all that is in them, but rested the seventh day; therefore the Lord blessed the sabbath day and consecrated it" (Exodus 20:11). God needed to rest. Creating the universe in less than a week would wear anybody out. However, this commandment is not about giving workers the weekend off, or a welcome way to relax while worshipping in church on the "day of rest." It's a serious law. Working on the Sabbath is a capital crime: "You must observe my Sabbaths. This will be a sign between me and you for the generations to come, so you may know that I am the Lord, who makes you holy. Observe the Sabbath, because it is holy to you. Anyone who desecrates it is to be put to death" (Exodus 31:13–14, NIV).

* * *

Really. If you go to work on the Lord's Day, you die.

Once again, this is not about morality, but about paying appropriate deference to God. But what does "desecrate" mean? What exactly constitutes work? What horrible act would you have to commit on that holy day of rest to earn the death penalty?

We don't have to guess. God gives us an example:

> When the Israelites were in the wilderness, they found a man gathering sticks on the sabbath day. Those who found him gathering sticks brought him to Moses, Aaron, and to the whole congregation. They put him in custody, because it was not clear what should be done to him. Then the Lord said to Moses, "The man shall be put to death; all the congregation shall stone him outside the camp." The whole congregation brought him outside the camp and stoned him to death, just as the Lord had commanded Moses. (NUMBERS 15:32–36)

A man was publicly executed for picking up sticks.

I've committed the same crime. Often when my Christian family was camping in the California mountains over the weekend, we boys would run into the forest to collect kindling wood. What were my parents thinking!? They probably assumed that gathering sticks for a campfire is no crime at all. It was a fun family experience. We needed to cook our food. Even if it were private property, at most it would have amounted to petty theft. It would certainly not merit the electric chair. Or stoning. No judge would sentence a person to the gas chamber for the trivial infraction of picking up sticks on Saturday.

The sticks were not the issue. In order to honor God, you can't carry *anything* on the Sabbath:

> But if you do not listen to me, to keep the sabbath day holy, and to carry in no burden through the gates of Jerusalem on the sabbath day, then I will kindle a fire in its gates; it shall devour the palaces of Jerusalem and shall not be quenched. (JEREMIAH 17:27)

What is the moral issue here? What crime was so terrible that a city had to be burned? Who is hurt if I carry a parcel? Someone might be hurt if I don't. It seems the only harm here is to the fragile ego of the unreasonable Lord: "If you don't pay attention to me, you have to die." (And that is no crime at all: neither an omnipotent nor fictional god can possibly be hurt.)

I thought the Ten Commandments were guides for ethical behavior, but some of them seem to be arbitrary rules for flattering the Lord Jealous "because I said so." The

God of the Old Testament can't measure his morality. He can't temper his temper.
He is preoccupied with pointless petty particulars.

"I am against your pillows!"

EZEKIEL 13:18–20 "Thus saith the Lord God; Woe to the women that sew
pillows to all armholes, and make kerchiefs upon the head of every stature
to hunt souls! Will ye hunt the souls of my people, and will ye save the
souls alive that come unto you? And will ye pollute me among my people
for handfuls of barley and for pieces of bread, to slay the souls that should
not die, and to save the souls alive that should not live, by your lying to
my people that hear your lies? Wherefore thus saith the Lord God; **Behold,
I am against your pillows**." KJV (*Scholars are not sure what "kesathoth"—
"pillow"—means. It appears only here. Some translations have "bands,"
"magic pads," "cushions," "bracelets," "wristbands." It would seem that
if God really believed there were women with "magic charms," he would
be against them—"I am against you fortune tellers!"—rather than the
pillows themselves. This seems rather silly and petty. That would be like
Voldemort telling Harry Potter, "I am against your magic wand!"*)

Cover up your poop. God might step in it

DEUTERONOMY 23:12–14 "Designate a place outside the camp where you
can go **to relieve yourself**. As part of your equipment have something to dig
with, and when you relieve yourself, dig a hole and cover up your **excrement**.
For the Lord your God moves about in your camp to protect you and to
deliver your enemies to you. Your camp must be holy, so that he will not
see among you anything indecent and turn away from you." NIV (*Does the
president of the U.S. go out and teach the troops how to build an outhouse?*)

If a soldier has a wet dream, don't let him in the camp

DEUTERONOMY 23:10–11 "If one of your men is unclean because of a
"**nocturnal emission**, he is to go outside the camp and stay there. But as
evening approaches he is to wash himself, and at sunset he may return
"to the camp." NIV

Don't smell like a priest

EXODUS 30:22–38 "Then the Lord said to Moses, 'Take the following fine
spices . . . Make these into a sacred anointing oil, a fragrant blend, the work
of a perfumer. It will be the sacred anointing oil. . . . Anoint Aaron and his
sons and consecrate them so they may serve me as priests. . . . Do not make
any incense with this formula for yourselves; consider it holy to the Lord.
**Whoever makes incense like it to enjoy its fragrance must be cut off from
their people.**'" NIV

No round haircuts

Leviticus 19:27 "You shall not round off the hair on your temples or mar the edges of your beard." RSV

No tattoos

Leviticus 19:28 "You shall not make any cuttings in your flesh on account of the dead or tattoo any marks upon you: I am the Lord." RSV

Make tassels on your clothes . . .

Deuteronomy 22:12 "Make tassels on the four corners of the cloak you wear." KJV

. . . and add fringes with blue cords

Numbers 15:37–39 "Speak to the Israelites and say to them: 'Throughout the generations to come you are to make tassels on the corners of your garments, with a blue cord on each tassel. You will have these tassels to look at and so you will remember all the commands of the Lord, that you may obey them and not prostitute yourselves by chasing after the lusts of your own hearts and eyes.'" KJV

Basket is cursed

Deuteronomy 28:17 "Cursed shall be your basket and your kneading-trough." RSV

Don't cook a goat in its mother's milk

Exodus 34:26 "Do not cook a young goat in its mother's milk." NIV (*This is the tenth commandment in the only list in Exodus called "The Ten Commandments" [*Exodus 34:28*] and engraved on stone tablets. It is still followed by observant Jews.*)

Mutton recipe. "Smells good."

Exodus 29:38–41 "Now this is that which thou shalt offer upon the altar; two lambs of the first year day by day continually. The one lamb thou shalt offer in the morning; and the other lamb thou shalt offer at even: And with the one lamb a tenth deal of flour mingled with the fourth part of an hin of beaten oil; and the fourth part of an hin of wine for a drink offering. And the other lamb thou shalt offer at even, and shalt do thereto according to the meat offering of the morning, and according to the drink offering thereof, for **a sweet savour**, an offering made by fire unto the Lord." KJV (*A hin was roughly equal to a gallon.*)

God has picky taste in the birds he created

Leviticus 11:13–19 "And these you shall have in abomination among the birds, they shall not be eaten, they are an abomination: the eagle, the vulture, the osprey, the kite, the falcon according to its kind, every raven according to its kind, the ostrich, the nighthawk, the sea gull, the hawk according to its kind, the owl, the cormorant, the ibis, the water hen, the pelican, the carrion vulture, the stork, the heron according to its kind, the hoopoe, and the bat." RSV (*The writers of the Old Testament did not know that bats are not birds.*)

You can eat grasshoppers and beetles, but no insects with four feet
LEVITICUS 11:20–23 "All winged insects that go upon all fours are an abomination to you. Yet among the winged insects that go on all fours you may eat those which have legs above their feet, with which to leap on the earth. Of them you may eat: the locust according to its kind, the bald locust according to its kind, the cricket according to its kind, and the grasshopper according to its kind. But all other winged insects which have four feet are an abomination to you." RSV (*Winged insects with four feet?*)

Shellfish are taboo
LEVITICUS 11:10–12 "But anything in the seas or the rivers that has not fins and scales, of the swarming creatures in the waters and of the living creatures that are in the waters, is an abomination to you. They shall remain an abomination to you; of their flesh you shall not eat, and their carcasses you shall have in abomination. Everything in the waters that has not fins and scales is an abomination to you." RSV (*This turns seafood restaurants into dens of iniquity.*)

Stay away from yeast
EXODUS 23:18 "Thou shalt not offer the blood of my sacrifice with **leavened** bread; neither shall the fat of my sacrifice remain until the morning." KJV

Don't mock a bald head, kids
2 KINGS 2:23–24 "And he [Elisha] went up from thence unto Bethel: and as he was going up by the way, there came forth little children out of the city, and mocked him, and said unto him, Go up, thou bald head; go up, thou bald head. And he turned back, and looked on them, and cursed them in the name of the Lord. And there came forth two she bears out of the wood, and tare forty and two children of them." KJV

Don't go to church with mutilated private parts
DEUTERONOMY 23:1 "No one whose **testicles** are crushed or whose **penis** is cut off shall be admitted to the assembly of the Lord." NRSV

Very picky offerings accepted

Exodus 25:1–7 "The Lord said to Moses, 'Tell the Israelites to bring me an offering. You are to receive the offering for me from everyone whose heart prompts them to give. These are the offerings you are to receive from them: gold, silver and bronze; blue, purple and scarlet yarn and fine linen; goat hair; ram skins dyed red and another type of durable leather; acacia wood; olive oil for the light; spices for the anointing oil and for the fragrant incense; and onyx stones and other gems to be mounted on the ephod and breastpiece.'" KJV

God liked Abel's offering better than Cain's

Genesis 4:3–5 "In the course of time Cain brought some of the fruits of the soil as an offering to the Lord. And Abel also brought an offering—fat portions from some of the firstborn of his flock. The Lord looked with favor on Abel and his offering, but on Cain and his offering **he did not look with favor**." KJV (*God was clearly not a vegetarian. If the worship is sincere, why should it matter exactly what a person chooses to sacrifice?*)

No cross-breeding

Leviticus 19:19 "Ye shall keep my statutes. Thou shalt not let thy cattle gender with a diverse kind." KJV

No cotton/linen blends

Leviticus 19:19 "Do not wear clothing woven of two kinds of material." NIV

Don't wear foreign clothing

Zephaniah 1:8 "And on the day of the Lord's sacrifice—'I will punish the officials and the king's sons and all who array themselves in foreign attire.'" RSV

No dwarfs, hunchbacks, or crushed testicles allowed

Leviticus 21:16–23 "The Lord said to Moses, 'Say to Aaron: "For the generations to come none of your descendants who has a **defect** may come near to offer the food of his God. No man who has any **defect** may come near: no man who is **blind** or **lame**, **disfigured** or **deformed**; no man with a **crippled** foot or hand, or who is a **hunchback** or a **dwarf**, or who has any eye **defect**, or who has **festering** or running **sores** or **damaged testicles**. No descendant of Aaron the priest who has any **defect** is to come near to present the food offerings to the Lord. He has a **defect**; he must not come near to offer the food of his God. He may eat the most holy food of his God, as well as the holy food; yet because of his **defect**, he must not go near the curtain or approach the altar, and so desecrate my sanctuary. I am the Lord, who makes them holy."'" KJV (*Whose fault is it if you are a dwarf?*)

God punishes a forest

EZEKIEL 20:45–48 "And the word of the Lord came to me: 'Son of man, set your face toward the south, preach against the south, and prophesy against the forest land in the Negeb; **say to the forest** of the Negeb, Hear the word of the Lord: Thus says the Lord God, Behold, I will kindle a fire in you, and it shall devour every green tree in you and every dry tree; the blazing flame shall not be quenched, and all faces from south to north shall be scorched by it. All flesh shall see that I the Lord have kindled it; it shall not be quenched.'" RSV (*God talks to trees.*)

Don't let your hair or clothes get messy

LEVITICUS 10:3–6 "Moses then said to Aaron, 'This is what the Lord spoke of when he said: "Among those who approach me I will be proved holy; in the sight of all the people I will be honored. "' . . . Then Moses said to Aaron and his sons Eleazar and Ithamar, 'Do not let your hair become unkempt and do not tear your clothes, or you will die and the Lord will be angry with the whole community.'"

3

Unjust

"I the Lord your God am a jealous God,
punishing children for the iniquity of parents,
to the third and fourth generation of those who reject me."
—DEUTERONOMY 5:9

What happened to those Ten Commandments, "the two tab-lets of the covenant, tablets of stone, written with the finger of God" (EXODUS 31:18)? Those original objects would be the most precious artifacts in the history of the human race. After going to so much trouble, shouldn't the powerful Lord Jealous have preserved his handwritten documents for all time? Why didn't he carve his thoughts in huge letters onto something more permanent, such as the cliff face at Half Dome in Yosemite? Or why not on the surface of the moon for all to see?

The Israelites indeed considered those tablets to be holy, and not just because they were the basis of Hebrew law. Those were their founding documents, the very establishment of the nation of Israel. The actual Constitution of the United States of America is on public display in the rotunda of the National Archives in Washington, D.C. Where are the Ten Commandments?

According to the writers of the Old Testament, God instructed the Israelites to build a special box to hold those treasured tablets. The Ark of the Covenant was an ornate gold-plated chest with golden angels on top (the Mercy Seat) hidden behind a curtain inside the Holy of Holies, the inner chamber of the huge traveling tent called the Tabernacle. God himself actually inhabited that Mercy Seat: "the ark of the covenant of the Lord of hosts, who is enthroned on the cherubim" (1 Samuel 4:4). Once a year, on Yom Kippur, the high priest was allowed to look at the Ark. So the writers tell us.

In reality, there almost certainly were no tablets. The Old Testament—especially the exploits of Moses on the smoking Mt. Sinai—is fictional, after all. If an Ark of the Covenant ever was made, it was empty—at least empty of the decalogue stones. It may have contained scrolls and other purported artifacts, but no divinely carved edicts cut from the side of a mountain. To protect this pretense, the religious leaders invented a fierce law to keep the common folk away from it. Just as the people were ordered to stay away from the peak where the commandments were inscribed, they were also prohibited from touching or looking at the Ark where they were ostensibly preserved.

Not only were worshippers barred from entering the Holy of Holies where the Ark was hidden, but when it was being moved it was covered with three large cloths. The common folk were instructed not to come any closer than "a distance of about two thousand cubits" (Joshua 3:4), more than a half mile away. Nobody actually saw the tablets or the Ark!

One day a devout and helpful man named Uzzah was driving the cart transporting the Ark. When he reached back to steady it after the oxen stumbled, he was struck dead by God (2 Samuel 6:6–7, and 1 Chronicles 13:9–10). Is it just to execute someone who makes a harmless mistake while trying to be respectful to the faith? The story was clearly invented to instill fear.

If the Commandments truly existed, why hide them? Why would God not want his people to see his work? The obvious explanation is that the Mount Sinai story was fictional. The religious leaders did not want the people to discover the deception. They needed their compliant congregation to remain enthralled by the awe and majesty of their faith.

In order to frighten the Israelites away from the empty box, a horror story is related in the book of 1 Samuel. God's chosen people were losing badly in their war with the Philistines—4,000 killed in one day—so in desperation they pulled their trump card. They relaxed the rule about looking at the box and marched into battle with the Ark of the Covenant itself. They carried "God Himself" to the front lines. When they got to the battlefield, the bemused Philistines simply grabbed the box and ran off with it—like Capture the Flag. The Israelites were devastated: "The Glory has departed from Israel, for the ark of God has been captured" (1 Samuel 4:22).

When the Philistines got their prize back to the Mediterranean coastal area, they started having weird problems, such as plagues, panic, death, rats, and tumors.

(Tumors? Were the Commandments radioactive?) Suspecting they might have stolen a truly sacred object, they decided to give it back. They put it on a cart, along with a "guilt offering" of golden mice and golden tumors. That's right—gold *tumors*. They attached two cows who had just given birth and who had never pulled a cart, and let them freely roam. Instead of heading back toward their crying calves, the cows hauled the cart eastward toward the nation of Israel. That was clear proof that the box was holy.

A little while later, some Israelite farmers outside the town of Bethshemesh spotted the approaching cart and recognized what it was. Their eyes lit up and they began rejoicing at the return of their nation's precious objects. So, of course, they broke up the cart to build a fire and "offered the cows as a burnt offering to the Lord" (1 SAMUEL 6:14).

What did God do at this joyous moment of praise and thanksgiving at the return of his holy Commandments to their rightful owners?

He smote the men of Bethshemesh, because they had looked into the ark of the Lord, even he smote of the people fifty thousand and threescore and ten men: and the people lamented, because the Lord had smitten many of the people with a great slaughter. (1 SAMUEL 6:19, KJV)

God slaughtered more than 50,000 of his worshipful people because a few of them peeked into the Ark.

Is that just?

The Hebrew text says it was 50,070 men, but some modern translations, such as the NIV and NRSV, suggest that the scribes made an error. They think it was only 70 men out of 50,000 who were killed in the great slaughter. We know the Old Testament writers exaggerated the size of Bethshemesh because there was no city in that area with that many inhabitants. But it makes no difference how many were massacred. It is horribly unjust to kill *any* number of people for simply looking at a box.

Bethshemesh means "House of the Sun," or "Temple of the Sun God." Shemesh— related to the Babylonian Sun God Shamash—was a Canaanite sun goddess who had been worshipped long before the Israelites came on the scene. It is not unlikely that the writers of the Old Testament were targeting the town for punishment simply because it had a pagan name. It defied the first commandment. It looks like this tale of injustice was motivated by jealousy.

To be unjust is to punish people for a crime they did not commit, or to punish people more severely than they deserve for their crimes. The injustice is especially egregious when it involves children.

Children punished for the crimes of their ancestors

DEUTERONOMY 5:8–9 [Ten Commandments] "You shall not make for yourself an image in the form of anything in heaven above or on the earth beneath or in the waters below. You shall not bow down to them or worship them; for I, the Lord your God, am a jealous God, **punishing the children for the sin of the parents** to the third and fourth generation of those who hate me." NIV (*Other verses contradict generational punishment: "The fathers shall not be put to death for the children, neither shall the children be put to death for the fathers: every man shall be put to death for his own sin." (DEUTERONOMY 24:16; see also 2 KINGS 14:6, JEREMIAH 31:29–30, EZEKIEL 18:20)*

EXODUS 34:6–7 "And the Lord passed by before him, and proclaimed, The Lord, The Lord God, merciful and gracious, longsuffering, and abundant in goodness and truth, Keeping mercy for thousands, forgiving iniquity and transgression and sin, and that will by no means clear the guilty; **visiting the iniquity of the fathers upon the children, and upon the children's children**, unto the third and to the fourth generation." KJV

NUMBERS 14:18 "The Lord is longsuffering, and of great mercy, forgiving iniquity and transgression, and by no means clearing the guilty, **visiting the iniquity of the fathers upon the children** unto the third and fourth generation." KJV

1 KINGS 21:28–29 "And the word of the Lord came to Elijah the Tishbite, saying, Seest thou how Ahab humbleth himself before me? because he humbleth himself before me, I will not bring the evil in his days: but **in his son's days will I bring the evil upon his house**." KJV

ISAIAH 14:21 "**Prepare slaughter for his children** for the iniquity of their fathers; that they do not rise, nor possess the land, nor fill the face of the world with cities." KJV

Descendants punished for the crime of their ancestors

JEREMIAH 16:10–11 "Wherefore hath the Lord pronounced all this great evil against us? or what is our iniquity? or what is our sin that we have committed against the Lord our God? . . . **Because your fathers have forsaken me**, saith the Lord, and have walked after other gods, and have served them, and have worshipped them, and have forsaken me, and have not kept my law." KJV

JEREMIAH 29:31–32 "This is what the Lord says about Shemaiah the Nehelamite: Because Shemaiah has prophesied to you, even though I did not send him, and has persuaded you to trust in lies, this is what the Lord says: **I will surely punish Shemaiah the Nehelamite and his descendants**." NIV

JEREMIAH 32:18 "Ah, Sovereign Lord, you have made the heavens and the earth by your great power and outstretched arm. Nothing is too hard for you. You show love to thousands but bring the **punishment for the parents' sins** into the laps of their children after them." NIV

God threatens to kill babies and fetuses

HOSEA 13:16 "The people of Samaria must bear their guilt, because they have rebelled against their God. They will fall by the sword; their **little ones will be dashed to the ground, their pregnant women ripped open**." NIV

Babies killed and wives raped to punish pride

ISAIAH 13:11–16 "I will put an end to the arrogance of the haughty. . . . **Their infants will be dashed to pieces** before their eyes; their houses will be looted and **their wives violated**." NIV

God sells children to others

JOEL 3:8 "And **I will sell your sons and your daughters** into the hand of the children of Judah, and they shall sell them to the Sabeans, to a people far off: for the Lord hath spoken it." KJV

Two sons killed on the same day, to punish the father

I SAMUEL 2:30–34 "Therefore the Lord, the God of Israel, declares: . . . those who despise me will be disdained. . . . And what happens to your two sons, Hophni and Phinehas, will be a sign to you—**they will both die on the same day**." NIV (*At least the sons are named, unlike Jephthah's poor daughter.*)

A child will die because Jeroboam was evil

I KINGS 14:9–12 "But hast done evil above all that were before thee: for thou hast gone and made thee other gods, and molten images, to provoke me to anger, and hast cast me behind thy back: Therefore, behold, I will bring evil upon the house of Jeroboam . . . when thy feet enter into the city, **the child shall die**." KJV

Sons and daughters killed

EZEKIEL 23:46–47 "For thus saith the Lord God; I will bring up a company upon them, and will give them to be removed and spoiled. And the company shall stone them with stones, and dispatch them with their swords; **they shall slay their sons and their daughters**, and burn up their houses with fire." KJV

God shows "no mercy" to the children of a prostitute

HOSEA 2:4–5 "And I will not have mercy upon her **children**; for they be the children of whoredoms. For their mother hath played the harlot: she that conceived them hath done shamefully." KJV

Bastards are unworthy

DEUTERONOMY 23:2 "A bastard shall not enter into the congregation of the Lord; even to his **tenth generation** shall he not enter into the congregation of the Lord." KJV (*Whose fault is it if your birth is "illicit"?*)

The eyes of disobedient children should be plucked out and eaten

PROVERBS 30:17 "The eye that mocketh at his father, and despiseth to obey his mother, the ravens of the valley shall pick it out, and the young eagles [NRSV: "vultures"] shall eat it." KJV

Egyptian children killed for the actions of their Pharaoh

EXODUS 11:4–6; 12:29 "And Moses said, Thus saith the Lord, About midnight will I go out into the midst of Egypt: And **all the firstborn in the land of Egypt shall die**, from the first born of Pharaoh that sitteth upon his throne, even unto the firstborn of the maidservant that is behind the mill; and all the firstborn of beasts. . . . And it came to pass, that at midnight **the Lord smote all the firstborn** in the land of Egypt, from the firstborn of Pharaoh that sat on his throne unto the firstborn of the captive that was in the dungeon; and all the firstborn of cattle." KJV

God ordered the rape of David's wives as a punishment for his sin . . .

2 SAMUEL 12:11 "Thus says the Lord, 'Behold, I will raise up evil against you out of your own house; and **I will take your wives before your eyes**, and give them to your neighbor, and he shall lie with your wives in the sight of this sun." RSV

. . . then killed the child for David's crime

2 SAMUEL 12:13–14 "David said to Nathan, 'I have sinned against the Lord.' And Nathan said to David, 'The Lord also has put away your sin; you shall not die. Nevertheless, because by this deed you have utterly scorned the Lord, **the child that is born to you shall die**.'" RSV

When David's wife criticizes his lewd dancing (exposing his genitals to other women), God curses her with barrenness

2 SAMUEL 6:20–23 "And Michal the daughter of Saul came out to meet David, and said, How glorious was the king of Israel to day, who uncovered himself to day in the eyes of the handmaids of his servants, as one of the vain fellows shamelessly uncovereth himself! And David said unto Michal,

It was before the Lord, which chose me before thy father, and before all his house, to appoint me ruler over the people of the Lord, over Israel: therefore will I play before the Lord. And I will yet be more vile than thus, and will be base in mine own sight: and of the maidservants which thou hast spoken of, of them shall I be had in honour. Therefore **Michal the daughter of Saul had no child unto the day of her death.**" KJV *(By the way, 2 SAMUEL 21:8 says Michal had five sons. Some translations replace "Michal" with "Merab," even though the Hebrew and Greek Septuagint have "Michal.")*

David acknowledges God's injustice
2 SAMUEL 24:17 "And David spake unto the Lord when he saw the angel that smote the people, and said, Lo, I have sinned, and I have done wickedly: **but these sheep, what have they done?** let thine hand, I pray thee, be against me, and against my father's house." KJV

God punishes the nation with a three-year famine because of Saul's actions
2 SAMUEL 21:1 "Then there was a famine in the days of David three years, year after year; and David enquired of the Lord. And the Lord answered, **It is for Saul, and for his bloody house**, because he slew the Gibeonites." KJV

Seven of Saul's sons and grandsons are killed to end the famine
2 SAMUEL 21:4–14 "And the Gibeonites said unto him [David] . . . The man that consumed us, and that devised against us that we should be destroyed from remaining in any of the coasts of Israel, **Let seven men of his sons be delivered unto us**, and we will hang them up unto the Lord. . . . And he delivered them into the hands of the Gibeonites, and they hanged them in the hill before the Lord: and **they fell all seven together, and were put to death** in the days of harvest, in the first days, in the beginning of barley harvest. . . . And after that **God was intreated for the land.**" KJV

God deliberately made bad laws in order to "horrify" his people
EZEKIEL 20:25–26 "So I gave them other **statutes that were not good** and laws through which they could not live; I defiled them through their gifts— the sacrifice of every firstborn—that I might fill them with horror so they would know that I am the Lord." NIV

God punishes indiscriminately, both the good and the bad, with his sword
EZEKIEL 21:3–5 "Thus says the Lord: Behold, I am against you, and will draw forth my sword out of its sheath, and **will cut off from you both righteous and wicked.** Because I will cut off from you both righteous and

wicked, therefore my sword shall go out of its sheath against all flesh from south to north." RSV

Women punished for the wrongdoing of another

GENESIS 20:18 "For **the Lord had closed all the wombs** of the house of Abim'elech because of Sarah, Abraham's wife." RSV

The prophet who believed the lie, not one who told the lie, was killed by a lion

1 KINGS 13:18–24 "The old prophet answered, 'I too am a prophet, as you are. And an angel said to me by the word of the Lord: "Bring him back with you to your house so that he may eat bread and drink water."' (**But he was lying to him.**) So the man of God returned with him and ate and drank in his house. While they were sitting at the table, the word of the Lord came to the old prophet who had brought him back. . . . 'This is what the Lord says: "You have defied the word of the Lord and have not kept the command the Lord your God gave you. . . . Therefore your body will not be buried in the tomb of your ancestors."'. . . As he went on his way, **a lion met him on the road and killed him**." NIV

A well-meaning but mistaken prophet was killed

JEREMIAH 28:15–17 "Then said the prophet Jeremiah unto Hananiah the prophet, Hear now, Hananiah; The Lord hath not sent thee; but thou makest this people to trust in a lie. Therefore thus saith the Lord; Behold, I will cast thee from off the face of the earth: **this year thou shalt die**, because thou hast taught rebellion against the Lord. So **Hananiah the prophet died the same year** in the seventh month." KJV

God deceives a prophet, then destroys him for his deception

EZEKIEL 14:9 "And if the prophet be deceived when he hath spoken a thing, **I the Lord have deceived that prophet**, and I will stretch out my hand upon him, and will destroy him from the midst of my people Israel." KJV (*No matter how this verse is interpreted, the injustice of the punishment is the same.*)

Discrimination against the handicapped

LEVITICUS 21:16–23 "The Lord said to Moses, 'Say to Aaron: "For the generations to come none of your descendants who has a **defect** may come near to offer the food of his God. No man who has any **defect** may come near: no man who is **blind** or **lame**, **disfigured** or **deformed**; no man with a **crippled** foot or hand, or who is a **hunchback** or a **dwarf**, or who has any

eye defect, or who has festering or running **sores** or **damaged testicles**. No descendant of Aaron the priest who has any **defect** is to come near to present the food offerings to the Lord. He has a **defect**; he must not come near to offer the food of his God. He may eat the most holy food of his God, as well as the holy food; yet because of his **defect**, he must not go near the curtain or approach the altar, and so **desecrate** my sanctuary. I am the Lord, who makes them holy."'" NIV (*Is shortness or a blemish a moral failing?*)

The poor pay the same tax as the rich

EXODUS 30:14–15 "Every one who is numbered in the census, from twenty years old and upward, shall give the Lord's offering. **The rich shall not give more**, and the poor shall not give less, than the half shekel, when you give the Lord's offering to make atonement for yourselves." RSV

Lot's wife killed for the "crime" of looking back at her former home

GENESIS 19:26 "But his wife looked back from behind him, and she became a pillar of salt." KJV

Capital punishment for cursing one's parents

EXODUS 21:17 "Whoever curses his father or his mother shall be put to death." RSV

Death penalty for an animal

LEVITICUS 20:15–16 "And if a man lie with a beast, he shall surely be put to death: and ye shall **slay the beast**. And if a woman approach unto any beast, and lie down thereto, thou shalt kill the woman, and the beast: they shall surely be put to death; their blood shall be upon them." KJV (*Bestiality is immoral, but why the death penalty? And why for the animal?*)

A fool should be beaten like a horse

PROVERBS 26:3 "A whip for the horse, a bridle for the ass, and a rod for the fool's back." KJV

Kill witches, for the crime of being witches

EXODUS 22:18 "Thou shalt not suffer a witch to live." KJV

Virgins are abducted, through war booty and kidnapping, to provide wives for a tribe of Israel

JUDGES 21:6–23 Now the Israelites grieved for the tribe of Benjamin, their fellow Israelites. . . . 'How can we provide wives for those who are left, since we have taken an oath by the Lord not to give them any of our daughters in marriage?' . . . So the assembly sent twelve thousand fighting men with instructions to go to Jabesh Gilead and put to the sword those living there, including the women and children. . . . 'Kill every male and every woman who is not a virgin.' They found among the people living in Jabesh Gilead four hundred young women who had never slept with a man. . . . But there were not enough for all of them. . . . So they instructed the Benjamites, saying, 'Go and hide in the vineyards and watch. When the young women of Shiloh come out to join in the dancing, rush from the vineyards and each of you seize one of them to be your wife.' . . . So that is what the Benjamites did. While the young women were dancing, each man caught one and carried her off to be his wife." NIV (This was all done because of a vow sworn to God.)

God killed a man for refusing to hand over his hard-earned goods to David. Then David married his wife

1 SAMUEL 25:5–39 "David said unto the young men, Get you up to Carmel, and go to Nabal, and greet him in my name: . . . Give, I pray thee, whatsoever cometh to thine hand unto thy servants, and to thy son David. . . . And Nabal answered David's servants, and said, Who is David? . . . Shall I then take my bread, and my water, and my flesh that I have killed for my shearers, and give it unto men, whom I know not whence they be? . . . And it came to pass about ten days after, that the Lord smote Nabal, that he died. . . . And David sent and communed with Abigail, to take her to him to wife." KJV

David gets to pick his punishment. He chooses a pestilence that kills 70,000

1 CHRONICLES 21:11–14 "Thus saith the Lord, Choose thee either three years' famine; or three months to be destroyed before thy foes, while that the sword of thine enemies overtaketh thee; or else three days the sword of the Lord, even the pestilence, in the land, and the angel of the Lord destroying throughout all the coasts of Israel. . . . And David said unto God, I am in a great strait: let me fall now into the hand of the Lord; for very great are his mercies: but let me not fall into the hand of man. So the Lord sent pestilence upon Israel: and there fell of Israel seventy thousand men." KJV

God punishes the environment for the supposed "wickedness" of the people

PSALM 107:33–34 "He turns rivers into a desert, springs of water into thirsty ground, a fruitful land into a salty waste, because of the wickedness of its inhabitants." RSV

God inflicts leprosy on King Uzziah for acting like a priest

2 CHRONICLES 26:19–21 "Uzziah, who had a censer in his hand ready to burn incense, became angry. While he was raging at the priests in their presence before the incense altar in the Lord's temple, leprosy broke out on his forehead. When Azariah the chief priest and all the other priests looked at him, they saw that he had leprosy on his forehead, so they hurried him out. . . . King Uzziah had **leprosy until the day he died**. He lived in a separate house—leprous, and banned from the temple of the Lord." NIV

No matter how good you have been, you will die from one transgression. "Am I unjust?"

EZEKIEL 18:24–26 "But if a righteous person turns from their righteousness and commits sin and does the same detestable things the wicked person does, will they live? **None of the righteous things that person has done will be remembered.** Because of the unfaithfulness they are guilty of and because of the sins they have committed, they will die. Yet you say, 'The way of the Lord is not just.' Hear, you Israelites: **Is my way unjust?** Is it not your ways that are unjust? If a righteous person turns from their righteousness and commits sin, they will die for it; because of the sin they have committed they will die." NIV

One mistake erases a lifetime of goodness

EZEKIEL 33:12–13 "The righteous person who sins will not be allowed to live even though they were formerly righteous. If I tell a righteous person that they will surely live, but then they trust in their righteousness and do evil, **none of the righteous things that person has done will be remembered;** they will die for the evil they have done." NIV

No democracy in the Old Testament. God sets up and removes kings

DANIEL 2:20–21 "Daniel answered and said, Blessed be the name of God for ever and ever: for wisdom and might are his: And he changeth the times and the seasons: **he removeth kings, and setteth up kings.**" KJV

No religious freedom

EXODUS 22:20 "Whoever sacrifices to any god other than the Lord must be destroyed." NIV

God sent lions to kill nonbelievers

2 KINGS 17:25 "When they first lived there, they did not worship the Lord; so he sent lions among them and they **killed some of the people.**" NIV (*It is unjust to kill over religious differences.*)

Death to nonbelievers

2 CHRONICLES 15:13 "All who would not seek the Lord, the God of Israel, were to be **put to death**, whether small or great, man or woman." NIV
(It is unjust to punish someone simply for their opinions.)

More death to nonbelievers

PSALM 78:21–22, 31 "When the Lord heard them, he was furious; his fire broke out against Jacob, and his wrath rose against Israel, for they did not believe in God or trust in his deliverance. . . . God's anger rose against them; he **put to death** the sturdiest among them, cutting down the young men of Israel." NIV

Nonbelievers' property (including wives) will be given away

JEREMIAH 8:9–10 "Since they have rejected the word of the Lord, what kind of wisdom do they have? Therefore **I will give their wives to other men** and their fields to new owners." NIV

God kills and persecutes those who do not listen to him

JEREMIAH 29:18–19 "And I will **persecute** them with the sword, with the famine, and with the pestilence, and will deliver them to be removed to all the kingdoms of the earth, to be a curse, and an astonishment, and an hissing, and a reproach, among all the nations whither I have driven them: Because **they have not hearkened** to my words, saith the Lord, which I sent unto them by my servants the prophets, rising up early and sending them; but **ye would not hear**, saith the Lord." KJV

A skeptic was trampled to death

2 KINGS 7:19–20 "The officer had said to the man of God, 'Look, even if the Lord should open the floodgates of the heavens, could this happen?' The man of God had replied, 'You will see it with your own eyes, but you will not eat any of it!' And that is exactly what happened to him, for the people **trampled** him in the gateway, and he **died**." NIV

Skeptics will be burned

JEREMIAH 5:12–14 "They have belied the Lord, and said, It is not he; neither shall evil come upon us; neither shall we see sword nor famine: And the prophets shall become wind, and the word is not in them: thus shall it be done unto them. Wherefore thus saith the Lord God of hosts, Because ye speak this word, behold, I will make my words in thy mouth **fire**, and this people wood, and it **shall devour them**." KJV

To punish someone less severely than is deserved by the crime is mercy. To punish them *more* severely is unjust.

> *And if ye walk contrary unto me, and will not hearken unto me; I will bring* **seven times more plagues** *upon you according to your sins. . . . Then I will walk contrary unto you also in fury; and I, even I, will chastise you* **seven times for your sins**. KJV (LEVITICUS 26:21, 26:28)

The Lord Jealous should listen to his own prophet: "The unjust knows no share" (ZEPHANIAH 3:5).

4

Unforgiving

"He is a jealous God; he will not forgive
your transgressions or your sins."
—Joshua 24:19

According to Genesis, Adam and Eve deeply offended God's authority. Because of that one act of disobedience, the *entire* human race must be punished into perpetuity. The Lord Jealous put the "fear of God" into his children by kicking them out of the house. He damned all of us. "Actions have consequences," the strict parent lectures his unruly children.

We sometimes hear that God is a forgiving parent, but the scriptures don't support that claim. The forgiveness that is sometimes mentioned in the Old Testament is almost always contingent on paying a price to appease the wrath of the Lord Jealous. Forgiveness is not something he freely gives: it has to be bought, usually with the blood ransom of animal sacrifice.

> *He shall remove all its fat, as the fat is removed from the offering of well-being, and the priest shall turn it into smoke on the altar for a pleasing odor to the Lord. Thus the priest shall make atonement on your behalf, and you shall be forgiven.* (Leviticus 4:31)

When God's anger is soothed by the "pleasing odor" of a burning animal, only then will he pardon your crimes.

If a father said to his child, "You angered me by opening your Christmas present early, but I will forgive you when I smell the smoke of your pet burning," we would howl with condemnation at such abusive parenting. As Richard Dawkins notes in the Foreword, Christians have inherited this blood-penalty mentality from the Old Testament: "Without the shedding of blood, there is no remission [of sins]." (HEBREWS 9:22) God simply cannot forgive unless something dies.

There are now more than seven billion people on the planet. In the history of our species, there have been about a hundred billion human beings, all destined to die. According to biblical theology, God wanted every one of us to exist, all tenth-of-a-trillion unique individuals, but instead of creating each of us individually, like he did with Adam, he decided to do it biologically. As if we were animals. He started with two people. Well, actually only one. Adam was molded from mud, then Eve was carved from one of his ribs as "a help meet for him."

Those two were created "ex nihilo" (or "ex dirt," "ex rib"), but the rest of us descended from those mega-great-grandparents by sexual reproduction, just as you would expect if we had evolved though natural selection. Let's ignore the fact that according to the process of evolution, there could not have been an Adam and Eve, a single set of proto-parents, and even if there were, they would have lived in Africa, not the Middle East. Many theologians, clergy, and scientifically informed believers no longer take Genesis literally; but some still think it is nonfiction, especially evangelical Christians in the United States and conservative Christians, Jews, and Muslims around the world. Literal or not, the story was presented as historical truth by the author.

Those two freshly minted people in the Garden of Eden were presumably created in a perfect state, because a perfect God cannot make an imperfect product. But almost immediately, Adam and Eve did something horrible. (Or I should say "Eve and Adam" did something horrible. Eve was the first to do wrong. Always blame the woman.) Isn't it strange that out of all 100 billion of us, the two who would actually go astray were the very first two? What are the odds?

The unforgivable crime they committed was heinous enough to be mentioned right at the start—in the beginning—of the Hebrew scriptures. They ate fruit from God's forbidden magic tree of knowledge, a mistake with epic consequences. But who made the mistake? Eve, by succumbing to the temptation to gain knowledge? Or God, who created a human being who would succumb to such a desire? If Eve were a perfect creation, how could she do wrong? If "free will" is the culprit, then why did a perfect woman exercise her "free will" to do wrong instead of right? Where did the "flaw" that resulted in the fall of the human race originate?

It sure looks like God was to blame, but the writers of the Old Testament thought it was Eve's fault. That doesn't make any ultimate sense, but that's what they tell us. After "The Fall," the rest of us were helplessly born with "original sin" because of the polluting actions of our evil ancestors. We inherited the flaw, just like you would expect if we descended genetically. Eve and Adam's actions tainted all future generations. Like a natural mutation.

Is "original sin" passed through our DNA? Instead of "selfish genes," will scientists soon discover "sinful genes" in the nucleus of our cells? Is it like the historical and unfixable accident that our retinas are backwards? Now here we are, millennia later, still suffering the consequences of an independent woman.

Talk about unforgiving! The harmless act they committed was unpardonable in God's angry heart. They were immediately expelled from the garden. The entrance to Eden was blocked by a threatening angel with a flaming sword:

> *And to the man he said, "Because you have listened to the voice of your wife, and have eaten of the tree about which I commanded you, 'You shall not eat of it,' cursed is the ground because of you; in toil you shall eat of it all the days of your life; thorns and thistles it shall bring forth for you; and you shall eat the plants of the field. By the sweat of your face you shall eat bread until you return to the ground, for out of it you were taken; you are dust, and to dust you shall return." . . . therefore the Lord God sent him forth from the garden of Eden, to till the ground from which he was taken. He drove out the man; and at the east of the garden of Eden* **he placed the cherubim, and a sword flaming and turning to guard the way to the tree of life***. (*GENESIS 3:17–24*)*

By the way, notice that there is no mention of eternal life in this story of the fall of the human race. No hell or heaven. Adam is considered a material being—"the ground from which you are taken"—and his death is a physical degradation—"for dust you are and to dust you will return"—as if humans were simply biological organisms. The concept of eternal Hell, a truly infinite lack of forgiveness, does not occur until the New Testament, thanks to Jesus.

But let's stick with the Old Testament. I'll talk about Jesus in Chapter 28.

God will not forgive sins

JOSHUA 24:19 "And Joshua said unto the people, Ye cannot serve the Lord: for he is an holy God; he is a jealous God; **he will not forgive** your transgressions nor your sins." KJV

Not willing to forgive

2 KINGS 24:3–4 "Surely these things happened to Judah according to the Lord's command, in order to remove them from his presence because of the sins of Manasseh and all he had done, including the shedding of innocent blood. For he had filled Jerusalem with innocent blood, and **the Lord was not willing to forgive**." NIV

Never willing to forgive

DEUTERONOMY 29:20 "Surely these things happened to Judah according to the Lord's command, in order to remove them from his presence because of the sins of Manasseh and all he had done, including the shedding of innocent blood. For he had filled Jerusalem with innocent blood, and **the Lord was not willing to forgive.**" NIV

Rebellious freethinkers are not forgiven

EXODUS 23:21 "See, I am sending an angel ahead of you to guard you along the way and to bring you to the place I have prepared. Pay attention to him and listen to what he says. Do not rebel against him; **he will not forgive** your rebellion, since my Name is in him." NIV

His forgiveness is "covered with a cloud"

LAMENTATIONS 3:42–44 "We have transgressed and have rebelled: **thou hast not pardoned.** Thou hast covered with anger, and persecuted us: thou hast slain, thou hast not pitied. Thou hast covered thyself with a cloud, that our prayer should not pass through." KJV

Merciless justice

EZEKIEL 24:13–14 "Because I tried to cleanse you but you would not be cleansed from your impurity, you will not be clean again until my wrath against you has subsided. I the Lord have spoken. The time has come for me to act. I will not hold back; **I will not have pity, nor will I relent**. You will be judged according to your conduct and your actions, declares the Sovereign Lord." NIV

"Do not forgive them!"

ISAIAH 2:6–9 "You, Lord, have abandoned your people. . . . Their land is full of idols; they bow down to the work of their hands, to what their fingers have made. So people will be brought low and everyone humbled—**do not forgive them**." NIV

Not forgiven until you die

ISAIAH 22:14 "The Lord of hosts has revealed himself in my ears: 'Surely **this iniquity will not be forgiven** you till you die,' says the Lord God of hosts." RSV

God will "laugh at your calamity"

PROVERBS 1:24–30 "Because I have called, and ye refused; I have stretched out my hand, and no man regarded; But ye have set at nought all my counsel, and would none of my reproof: **I also will laugh at your calamity**; I will mock when your fear cometh; When your fear cometh as desolation, and your destruction cometh as a whirlwind; when distress and anguish cometh upon you. Then shall they call upon me, but **I will not answer**; they shall seek me early, but **they shall not find me**: For that they hated knowledge, and did not choose the fear of the Lord: They would none of my counsel: they despised all my reproof." KJV

Kill without pity

EZEKIEL 9:3–10 "And the Lord said unto him, Go through the midst of the city, through the midst of Jerusalem, and set a mark upon the foreheads of the men that sigh and that cry for all the abominations that be done in the midst thereof. And to the others he said in mine hearing, Go ye after him through the city, and smite: **let not your eye spare, neither have ye pity**: Slay utterly old and young, both maids, and little children, and women. . . . The Lord hath forsaken the earth, and the Lord seeth not. And as for me also, **mine eye shall not spare, neither will I have pity**, but I will recompense their way upon their head." KJV

Don't even pray for these people

JEREMIAH 11:14 "Therefore do not pray for this people, or lift up a cry or prayer on their behalf, for I **will not listen when they call to me in the time of their trouble**." RSV

Don't bother fasting or worshipping—God will still kill you

JEREMIAH 14:12 "Though they fast, **I will not hear their cry**, and though they offer burnt offering and cereal offering, I will not accept them; but I will consume them by the sword, by famine, and by pestilence." RSV

Even if the patriarchs intercede for you, they are wasting their time

JEREMIAH 15:1 "Then the Lord said to me, 'Though Moses and Samuel stood before me, yet **my heart would not turn toward this people**. Send them out of my sight, and let them go!'" RSV

Jeremiah expects God not to forgive an attempted assassination

JEREMIAH 18:23 "Yet, thou, O Lord, knowest all their plotting to slay me. **Forgive not their iniquity, nor blot out their sin from thy sight**. Let them be overthrown before thee; deal with them in the time of thine anger." RSV

"I will not spare you"

EZEKIEL 7:3–4 "The end is now upon you, and I will unleash my anger against you. I will judge you according to your conduct and repay you for all your detestable practices. **I will not look on you with pity; I will not spare you**." NIV

"No bastards allowed in church" (or their descendants) until the 10th generation

DEUTERONOMY 23:2 "A bastard shall not enter into the congregation of the Lord; **even to his tenth generation** shall he not enter into the congregation of the Lord." KJV (*Scholars are not sure what the word "mamzer" means. It could mean illegitimate, or inter-ethnic. But whatever it means, it is not the child's fault. And certainly not the fault of any subsequent generation. And who was keeping track? Do you know who your tenth-generation ancestors were, or if any of them were bastards? My mother was "illegitimate," so why was I allowed in church?*)

Perpetual punishment

EXODUS 20:5 "Thou shalt not bow down thyself to them, nor serve them: for I the Lord thy God am a jealous God, visiting the iniquity of the fathers upon the children unto the **third and fourth generation** of them that hate me." KJV (*The next verse says "but showing love to a thousand generations of those who love me and keep my commandments." There could be a thousand generations of one family who never sin? That is 25,000 years! That means the world cannot end for at least another 20,000 years.*)

In the Old Testament, forgiveness is purchased by making a sacrifice of something you own, usually an animal.

God's forgiveness is purchased with blood

EXODUS 29:36 "And thou shalt offer every day a bullock for a **sin offering for atonement**: and thou shalt cleanse the altar, when thou hast made an atonement for it, and thou shalt anoint it, to sanctify it." KJV

LEVITICUS 4:20 "Thus shall he do with the bull; as he did with the bull of the sin offering, so shall he do with this; and the priest shall make atonement for them, and **they shall be forgiven**." RSV

LEVITICUS 4:26 "And all its fat he shall burn on the altar, like the fat of the sacrifice of peace offerings; so the priest shall make atonement for him for his sin, and **he shall be forgiven**." RSV

LEVITICUS 4:35 "And all its fat he shall remove as the fat of the lamb is removed from the sacrifice of peace offerings, and the priest shall burn it on the altar, upon the offerings by fire to the Lord; and the priest shall make atonement for him for the sin which he has committed, and **he shall be forgiven**." RSV

LEVITICUS 5:16 "He shall also make restitution for what he has done amiss in the holy thing, and shall add a fifth to it and give it to the priest; and the priest shall make atonement for him with the ram of the guilt offering, and **he shall be forgiven**." RSV

LEVITICUS 5:18–19 "He shall bring to the priest a ram without blemish out of the flock, valued by you at the price for a guilt offering, and the priest shall make atonement for him for the error which he committed unwittingly, and **he shall be forgiven**. It is a guilt offering; he is guilty before the Lord." RSV

LEVITICUS 6:6–7 "And he shall bring to the priest his guilt offering to the Lord, a ram without blemish out of the flock, valued by you at the price for a guilt offering; and the priest shall make atonement for him before the Lord, and **he shall be forgiven** for any of the things which one may do and thereby become guilty." RSV

LEVITICUS 19:22 "And the priest shall make atonement for him with the ram of the guilt offering before the Lord for his sin which he has committed; and the sin which he has committed **shall be forgiven him**." RSV

NUMBERS 15:25 "And the priest shall make an **atonement** for all the congregation of the children of Israel, and it **shall be forgiven** them; for it is ignorance: and they shall bring their offering, a sacrifice made by fire unto the Lord, and their sin offering before the Lord, for their ignorance." KJV

How is purchasing forgiveness different from bribing a judge?

5

Control Freak

*"I know, O Lord, that the way of human beings is not in their control,
that mortals as they walk cannot direct their steps."*
—JEREMIAH 10:23

There are very few moral principles in the Old Testament—very little guidance toward leading mature ethical lives. The Lord Jealous is more concerned with micromanaging the daily lives of the early Israelites to the tiniest details than he is with teaching his children how to think for themselves. "Lean not unto thine own understanding. In all thy ways acknowledge him, and he shall direct thy paths." (PROVERBS 3:5–6, KJV).

God is a helicopter parent. He meddles with his children's eating habits, washing rituals, travel routes, clothing choices, hair styles, artwork, underwear, sex lives, and toilet habits. He is a micro manager, a nagging boss. He demands to be worshipped, but his people cannot even choose how to express their love; he must be admired in very specific ways. "Yes, that's how I like it." He especially enjoys controlling their religious rituals by frightening them with graphic threats and carefully crafted curses if they do it wrong.

What kind of practical advice do we find in the Old Testament? The God of the universe, the cosmic source of wisdom, spends six entire chapters in Exodus, the second book of the bible, on minutely detailed instructions on how to build a tent for his glory. That's right. The "Holy Bible" that you find in your hotel room can give you desperately needed guidance on how to construct a wandering desert big top.

Not only were the Ten Commandments stored in the elaborate Ark of the Covenant, but the Ark itself was hidden behind costly curtains in a male-only secret space, accessible to the high priest alone. The Holy of Holies was the inner chamber of a massive opulent mobile tent called the Tabernacle, the Israelites' traveling temple. God is such a control freak that he even specifies the name of the general contractor.

Beginning with the direct orders at Exodus 25:8–9—"And have them make me a sanctuary, so that I may dwell among them. In accordance with all that I show you concerning the pattern of the tabernacle and of all its furniture, so you shall make it"—and ending with the OCD words at Exodus 31:11—"They shall do just as I have commanded you"—those six long chapters deal in painful detail with:

- the Ark of the Covenant
- the Mercy Seat, with cherubims
- table of shittim wood
- dishes, spoons, tableware
- candlestick
- curtains
- tent covering of ram skin
- tent construction of shittim wood, overlaid with gold
- door made of scarlet and linen
- elaborate altar (more shittim wood)
- brass pan to receive the ashes
- 50-cubit courtyard with pillars and linen hangings
- courtyard gate with scarlet and linen
- brass tableware
- precise tailoring specifications for the expensive priestly garments (a whole chapter)
- breastplate and mitre
- careful details on how to kill the bull and the ram ("seethe his flesh in the holy place")
- how to cook the lamb to be sacrificed on the altar
- animals to be continually burned at the door
- another ornate altar outside the door
- fancy brass wash basin, for the priests' hands and feet
- how to make holy oil and incense, for priests only
- how to fundraise for the project: "And thou shalt take the atonement money of the children of Israel, and shalt appoint it for the service of the tabernacle of the congregation."
- God actually names the contractor to use for the construction

Here are a few of God's control-freak specifications in detail:

Ten verses of holy scripture detailing how to make a showy candlestick

EXODUS 25:31–40 "And thou shalt make a **candlestick** of pure gold: of beaten work shall the **candlestick** be made: his shaft, and his branches, his bowls, his knops, and his flowers, shall be of the same. And six branches shall come out of the sides of it; three branches of the **candlestick** out of the one side, and three branches of the **candlestick** out of the other side: Three bowls made like unto almonds, with a knop and a flower in one branch; and three bowls made like almonds in the other branch, with a knop and a flower: so in the six branches that come out of the **candlestick**. And in the **candlesticks** shall be four bowls made like unto almonds, with their knops and their flowers. And there shall be a knop under two branches of the same, and a knop under two branches of the same, and a knop under two branches of the same, according to the six branches that proceed out of the **candlestick**. Their knops and their branches shall be of the same: all it shall be one beaten work of pure gold. And thou shalt make the seven **lamps** thereof: and they shall light the **lamps** thereof, that they may give light over against it. And the tongs thereof, and the **snuffdishes** thereof, shall be of pure gold. Of a talent of pure gold shall he make it, with all these **vessels**. And look that thou make them after their pattern, which was shewed thee in the mount." KJV (*God can speak volumes about lampstands, but can't afford a single verse against sexually molesting children.*)

God the interior decorator. Thirteen whole verses about fancy draperies

EXODUS 26:1–13 "Moreover thou shalt make the tabernacle with ten **curtains** of fine twined linen, and blue, and purple, and scarlet: with cherubims of cunning work shalt thou make them. The length of one **curtain** shall be eight and twenty cubits, and the breadth of one **curtain** four cubits: and every one of the **curtains** shall have one measure. The five **curtains** shall be coupled together one to another; and other five **curtains** shall be coupled one to another. And thou shalt make loops of blue upon the edge of the one **curtain** from the selvedge in the coupling; and likewise shalt thou make in the uttermost edge of another **curtain**, in the coupling of the second. Fifty loops shalt thou make in the one **curtain**, and fifty loops shalt thou make in the edge of the **curtain** that is in the coupling of the second; that the loops may take hold one of another. And thou shalt make fifty taches of gold, and couple the **curtains** together with the taches: and it shall be one tabernacle. And thou shalt make **curtains** of goats' hair to be a covering upon the tabernacle: eleven **curtains** shalt thou make. The length of one **curtain** shall be thirty cubits, and the breadth of one **curtain** four cubits: and the eleven **curtains** shall be all of one measure. And thou shalt couple five **curtains** by themselves, and six **curtains** by themselves, and shalt double the sixth **curtain** in the forefront of the tabernacle. And thou shalt make fifty loops on the edge of the one **curtain** that is outmost in the coupling, and fifty loops in the edge of the **curtain** which coupleth the second. And thou shalt make fifty taches of brass, and put the taches into the loops, and couple the tent together, that it may be one. And the remnant that remaineth of the **curtains** of the tent, the half **curtain** that remaineth, shall hang over the backside of the tabernacle. And a cubit on the one side, and a cubit on the other side of that which remaineth in the length of the **curtains** of the tent, it shall hang over the sides of the tabernacle on this side and on that side, to cover it." KJV

Don't forget the tableware

Exodus 27:19 "All the vessels of the tabernacle in all the service thereof, and all the pins thereof, and all the pins of the court, shall be of brass." KJV (*Extravagant, like the Vatican. Couldn't they use cheaper spoons to save some money for the poor?*)

Boxer shorts! A whole *chapter* for fancy garments for one man and his sons

Exodus 28:4–42 "They are to make these **sacred garments** for your brother Aaron and his sons, so they may serve me as priests. Have them use **gold**, and blue, purple and scarlet yarn, and fine linen. Make the **ephod** of **gold**, and of blue, purple and scarlet yarn, and of finely twisted linen—the work of skilled hands. It is to have two **shoulder pieces** attached to two of its corners, so it can be fastened. Its skillfully woven waistband is to be like it—of one piece with the ephod and made with **gold**, and with blue, purple and scarlet yarn, and with finely twisted **linen**. Take two onyx stones and engrave on them the names of the sons of Israel in the order of their birth—six names on one stone and the remaining six on the other. Engrave the names of the sons of Israel on the two stones the way a gem cutter engraves a seal. Then mount the stones in **gold** filigree settings and fasten them on the **shoulder pieces** of the **ephod** as memorial stones for the sons of Israel. . . . Make **gold** filigree settings and two braided **chains** of pure **gold**, like a rope, and attach the **chains** to the settings. Fashion a **breastpiece** for making decisions—the work of skilled hands. Make it like the ephod: of **gold**, and of blue, purple and scarlet yarn, and of finely twisted **linen**. It is to be square—a span long and a span wide—and folded double. Then mount four rows of precious stones on it. The first row shall be carnelian, chrysolite and beryl; the second row shall be turquoise, lapis lazuli and emerald; the third row shall be jacinth, agate and amethyst; the fourth row shall be topaz, onyx and jasper. Mount them in **gold** filigree settings. There are to be twelve stones, one for each of the names of the sons of Israel, each engraved like a seal with the name of one of the twelve tribes. For the **breastpiece** make braided **chains** of pure **gold**, like a rope. Make two gold rings for it and fasten them to two corners of the **breastpiece**. Fasten the two **gold chains** to the rings at the corners of the **breastpiece**, and the other ends of the **chains** to the two settings, attaching them to the shoulder pieces of the **ephod** at the front. Make two **gold** rings and attach them to the other two corners of the breastpiece on the inside edge next to the ephod. Make two more gold rings and attach them to the bottom of the shoulder pieces on the front of the ephod, close to the seam just above the waistband of the ephod. The rings of the **breastpiece** are to be tied to the rings of the **ephod** with blue cord, connecting it to the waistband, so that the breastpiece will not swing out from the ephod. . . . Also put the Urim and the Thummim in the **breastpiece**, so they may be over Aaron's heart whenever he enters the presence of the Lord. . . . Make the robe of the **ephod** entirely of blue cloth, with an opening for the head in its center. There shall be a woven edge like a collar around this opening, so that it will not tear. Make pomegranates of blue, purple and scarlet yarn around the hem of the robe, with **gold bells** between them. The **gold bells** and the pomegranates are to alternate around the hem of the robe. . . . The sound of the **bells** will be heard when he enters the Holy Place before the Lord and when he comes out, so that he will not die. Make a plate of pure **gold** and engrave on it as on a seal: holy to the Lord. Fasten a blue cord to it to attach it to the **turban**; it is to be on the front of the **turban**. . . . Weave the **tunic** of fine **linen** and make the **turban** of fine **linen**. The sash is to be the work of an embroiderer. Make **tunics**, **sashes** and **caps** for Aaron's sons to give them dignity and honor. . . . Make **linen undergarments** as a covering for the body, reaching from the waist to the thigh. Aaron and his sons must wear them whenever they enter the tent of meeting or approach the altar to minister in the Holy Place, so that they will not incur guilt and die. This is to be a lasting ordinance for Aaron and his descendants." NIV (*Hans Christian Andersen would have been proud of this passage.*)

God orders a personal washbasin for the priests

EXODUS 30:17–21 "The Lord said to Moses, 'You shall also make a laver of bronze, with its base of bronze, for washing. And you shall put it between the tent of meeting and the altar, and you shall put water in it, with which Aaron and his sons shall wash their hands and their feet. When they go into the tent of meeting, or when they come near the altar to minister, to burn an offering by fire to the Lord, they shall wash with water, lest they die.

They shall wash their hands and their feet, lest they die: it shall be a statute for ever to them, even to him and to his descendants throughout their generations.'" RSV

The God of the universe takes time to explain how to butcher a bull

EXODUS 29:10–14 "And thou shalt cause a bullock to be brought before the tabernacle of the congregation: and Aaron and his sons shall put their hands upon the head of the bullock. And thou shalt **kill the bullock** before the Lord, by the door of the tabernacle of the congregation. And thou shalt take of the blood of the bullock, and put it upon the horns of the altar with thy finger, and pour all the blood beside the bottom of the altar. And thou shalt take all the **fat** that covereth the **inwards**, and the **caul** that is above the **liver**, and the two **kidneys**, and the **fat** that is upon them, and burn them upon the altar. But the flesh of the bullock, and his **skin**, and his **dung**, shalt thou burn with fire without the camp: it is a sin offering." KJV

God picks the general contractors. No competitive bidding

EXODUS 31:1–6 "And the Lord spake unto Moses, saying, See, I have called by name **Bezaleel the son of Uri**, the son of Hur, of the tribe of Judah: And I have filled him with the spirit of God, in wisdom, and in understanding, and in knowledge, and in all manner of workmanship, To devise cunning works, to work in gold, and in silver, and in brass, And in cutting of stones, to set them, and in carving of timber, to work in all manner of workmanship. And I, behold, I have given with him **Aholiab, the son of Ahisamach,** of the tribe of Dan: and in the hearts of all that are wise hearted I have put wisdom, that they may make all that I have commanded thee." KJV

EXODUS 36:1 "Then wrought **Bezaleel** and **Aholiab**, and every wise hearted man, in whom the Lord put wisdom and understanding to know how to work all manner of work for the service of the sanctuary, according to all that **the Lord had commanded**." KJV (*I wonder if Bezaleel paid the Old Testament writers to plug their company. This reads like a promotional brochure for the construction firm.*)

God is not just a control freak; he is a creatively sadistic taskmaster. DEUTERONOMY 28:15–68 presents us with a jumbo menu of exquisitely tasty horrors God has prepared for those who disobey him. The list includes curses, disaster, panic, frustration, pestilence, consumption, fever, inflammation, heat, drought, blight, mildew, dust, boils, ulcers, scurvy, itch, madness, blindness, confusion of mind, abuse, robbery, butchery, worms, cicadas, locusts, aliens, nakedness, cannibalism, diseases, dread, trembling heart, and languishing spirit. (See Chapter 15 for the entire quote.)

Here are a few more examples of God's Type-A micromanagement:

God personally directed troop movements over specific terrain

DEUTERONOMY 2:2–24 "And the Lord spake unto me, saying, Ye have compassed this mountain long enough: **turn you northward**. And command thou the people, saying, Ye are to **pass through the coast** of your brethren the children of Esau, which dwell in Seir. . . . And when we passed by from our brethren the children of Esau, which dwelt in Seir, through the way of the plain from Elath, and from Eziongaber, we turned and passed by the way of the wilderness of Moab. And the Lord said unto me, Distress not the Moabites. . . . Now rise up, said I, and **get you over the brook Zered**. And we went over the brook Zered. . . . The Lord spake unto me, saying, Thou art **to pass over through Ar, the coast of Moab**, this day: And when thou comest nigh over against the children of Ammon, distress them not. . . . Rise ye up, take your journey, and **pass over the river Arnon**." KJV (*How would you like God as your backseat driver?*)

A whole chapter on wet dreams, semen, and menstrual blood

LEVITICUS 15:1–33 "The Lord said to Moses and Aaron, 'Speak to the Israelites and say to them: "When any man has an unusual **bodily discharge**, such a discharge is unclean. Whether it continues flowing from his body or is blocked, it will make him unclean. This is how his **discharge** will bring about uncleanness: Any bed the man with a discharge lies on will be unclean, and anything he sits on will be unclean. Anyone who touches his bed must wash their clothes and bathe with water, and they will be unclean till evening. Whoever sits on anything that the man with a **discharge** sat on must wash their clothes and bathe with water, and they will be unclean till evening. Whoever touches the man who has a **discharge** must wash their clothes and bathe with water, and they will be unclean till evening. If the man with the **discharge** spits on anyone who is clean, they must wash their clothes and bathe with water, and they will be unclean till evening. Everything the man sits on when riding will be unclean. . . . When a man has an **emission of semen**, he must bathe his whole body with water, and he will be unclean till evening. Any clothing or leather that has **semen** on it must be washed with water, and it will be unclean till evening. When a man has **sexual relations** with a woman and there is an **emission of semen**, both of them must bathe with water, and they will be **unclean** till evening. When a woman has her **regular flow of blood**, the impurity of her **monthly period** will last seven days, and anyone who touches her will be unclean till evening. . . . If a man has **sexual relations** with her and her monthly flow touches him, he will be unclean for seven days; any bed he lies on will be unclean. . . . You must keep the Israelites separate from things that make them unclean, so they will not die in their uncleanness for defiling my dwelling place, which is among them. These are the regulations for a man with a **discharge**, for anyone made unclean by an **emission of semen**, for a woman in her **monthly period**, for a man or a woman with a discharge, and for a man who has **sexual relations** with a woman who is ceremonially unclean."'" NIV (*Notice that a woman's period is called an "impurity" [NRSV: "infirmity"].*)

He drew the national borders

DEUTERONOMY 32:8–9 "When the Most High [Elyon] divided to the nations their inheritance, when he separated the sons of Adam, he **set the bounds of the people** according to the number of the children of Israel. For the Lord's portion is his people; Jacob is the lot of his inheritance." KJV (*Here the "Most High" is "Elyon" in the Hebrew, a pre-Israelite name, and shows him dividing the land among his sons. "The Lord" god of Israel was one of the sons of Elyon. This shows that the early Israelites were indeed polytheistic.*)

Don't chisel your altars. It is profanity

EXODUS 20:25 "If you make an altar of stones for me, do not build it with dressed stones, for you will defile it if you use a tool on it." NIV (*This was spoken immediately after the Ten Commandments in Exodus 20, so it must be very important.*)

Don't eat an animal that hasn't been killed

DEUTERONOMY 14:21 "Do not eat anything you find already dead. You may give it to the foreigner residing in any of your towns, and they may eat it, or you may sell it to any other foreigner. But you are a people holy to the Lord your God." NIV

In general, God makes it very clear that he is in total control of everything, including random chance.

God has designs and plans

ISAIAH 14:24 "The Lord Almighty has sworn, 'Surely, as **I have planned**, so it will be, and as I have **purposed**, so it will happen.'" NIV

God does it all, including "evil"

ISAIAH 45:6–7 "That they may know from the rising of the sun, and from the west, that there is none beside me. I am the Lord, and there is none else. I form the light, and create darkness: **I make peace, and create evil: I the Lord do all these things**." KJV (*Some translations have "calamity" or "woe"* *in place of "evil," though that makes little difference. The word is "rah," which means moral evil.)*

It doesn't matter what you think. God will do what he wants

ISAIAH 55:8–11: "For **my thoughts are not your thoughts**, neither are your ways my ways, saith the Lord. For as the heavens are higher than the earth, so are my ways higher than your ways, and my thoughts than your thoughts. For as the rain cometh down, and the snow from heaven, and returneth not thither, but watereth the earth, and maketh it bring forth and bud, that it may give seed to the sower, and bread to the eater: So shall my word be that goeth forth out of my mouth: it shall not return unto me void, but it shall **accomplish that which I please**, and it shall prosper in the thing whereto I sent it." KJV

God controls who lives and who dies, and who becomes rich or poor

1 SAMUEL 2:6–7 "The Lord brings **death** and **makes alive**; he brings down to the grave and raises up. The Lord sends **poverty** and **wealth**; he humbles and he exalts." NIV

JOB 12:10 "**In his hand** is the life of every creature and the breath of all mankind." NIV

God rules over all the nations

2 CHRONICLES 20:6 "O Lord, God of our fathers, art thou not God in heaven? **Dost thou not rule over all the kingdoms of the nations?** In thy hand are power and might, so that none is able to withstand thee." RSV

PSALM 22:28 "For the kingdom is the Lord's: and **he is the governor among the nations**." KJV

PSALM 99:1 "**The Lord reigns**, let the nations tremble; he sits enthroned between the cherubim, let the earth shake." NIV

People are "nothing." God does what he wants

DANIEL 4:35 "All the peoples of the earth are regarded as nothing. **He does as he pleases** with the powers of heaven and the peoples of the earth. No one can hold back his hand or say to him: 'What have you done?'" NIV

Nothing happens by chance. God controls everything

PROVERBS 16:33 "The lot is cast into the lap, but its every decision is from the Lord." NIV

Vindictive

"I will take vengeance, and I will spare no man."
—Isaiah 47:3

One of the reasons Protestants split off from Catholics was the issue of the priesthood. Catholics insist there are human intermediaries between the people and God: a higher class of priests, bishops, archbishops, cardinals, popes, and saints. The Church was charging money for the privilege of going through one of these special people to petition God. It got really bad when they began selling indulgences, which were like "Get out of jail" tickets to buy your way out of hell. The Roman Catholic Church, to this day, maintains the elevated status of "ordained" human beings who inhabit a loftier status of humanity, closer to God.

Martin Luther and other Reformation thinkers challenged this classist hierarchy. They rebelled against the supreme authority of the Church and insisted that each human being has direct access to God. Baptists are one of the groups that adhere to the doctrine of The Priesthood of All Believers.

So it is curious that Protestants do not join me in denouncing the vindictive God of the Old Testament for brutally crushing a similar Reformation attempt while the Israelites were wandering in the wilderness. The squashing (literally) of that rebellion was worse than any torture of the Inquisition. It was unimaginably cruel, and of truly "biblical proportions."

* * *

In the 16th chapter of the book of Numbers (so called because it contains a couple of censuses), we read the story of Korah, a precursor to Martin Luther. Moses was the ordained leader of the Israelites, and all of God's instructions came exclusively through him and his brother Aaron, the high priest. A nice nepotism. God spoke directly to Moses, and Aaron was allowed to approach the Holy of Holies where God was enthroned. Like the crowd that was roped off from Mount Sinai, the common people had to humbly rely on those two intermediaries for guidance and blessings from the deity.

A man named Korah and 250 leaders of the Levite tribe thought that was not right. Why can't God speak to *any* human being? Like Martin Luther addressing the pope and cardinals, Korah said to Moses and Aaron:

> You have gone too far! All the congregation are holy, every one of them, and the Lord is among them. So why then do you exalt yourselves above the assembly of the Lord? (NUMBERS 16:3)

Good question. Why do clergy exalt themselves above the congregation? People who are being led have the natural right to ask: "Who gave *you* the authority?" The rebellious Protestants, who also believed that "all the congregation are holy," asked that very question of the Holy Roman Church.

Moses might have replied, "I respect your honest question, but we are going through tough times right now, times that require a temporary military structure with top-down authority. Please be patient. When we get settled in the Promised Land, we will discuss your well-intentioned concerns." Instead, he fell down on his face and said, "In the morning the Lord will make known who is his, and who is holy, and who will be allowed to approach him. . . . You Levites have gone too far!" (NUMBERS 16:5-7).

God told Moses to tell the Israelites: "Turn away from the tents of these wicked men, and touch nothing of theirs, or you will be swept away for all their sins" (NUMBERS 16:26). Moses, like all autocrats and popes throughout history, labeled his detractors "wicked men." Their honest question was called a "sin."

What happens next needs Hollywood special effects to visualize:

> As soon as he finished speaking all these words, the ground under them was split apart. The earth opened its mouth and swallowed them up, along with their households—everyone who belonged to Korah and all their goods. So they with all that belonged to them went down alive into Sheol; the earth closed over them, and they perished from the midst of the assembly. (NUMBERS 16:28-33)

The earth cracked open and swallowed good, thinking protestants, because "these men have despised the Lord." Talk about vindictive! Korah was not an unbelieving pagan. He and his followers were part of God's chosen people who wanted to be closer to their Lord, just like Luther, Calvin, Zwingli, and Servetus, and just like most believers today who pray directly to God rather than rely on intermediaries. History shows us how the popes tried to "swallow alive" the insubordinate reformers who challenged their supreme authority. But don't blame the Roman Catholic Church. The pope was actually acting more biblically, in a more godly manner, more like Moses than the Protestants. If you want to be God-like, you must be autocratic, cruel, and vindictive.

God of vengeance

PSALM 94:1 "O Lord, the **God of vengeance**, O **God of vengeance**, let your glorious justice shine forth!" NLT

"I will take revenge"

DEUTERONOMY 32:35 "The Lord says, . . . 'I will take **revenge**; I will pay them back. In due time their feet will slip. Their day of disaster will arrive, and their destiny will overtake them.'" NLT

Sword of vengeance

LEVITICUS 26:25 "And I will bring a sword upon you, that shall **execute vengeance** for the covenant; and if you gather within your cities I will send pestilence among you, and you shall be delivered into the hand of the enemy." RSV

Garments of vengeance

ISAIAH 59:17 "He put on righteousness as a breastplate, and a helmet of salvation upon his head; he put on **garments of vengeance** for clothing, and wrapped himself in fury as a mantle." RSV

Payback time for God's enemies

LAMENTATIONS 3:64–66 "**Pay them back what they deserve**, Lord, for what their hands have done. Put a veil over their hearts, and may your curse be on them! Pursue them in anger and destroy them from under the heavens of the Lord." NIV

Payback time for the Amalekites

1 SAMUEL 15:1–2 "One day Samuel said to Saul, 'It was the Lord who told me to anoint you as king of his people, Israel. Now listen to this message from the Lord! This is what the Lord of Heaven's Armies has declared: **I have decided to settle accounts** with the nation of Amalek for opposing Israel when they came from Egypt.'" NLT

Payback time for the Babylonians

PSALM 137:8–9 "O daughter of Babylon, who art to be destroyed; happy shall he be, that **rewardeth thee as thou hast served us**. Happy shall he be, that taketh and dasheth thy little ones against the stones." KJV

Speaking to (female) Babylon

ISAIAH 47:3–4 "Your nakedness shall be uncovered, and your shame shall be seen. **I will take vengeance**, and I will spare no man. Our Redeemer— the Lord of hosts is his name—is the Holy One of Israel." RSV (*"Uncover nakedness" is a euphemism for sexual assault. This means Babylon will be raped.*)

Armed vengeance against the Midianites

NUMBERS 31:3 "And Moses spake unto the people, saying, Arm some of yourselves unto the war, and let them go against the Midianites, and **avenge** the Lord of Midian." KJV

Weapons of vengeance: arrows drunk with blood

DEUTERONOMY 32:41–42 "See now that I, even I, am he, and there is no god beside me. . . . [I]f I whet my glittering sword, and my hand takes hold on judgment, **I will take vengeance** on my adversaries, and will requite those who hate me. I will make my **arrows drunk with blood**, and my sword shall devour flesh—with the blood of the slain and the captives." RSV

Vengeance on enemies

DEUTERONOMY 32:43 "Rejoice, you nations, with his people, for he will **avenge** the blood of his servants; he will take **vengeance** on his enemies and make atonement for his land and people." NIV

"I'll do to them what they did to me"

DEUTERONOMY 32:21 "They have stirred me to jealousy with what is no god; they have provoked me with their idols. **So I will stir them to jealousy** with those who are no people; I will provoke them with a foolish nation." RSV

Decapitating revenge

2 SAMUEL 4:8 "They brought the head of Ish-Bosheth to David at Hebron and said to the king, 'Here is the head of Ish-Bosheth son of Saul, your enemy, who tried to kill you. This day **the Lord has avenged** my lord the king against Saul and his offspring.'" NIV

Don't you dare turn away from God

JOSHUA 22:23 "For building an altar to turn away from following the Lord; or if we did so to offer burnt offerings or cereal offerings or peace offerings on it, may the Lord himself take **vengeance**." RSV

God caused a drought because his temple was in ruins

HAGGAI 1:9–11 "**Because of my house**, which remains a ruin, while each of you is busy with your own house. Therefore, because of you the heavens have withheld their dew and the earth its crops. I called for a drought on the fields and the mountains, on the grain, the new wine, the olive oil and everything else the ground produces, on people and livestock, and on all the labor of your hands." NIV

God's "Day of Vengeance"

ISAIAH 34:8 "For the Lord has a **day of vengeance**, a year of recompense for the cause of Zion." RSV

Vengeance with terrible consequences

ISAIAH 35:4 "Say to those who are of a fearful heart, 'Be strong, fear not! Behold, your God will come with **vengeance**, with the recompense of God. He will come and save you.'" RSV

Day of Vengeance

JEREMIAH 46:10 "That day is the day of the Lord God of hosts, a **day of vengeance**, to avenge himself on his foes. The sword shall devour and be sated, and drink its fill of their blood." RSV

Destructive payback for Babylon

JEREMIAH 50:15 "For this is the **vengeance** of the Lord: take **vengeance** on her, do to her as she has done." RSV

Vengeance for a temple

JEREMIAH 50:28 "Hark! they flee and escape from the land of Babylon, to declare in Zion the **vengeance** of the Lord our God, vengeance for his temple." RSV

Sharpen your arrows!

JEREMIAH 51:11 "Sharpen the arrows! Take up the shields! The Lord has stirred up the spirit of the kings of the Medes, because his purpose concerning Babylon is to destroy it, for that is the **vengeance of the Lord, the vengeance for his temple**." RSV

Blood revenge

EZEKIEL 24:8 "To rouse my wrath, to take **vengeance**, I have set on the bare rock the blood she has shed, that it may not be covered." RSV

Great vengeance on the Philistines

EZEKIEL 25:14–17 "And I will lay my **vengeance** upon Edom by the hand of my people Israel; and they shall do in Edom according to my anger and according to my wrath; and they shall know my **vengeance**, says the Lord God. Thus says the Lord God: Because the Philistines acted revengefully and took vengeance with malice of heart to destroy in never-ending enmity; therefore thus says the Lord God, Behold, I will stretch out my hand against the Philistines, and I will cut off the Cher'ethites, and destroy the rest of the seacoast. I will execute **great vengeance** upon them with wrathful chastisements. Then they will know that I am the Lord, when I lay my **vengeance** upon them." RSV

Multi-national vengeance

MICAH 5:15 "And in anger and wrath I will execute **vengeance** upon the nations that did not obey." RSV

Avenged by an "evil spirit" from God

JUDGES 9:23–24 "But God sent an evil spirit between Abimelech and the lords of Shechem; and the lords of Shechem dealt treacherously with Abimelech. This happened so that the violence done to the seventy sons of Jerubbaal might be **avenged** and their blood be laid on their brother Abimelech." NRSV

Vindictive "suicide bomber" for God

JUDGES 16:28–30 "And Samson called unto the Lord, and said, O Lord God, remember me, I pray thee, and strengthen me, I pray thee, only this once, O God, that I may be at once **avenged** of the Philistines for my two eyes. . . . And he bowed himself with all his might; and the house fell upon the lords, and upon all the people that were therein. So the dead which he slew at his death were more than they which he slew in his life." KJV

Furious vengeance

NAHUM 1:2 "God is jealous, and the Lord **revengeth**; the Lord **revengeth**, and is furious; the Lord will take **vengeance** on his adversaries, and he reserveth wrath for his enemies." KJV

Vicarious vengeance

1 SAMUEL 24:12 "The Lord judge between me and thee, and **the Lord avenge** me of thee: but mine hand shall not be upon thee." KJV

Royal vengeance

2 SAMUEL 18:19, 31 "Then said Ahimaaz the son of Zadok, Let me now run, and bear the king tidings, how that **the Lord hath avenged** him of his enemies. . . . And, behold, Cushi came; and Cushi said, Tidings, my lord the king: for the Lord hath **avenged** thee this day of all them that rose up against thee." KJV

Godly vengeance

2 SAMUEL 22:48 "It is God that **avengeth** me, and that bringeth down the people under me." KJV

7

𝔅loodthirsty

"The Lord has a sword; it is sated with blood."
—Isaiah 34:6

𝔍n the previous chapter, we read about Korah's doomed revolt against the theocratic autocracy of Moses. Personally, I was rooting for Korah's team—maybe because I was raised Protestant—but what can you do when the other team's arsenal includes surgical earthquake strikes?

I think God's response was heavy-handed. But it is not just me. The Israelites who witnessed it first-hand objected to Moses's leadership style:

On the next day, however, the whole congregation of the Israelites rebelled against Moses and against Aaron, saying, "You have killed the people of the Lord." (Numbers 16:41)

That's right, Moses. You killed your own people! Shouldn't we be saving our forces for the heathens we will soon encounter in the Promised Land?

Bad move. You don't wag a finger at a furious warlord who just expended magnum force. It just gives him another chance to show off.

*And when the congregation had assembled against them, Moses and Aaron turned toward the tent of meeting; the cloud had covered it and **the glory of the Lord appeared**. Then Moses and Aaron came to the front of the tent of meeting, and the Lord spoke to Moses, saying, "Get away from this congregation, **so that I may consume them in a moment**." And they fell on their faces. Moses said to Aaron, "Take your censer, put fire on it from the altar and lay*

incense on it, and carry it quickly to the congregation and make atonement
for them. For wrath has gone out from the Lord; the plague has begun." . . .
Those who died by the plague were fourteen thousand seven hundred, *besides*
*those who died in the affair of Korah. (*NUMBERS 16:42–49*)*

Almost 15,000 of God's chosen people were killed by a super-fast virus, simply for voicing disagreement. The U.S. Constitution guarantees the freedom to "petition the government for a redress of grievances," but don't try that against a bloodthirsty God.

"Bloodthirsty" does not mean simply a thirst for blood. It includes a desire to kill or maim by any method: stabbing, stoning, hanging, drowning, burning, famine, plagues, etc. Synonyms include "eager to kill or hurt," "murderous," "homicidal," and "violent."

But we do find buckets of blood splashed over the pages of the Old Testament, and there is a good reason. Blood was the price for atonement. The 17th chapter of Leviticus, which deals with the sacrifice of animals, explains why:

For the life of the flesh is in the blood; and I have given it to you for making
atonement for your lives on the altar; for, as life, **it is the blood that makes**
atonement. *(*LEVITICUS 17:11*)*

The killing of an animal to extract its blood and "get right with God" was a very early Israelite practice. In fact, immediately after the Ten Commandments were recited in EXODUS 20, the first order God gave to his people was: "Kill something."

The Lord said to Moses: Thus you shall say to the Israelites: "You have seen
for yourselves that I spoke with you from heaven. You shall not make gods of
silver alongside me, nor shall you make for yourselves gods of gold. You need
make for me only an altar of earth and **sacrifice on it your burnt offerings**
and your offerings of well-being, **your sheep and your oxen***; in every place*
where I cause my name to be remembered I will come to you and bless you."
*(*EXODUS 20:22–24*)*

God wanted praise, and what better way to get it than by killing? Shedding blood was how "I cause my name to be remembered," he told us. (See also EZEKIEL 38:22–23, below.)

After the Ten Commandments and the mandate to slaughter animals, the next thing the Lord Jealous talked about was how to buy and sell slaves. He then lectured for three more chapters about numerous laws. Finally, when the day of droning pronouncements was over, what was the first thing the people did?

He [Moses] rose early in the morning, and built an altar at the foot of the
mountain, and set up twelve pillars, corresponding to the twelve tribes of

Israel. He sent young men of the people of Israel, who **offered burnt offerings and sacrificed oxen** *as offerings of well-being to the Lord. Moses took half of the blood and put it in basins, and* **half of the blood he dashed against the altar.** *(*EXODUS 24:4–6*)*

After receiving the commandments from the mountain, the people celebrated, but not with a beer party. They threw a blood party.

Compared with God, Dracula was a teetotaler. Here are Old Testament passages that specifically mention blood—mostly human blood.

"Drink the blood"

EZEKIEL 39:17–18 "And, thou son of man, thus saith the Lord God; Speak unto every feathered fowl, and to every beast of the field, Assemble yourselves, and come; gather yourselves on every side to my sacrifice that I do sacrifice for you, even a great sacrifice upon the mountains of Israel, that ye may eat flesh, and **drink blood.** Ye shall eat the flesh of the mighty, and **drink the blood** of the princes of the earth, of rams, of lambs, and of goats, of bullocks, all of them fatlings of Bashan." KJV

His sword is soaked with blood

ISAIAH 34:5–7 "For my sword has drunk its fill in the heavens; behold, it descends for judgment upon Edom, upon the people I have doomed. **The Lord has a sword; it is sated with blood**, it is gorged with fat, with the blood of lambs and goats, with the fat of the kidneys of rams. For the Lord has a sacrifice in Bozrah, a great slaughter in the land of Edom. Wild oxen shall fall with them, and young steers with the mighty bulls. Their land shall be **soaked with blood**, and their soil made rich with fat." RSV

Drunk with blood

JEREMIAH 46:10 "For this is the day of the Lord God of hosts, a day of vengeance, that he may avenge him of his adversaries: and the sword shall devour, and it shall be satiate and made **drunk with their blood.**" KJV

"My arrows are drunk with blood." Praise God!

DEUTERONOMY 32:39–43 "'See now that I myself am he! There is no god besides me. I put to death and I bring to life. . . . **I will make my arrows drunk with blood**, while my sword devours flesh: the **blood** of the slain and the captives, the heads of the enemy leaders.' Rejoice, you nations, with his people, for he will avenge the **blood** of his servants; he will take vengeance on his enemies and make atonement for his land and people." NIV

Mountains soaked with blood

ISAIAH 34:2–3 "The Lord is angry with all nations; his wrath is on all their armies. He will totally destroy them, he will give them over to slaughter. Their slain will be thrown out, their dead bodies will stink; the mountains will be **soaked with their blood**." NIV

God wants YOU to shed blood

JEREMIAH 48:1, 10 "Thus says the Lord of hosts, the God of Israel. . . . Cursed is he who does the work of the Lord with slackness; and cursed is he who **keeps back his sword from bloodshed**." RSV

Blood required at your hand

EZEKIEL 3:16, 20 "And it came to pass at the end of seven days, that the word of the Lord came unto me, saying. . . . Again, When a righteous man doth turn from his righteousness, and commit iniquity, and I lay a stumbling-block before him, he shall die: because thou hast not given him warning, he shall die in his sin, and his righteousness which he hath done shall not be remembered; but **his blood will I require** at thine hand." KJV

Pestilence and blood

EZEKIEL 5:17 "So will I send upon you famine and evil beasts, and they shall bereave thee: and pestilence and **blood** shall pass through thee; and I will bring the sword upon thee. I the Lord have spoken it." KJV

More pestilence and blood

EZEKIEL 14:19 "Or if I send a pestilence into that land, and pour out my wrath upon it with **blood**, to cut off from it man and beast." RSV

Blood upon (female) Jerusalem

EZEKIEL 16:38 "And I will judge you as women who break wedlock and shed blood are judged, and bring upon you the **blood** of wrath and jealousy." RSV

Blood shall pursue you

EZEKIEL 35:6 "Therefore, as I live, saith the Lord God, I will prepare thee unto **blood**, and **blood** shall pursue thee: sith thou hast not hated **blood**, even **blood** shall pursue thee." KJV (*"Sith" meant "since."*)

Drench Egypt with blood

EZEKIEL 32:6 "I will drench the land even to the mountains with your **flowing blood**; and the watercourses will be full of you." RSV

Blood in the streets

EZEKIEL 28:22–23 "Thus saith the Lord God; Behold, I am against thee, O Zidon; and I will be glorified in the midst of thee: and they shall know that I am the Lord, when I shall have executed judgments in her, and shall be sanctified in her. For I will send into her pestilence, and **blood** into her streets; and the wounded shall be judged in the midst of her by the sword upon her on every side; and they shall know that I am the Lord." KJV

Pleading with pestilence and blood

EZEKIEL 38:22–23 "And I will plead against him with pestilence and with **blood**; and I will rain upon him, and upon his bands, and upon the many people that are with him, an overflowing rain, and great hailstones, fire, and brimstone. Thus will I magnify myself, and sanctify myself; and I will be known in the eyes of many nations, and they shall know that I am the Lord." KJV

Blood on a rock

EZEKIEL 24:8 "For this is what the Sovereign Lord says: . . . To stir up wrath and take revenge I put her **blood** on the bare rock, so that it would not be covered." NIV

Blood on the wall

2 KINGS 9:33–37 "'Throw her down!' Jehu said. So they threw her down, and some of her **blood spattered the wall** and the horses as they trampled her underfoot. . . . 'This is the word of the Lord that he spoke through his servant Elijah the Tishbite: On the plot of ground at Jezreel dogs will devour Jezebel's flesh. Jezebel's body will be like dung on the ground in the plot at Jezreel, so that no one will be able to say, "This is Jezebel."'" NIV

Incest blood

LEVITICUS 20:11–12 "The man who lies with his father's wife has uncovered his father's nakedness; both of them shall be put to death, their **blood** is upon them. If a man lies with his daughter-in-law, both of them shall be put to death; they have committed incest, their **blood** is upon them." RSV

Homosexual blood

LEVITICUS 20:13 "If a man also lie with mankind, as he lieth with a woman, both of them have committed an abomination: they shall surely be put to death; their **blood** shall be upon them." KJV

Bestiality blood

LEVITICUS 20:16 "And if a woman approach unto any beast, and lie down thereto, thou shalt kill the woman, and the beast: they shall surely be put to death; their **blood** shall be upon them." KJV

Medium blood

Leviticus 20:27 "A man or a woman who is a medium or a wizard shall be put to death; they shall be stoned with stones, their **blood** shall be upon them." RSV

Children's blood

Leviticus 20:9 "For every one who curses his father or his mother shall be put to death; he has cursed his father or his mother, his **blood** is upon him." RSV

King David's last word, spoken to his son Solomon

1 Kings 2:9 "But now, do not consider him innocent. You are a man of wisdom; you will know what to do to him. Bring his gray head down to the grave in **blood**." NIV

Blood and fire

Joel 2:30 "And I will give portents in the heavens and on the earth, **blood** and fire and columns of smoke." RSV

Blood poured out like dust

Zephaniah 1:17 "I will bring such distress on all people that they will grope about like those who are blind, because they have sinned against the Lord. Their **blood** will be poured out like dust and their entrails like dung." NIV

Blood poured out on the earth

Isaiah 63:6 "I trod down the peoples in my anger, I made them drunk in my wrath, and I **poured out their lifeblood** on the earth." RSV

Other chapters in this book document God's homicidal actions, especially Chapter 4, "Unforgiving"; Chapter 12, "Infanticidal"; and Chapter 13, "Genocidal." Let's look at a few more examples of bloodthirstiness.

Slaughter without mercy

Lamentations 2:17–22 "Lord has done what he planned; he has fulfilled his word, which he decreed long ago. He has overthrown you without pity. . . . Young and old lie together in the dust of the streets; my young men and young women have fallen by the sword. You have slain them in the day of your anger; **you have slaughtered them without pity**. As you summon to a feast day, so you summoned against me terrors on every side. In the day of the Lord's anger no one escaped or survived; those I cared for and reared my enemy has destroyed." NIV

Death for hitting your parents

EXODUS 21:15 "Whoever strikes his father or his mother shall be **put to death**." RSV

Death for prostitution

LEVITICUS 21:9 "If a priest's daughter defiles herself by becoming a prostitute, she disgraces her father; she must be **burned in the fire**." NIV

Death for adultery

LEVITICUS 20:10 "If a man commits adultery with the wife of his neighbor, both the adulterer and the adulteress shall be **put to death**." RSV

Death for disobeying the clergy

DEUTERONOMY 17:12 "Anyone who shows contempt for the judge or for the priest who stands ministering there to the Lord your God is to be **put to death**. You must purge the evil from Israel." NIV

Death to nonbelievers

2 CHRONICLES 15:13 "All who would not seek the Lord, the God of Israel, were to be **put to death**, whether small or great, man or woman." NIV

Death to other religious followers

EXODUS 22:20 "Whoever sacrifices to any god, save to the Lord only, shall be **utterly destroyed**." RSV

Death for blasphemy

LEVITICUS 24:13–16 "Then the Lord said to Moses: 'Take the blasphemer outside the camp. All those who heard him are to lay their hands on his head, and the entire assembly is to **stone him**. Say to the Israelites: "Anyone who curses their God will be held responsible; anyone who blasphemes the name of the Lord is to be **put to death**. The entire assembly must **stone them**. Whether foreigner or native-born, when they blaspheme the Name they are to be **put to death**."'" NIV

Death to false prophets

DEUTERONOMY 18:20 "But the prophet who presumes to speak a word in my name which I have not commanded him to speak, or who speaks in the name of other gods, **that same prophet shall die**." RSV

Death to non-priests who approach the Tabernacle

NUMBERS 1:51 "When the tabernacle is to set out, the Levites shall take it down; and when the tabernacle is to be pitched, the Levites shall set it up. And if any one else comes near, he shall be **put to death**." RSV

Death to any woman who is not a virgin on her wedding night

DEUTERONOMY 22:20–21 "But if the thing is true, that the tokens of virginity were not found in the young woman, then they shall bring out the young woman to the door of her father's house, and the men of her city shall **stone her to death** with stones, because she has wrought folly in Israel by playing the harlot in her father's house; so you shall purge the evil from the midst of you." RSV

Death to children of those hostile to God

LEVITICUS 26:21–22 "If you remain hostile toward me and refuse to listen to me, I will multiply your afflictions seven times over, as your sins deserve. I will send wild animals against you, and they will **rob you of your children**, destroy your cattle and make you so few in number that your roads will be deserted." NIV

Death to a whole town that worships another god

DEUTERONOMY 13:12–16 "If thou shalt hear say in one of thy cities, which the Lord thy God hath given thee to dwell there, saying. . . . Let us go and serve other gods, which ye have not known; Then shalt thou enquire, and make search, and ask diligently; and, behold, if it be truth, and the thing certain, that such abomination is wrought among you; Thou shalt surely **smite the inhabitants of that city with the edge of the sword**, destroying it utterly, and all that is therein, and the cattle thereof, with the edge of the sword. And thou shalt gather all the spoil of it into the midst of the street thereof, and shalt burn with fire the city, and all the spoil thereof every whit, for the Lord thy God." KJV

Death to Babylon

JEREMIAH 50:18–27 "Therefore this is what the Lord Almighty, the God of Israel, says: 'I will punish the king of Babylon and his land. . . . **Pursue, kill and completely destroy them**,' declares the Lord. 'Do everything I have commanded you. The noise of battle is in the land, the noise of great destruction! . . . The Lord has opened his arsenal and brought out the weapons of his wrath, for the Sovereign Lord Almighty has work to do . . . pile her up like heaps of grain. **Completely destroy her** and leave her no remnant. . . . Woe to them! For their day has come, the time for them to be punished.'" NIV

Death to the Assyrians

2 KINGS 19:35 "And that night the angel of the Lord went forth, and slew a hundred and eighty-five thousand in the camp of the Assyrians; and when men arose early in the morning, behold, these were **all dead bodies**." RSV

Queen Esther demanded the slaughter of Persians . . .

ESTHER 9:5–6 "The Jews struck down all their enemies with the sword, **killing and destroying them**, and they did what they pleased to those who hated them. In the citadel of Susa, the Jews killed and destroyed five hundred men." NIV

. . . but she wanted *more* joyful death

ESTHER 9:13–17 "'If it pleases the king,' Esther answered, 'give the Jews in Susa permission to carry out this day's edict tomorrow also, and let Haman's ten sons be impaled on poles.' So the king commanded that this be done. An edict was issued in Susa, and **they impaled the ten sons of Haman**. The Jews in Susa came together on the fourteenth day of the month of Adar, and they **put to death in Susa three hundred men**, but they did not lay their hands on the plunder. Meanwhile, the remainder of the Jews who were in the king's provinces also assembled to protect themselves and get relief from their enemies. **They killed seventy-five thousand** of them but did not lay their hands on the plunder. This happened on the thirteenth day of the month of Adar, and on the fourteenth they rested and made it a day of feasting and joy." NIV (*Since the Book of Esther does not mention God, it might be argued that The Lord Jealous was not responsible for those 76,000 deaths. However, the Jews were God's chosen people in captivity as a punishment for not loving him enough. They included this book in their bible as a positive story of survival and blessing. The Jews greeted the slaughter with "joy," and to this day they celebrate the Festival of Purim commemorating that bloody massacre.*)

Death to the prophets of Baal

1 KINGS 18:39–40 "And when all the people saw it, they fell on their faces; and they said, 'The Lord, he is God; the Lord, he is God.' And Eli'jah said to them, 'Seize the prophets of Ba'al; let not one of them escape.' And they seized them; and Eli'jah brought them down to the brook Kishon, and **killed them there**." RSV

Death in the streets

EZEKIEL 9:4–6 "And the Lord said unto him . . . Go ye after him through the city, and smite: let not your eye spare, neither have ye pity: **Slay utterly old and young, both maids, and little children, and women**: but come not near any man upon whom is the mark." KJV

Death in the mountains, hills, valleys, and waterways

EZEKIEL 35:7–8 "I will make Mount Se'ir a waste and a desolation; and I will cut off from it all who come and go. And **I will fill your mountains with** the slain; on your hills and in your valleys and in all your ravines those slain with the sword shall fall." RSV

Kill your brothers and friends to get a blessing

Exodus 32:27–29 "Thus saith the Lord God of Israel, Put every man his sword by his side, and go in and out from gate to gate throughout the camp, and **slay every man his brother**, and every man his companion, and every man his neighbour. And the children of Levi did according to the word of Moses: and **there fell of the people that day about three thousand men**. For Moses had said, Consecrate yourselves today to the Lord, even every man upon his son, and upon his brother; that he may bestow upon you a blessing this day." KJV

Decapitate those who happen to worship the wrong god

Numbers 25:4–5 "And the Lord said unto Moses, Take all the **heads** of the people, and hang them up before the Lord against the sun, that the fierce anger of the Lord may be turned away from Israel. And Moses said unto the judges of Israel, **Slay ye every one his men** that were joined unto Baalpeor." KJV

Death by thirds

Ezekiel 5:11–16 "Wherefore, as I live, saith the Lord God; Surely, because thou hast defiled my sanctuary with all thy detestable things, and with all thine abominations, therefore will I also diminish thee; neither shall mine eye spare, neither will I have any pity. **A third part of thee shall die with the pestilence**, and with famine shall they be consumed in the midst of thee: and **a third part shall fall by the sword** round about thee; and **I will scatter a third part into all the winds**, and I will draw out a sword after them. . . . I the Lord have spoken it. When I shall send upon them the evil arrows of famine, which shall be for their destruction, and which I will send to destroy you: and I will increase the famine upon you, and will break your staff of bread." KJV

Pacifist killed by a lion

1 Kings 20:35–36 "And a certain man of the sons of the prophets said to his fellow at the command of the Lord, 'Strike me, I pray.' But the man refused to strike him. Then he said to him, 'Because you have not obeyed the voice of the Lord, behold, as soon as you have gone from me, a lion shall kill you.' And as soon as he had departed from him, **a lion met him and killed him**." RSV

God will "tear like a lion"

HOSEA 13:4–9 "But I have been the Lord your God ever since you came out of Egypt. You shall acknowledge no God but me, no Savior except me. I cared for you in the wilderness, in the land of burning heat. When I fed them, they were satisfied; when they were satisfied, they became proud; then they forgot me. So I will be like a lion to them, like a leopard I will lurk by the path. Like a bear robbed of her cubs, **I will attack them and rip them open**; like a lion **I will devour them**—a wild animal **will tear them apart**. You are **destroyed**, Israel, because you are against me, against your helper." NIV

Slaughter a lamb for every sinner

2 CHRONICLES 30:17 "For there were many in the assembly who had not sanctified themselves; therefore the Levites had to **kill the passover lamb** for every one who was not clean, to make it holy to the Lord." RSV

Smashing pep talk to Israel: "You are my battle axe"

JEREMIAH 51:20–23 "Thou art my battle axe and weapons of war: for with thee will I break in pieces the nations, and with thee will **I destroy kingdoms**; And with thee will I break in pieces the horse and his rider; and with thee will I break in pieces the chariot and his rider; With thee also **will I break in pieces man and woman**; and with thee will I **break in pieces** old and young; and with thee will I **break in pieces** the young man and the maid; I will also **break in pieces** with thee the shepherd and his flock; and with thee will I **break in pieces** the husbandman and his yoke of oxen; and with thee will I **break in pieces** captains and rulers." KJV

As promised, here are a few dozen passages dealing with animal sacrifice. You don't need to read them all. Just scan for the word "blood." When you are finished, you can wash your hands.

Bloody animal sacrifice

EXODUS 29:15–16 "Thou shalt also take one ram; and Aaron and his sons shall put their hands upon the head of the ram. And thou shalt slay the ram, and thou shalt take his **blood**, and sprinkle it round about upon the altar." KJV

EXODUS 30:10 "And Aaron shall make an atonement upon the horns of it once in a year with the **blood** of the sin offering of atonements: once in the year shall he make atonement upon it throughout your generations: it is most holy unto the Lord." KJV

Leviticus 1:5 "And he shall kill the bullock before the Lord: and the priests, Aaron's sons, shall bring the **blood**, and **sprinkle the blood** round about upon the altar that is by the door of the tabernacle of the congregation." KJV

Leviticus 1:10–11 "And if his offering be of the flocks, namely, of the sheep, or of the goats, for a burnt sacrifice; he shall bring it a male without blemish. And he shall kill it on the side of the altar northward before the Lord: and the priests, Aaron's sons, shall **sprinkle his blood** round about upon the altar." KJV

Leviticus 1:15 "And the priest shall bring it unto the altar, and wring off his head, and burn it on the altar; and the **blood** thereof shall be wrung out at the side of the altar." KJV

Leviticus 3:2 "And he shall lay his hand upon the head of his offering, and kill it at the door of the tabernacle of the congregation: and Aaron's sons the priests shall **sprinkle the blood** upon the altar round about." KJV

Leviticus 3:8 "And he shall lay his hand upon the head of his offering, and kill it before the tabernacle of the congregation: and Aaron's sons **shall sprinkle the blood** thereof round about upon the altar." KJV

Leviticus 3:13 "And he shall lay his hand upon the head of it, and kill it before the tabernacle of the congregation: and the sons of Aaron shall **sprinkle the blood** thereof upon the altar round about." KJV

Leviticus 4:5 "And the priest that is anointed shall take of the bullock's **blood**, and bring it to the tabernacle of the congregation." KJV

Leviticus 4:7 "And the priest shall put some of the **blood** upon the horns of the altar of sweet incense before the Lord, which is in the tabernacle of the congregation; and shall pour all the **blood** of the bullock at the bottom of the altar of the burnt offering, which is at the door of the tabernacle of the congregation." KJV

Leviticus 4:16–18 "And the priest that is anointed shall bring of the bullock's **blood** to the tabernacle of the congregation: And the priest shall dip his finger in some of the **blood**, and sprinkle it seven times before the Lord, even before the vail. And he shall put some of the **blood** upon the horns of the altar which is before the Lord, that is in the tabernacle of the congregation, and shall pour out all the **blood** at the bottom of the altar of the burnt offering, which is at the door of the tabernacle of the congregation." KJV

LEVITICUS 5:9 "And he shall **sprinkle of the blood** of the sin offering upon the side of the altar; and the rest of the blood shall be wrung out at the bottom of the altar: it is a sin offering." KJV

LEVITICUS 7:14 "And of it he shall offer one out of the whole oblation for an heave offering unto the Lord, and it shall be the priest's that **sprinkleth the blood** of the peace offerings." KJV

LEVITICUS 8:30 "And Moses took of the anointing oil, and of the **blood** which was upon the altar, and sprinkled it upon Aaron, and upon his garments, and upon his sons, and upon his sons' garments with him." KJV

LEVITICUS 9:12 "And he slew the burnt offering; and Aaron's sons presented unto him the **blood**, which he sprinkled round about upon the altar." KJV

LEVITICUS 9:18 "He slew also the bullock and the ram for a sacrifice of peace offerings, which was for the people: and Aaron's sons presented unto him the **blood**, which he sprinkled upon the altar round about." KJV

LEVITICUS 16:27 "And the bullock for the sin offering, and the goat for the sin offering, whose **blood** was brought in to make atonement in the holy place, shall one carry forth without the camp; and they shall burn in the fire their skins, and their flesh, and their dung." KJV

LEVITICUS 17:6 "And the priest shall **sprinkle the blood** upon the altar of the Lord at the door of the tabernacle of the congregation, and burn the fat for a sweet savour unto the Lord." KJV

NUMBERS 18:17 "But the firstling of a cow, or the firstling of a sheep, or the firstling of a goat, thou shalt not redeem; they are holy: thou shalt **sprinkle their blood** upon the altar, and shalt burn their fat for an offering made by fire, for a sweet savour unto the Lord." KJV

2 CHRONICLES 29:22–24 "So they killed the bullocks, and the priests received the **blood**, and sprinkled it on the altar: likewise, when they had killed the rams, they **sprinkled the blood** upon the altar: they killed also the lambs, and they **sprinkled the blood** upon the altar. And they brought forth the he goats for the sin offering before the king and the congregation; and they laid their hands upon them: And the priests killed them, and they made reconciliation with their **blood** upon the altar, to make an atonement for all Israel: for the king commanded that the burnt offering and the sin offering should be made for all Israel." KJV

Fingers dripping with blood

EXODUS 29:10–12 "Then you shall bring the bull before the tent of meeting. Aaron and his sons shall lay their hands upon the head of the bull, and you shall kill the bull before the Lord, at the door of the tent of meeting, and shall take part of the **blood** of the bull and put it upon the horns of the altar with your **finger**, and the rest of the **blood** you shall pour out at the base of the altar." RSV

LEVITICUS 4:6 "And the priest shall dip his **finger in the blood** and sprinkle part of the blood seven times before the Lord in front of the veil of the sanctuary." RSV

LEVITICUS 4:17 "And the priest shall dip his **finger in the blood** and sprinkle it seven times before the Lord in front of the veil." RSV

LEVITICUS 4:25 "Then the priest shall take some of the **blood** of the sin offering with his **finger** and put it on the horns of the altar of burnt offering, and pour out the rest of its **blood** at the base of the altar of burnt offering." RSV

LEVITICUS 4:30 "And the priest shall take some of its **blood** with his **finger** and put it on the horns of the altar of burnt offering, and pour out the rest of its **blood** at the base of the altar." RSV

LEVITICUS 4:34 "Then the priest shall take some of the **blood** of the sin offering with his **finger** and put it on the horns of the altar of burnt offering, and pour out the rest of its **blood** at the base of the altar." RSV

LEVITICUS 8:15 "And Moses killed it, and took the **blood**, and with his **finger** put it on the horns of the altar round about, and purified the altar, and poured out the **blood** at the base of the altar, and consecrated it, to make atonement for it." RSV

LEVITICUS 8:23–24 "And Moses killed it, and took some of its **blood** and put it on the tip of Aaron's right ear and on the **thumb** of his right hand and on the great **toe** of his right foot. And Aaron's sons were brought, and Moses put some of the **blood** on the tips of their right ears and on the **thumbs** of their right hands and on the great **toes** of their right feet; and Moses threw the **blood** upon the altar round about." RSV

LEVITICUS 9:9 "And the sons of Aaron presented the **blood** to him, and he dipped his **finger in the blood** and put it on the horns of the altar, and poured out the **blood** at the base of the altar." RSV

LEVITICUS 14:14 "And the priest shall take some of the **blood** of the trespass offering, and the priest shall put it upon the tip of the right ear of him that is to be cleansed, and upon the **thumb** of his right hand, and upon the great **toe** of his right foot." KJV

LEVITICUS 16:14–15 "And he shall take some of the **blood** of the bull, and sprinkle it with his **finger** on the front of the mercy seat, and before the mercy seat he shall **sprinkle the blood with his finger** seven times. Then he shall kill the goat of the sin offering which is for the people, and bring its

blood within the veil, and do with its **blood** as he did with the **blood** of the bull, sprinkling it upon the mercy seat and before the mercy seat." RSV

LEVITICUS 16:18–19 "Then he shall go out to the altar which is before the Lord and make atonement for it, and shall take some of the **blood** of the bull and of the **blood** of the goat, and put it on the horns of the altar round about. And he shall sprinkle some of the **blood** upon it with his **finger** seven times, and cleanse it and hallow it from the uncleannesses of the people of Israel." RSV

NUMBERS 19:1–5 "Now the Lord said to Moses and to Aaron, '. . . and Elea'zar the priest shall take some of her **blood with his finger**, and sprinkle some of her **blood** toward the front of the tent of meeting seven times. And the heifer shall be burned in his sight; her skin, her flesh, and her **blood**, with her dung, shall be burned.'" RSV

2 CHRONICLES 35:11 "And they killed the passover, and the priests **sprinkled the blood** from their **hands**, and the Levites flayed them." KJV

If the Old Testament had been marketed as a horror story—like a Stephen King novel—we might think differently about it. We applaud King's talent if not the actions of his characters. Those who read his belief-suspending books can appreciate the literary value of that genre. We wink as we wince. We could make allowances for the crude or even camp writing style of the Old Testament authors if we thought their aim was to entertain by shocking. But the real horror story—the one that made Nietzsche say he needed to put on gloves before reading it—is that those writers were not pretending, and neither were the readers. Today, anyone who takes the Old Testament seriously and does not wink or wince at the gratuitous splattering of blood is a troubled person.

Ethnic Cleanser

"You shall drive out all the inhabitants of the land from before you . . .
for I have given you the land to possess."
—NUMBERS 33:52–53

Ethnic cleansing is the systematic ridding from a geographic area of an unwanted ethnic or religious group. The intention is to create a territory inhabited by a "pure" people of a single religion, culture, or ethnicity. Ethnic cleansing usually includes destroying or desecrating temples and altars, sometimes burning or razing buildings, farms, livestock, orchards, and cities. It is a hateful attempt to wipe from the map the memory of the "bad" people, the vermin, the subhumans.

The most brutal way to accomplish ethnic cleansing is by genocide. While ethnic cleansing targets an area to be cleared, genocide targets a group of people to be killed. Genocide is pesticide. In Chapter 13 we will read of the annihilation of entire groups of people committed or commanded by the God of the Old Testament in order to purify the Promised Land and punish Israel's neighbors. That chapter could be incorporated here under Ethnic Cleanser, but this chapter deals mainly with the expulsion of a population from the territory as well as the destruction of their towns, altars, and temples.

This can be accomplished by running off the "savages," as happened with the lucky native Americans who were not massacred but chased off their ancestral land in numerous trails of tears. My own tribe, the Delaware Indians (Lenni Lenape), was forced to make eight migrations, starting in Manhattan (a Lenape word) and New Jersey, before we finally settled in Indian Territory in what is now Oklahoma. This was all because of the doctrine of Manifest Destiny preached by Christian Europeans who admired the God of the Old Testament and pretended that they had also been granted a property on which to build a holy "city on a hill." The conquest of the Americas was no different from the Jews staking out their own Holy Land in the Middle East, a territory that had to be purged of all impurity.

Sometimes the Lord Jealous threatened his own people with ethnic cleansing, and we will see that scare tactic below. If the Israelites do not love their god, he will wipe them out like the heathens.

Saul was the first king of the united kingdom of Israel and Judah. After he was deposed, he was followed by King David. Can you imagine why he was booted out of office? What horrible crime would a king have to commit to be removed from the throne?

King Saul was sacked because he was not a good enough ethnic cleanser. The 15th chapter of the book of 1 Samuel tells the story. The Lord Jealous commanded Saul:

> Go and attack Amalek, and utterly destroy all that they have; do not spare them, but kill both man and woman, child and infant, ox and sheep, camel and donkey. (1 SAMUEL 15:3)

Saul, who loved God, didn't blink at that genocidal order. He dutifully did what he was told:

> Saul defeated the Amalekites, from Havilah as far as Shur, which is east of Egypt. He took King Agag of the Amalekites alive, but utterly destroyed all the people with the edge of the sword. (1 SAMUEL 15:7–8)

He did a praiseworthy job of massacring children and their parents, as well as slaughtering livestock. But he made a small mistake: he kept a few choice animals alive, "the best of the sheep and of the cattle and of the fatlings, and the lambs" (1 SAMUEL 15:9).

Never mind that all the humans were butchered. God became angry with Saul for sparing a few *sheep*.

> I regret that I made Saul king, for he has turned back from following me, and has not carried out my commands. (1 SAMUEL 15:11)

This is curious. The God of The Old Testament usually allowed his people to keep the spoils of war. At times he commanded it, like when he told them to kill all the Midianites, "but all the young girls who have not known a man by sleeping with him, keep alive for yourselves" (NUMBERS 31:18). They could keep virgins as war booty, but not oxen? Either God is inconsistent or he thought the Amalekites were so horribly depraved that even their *animals* were infected. Maybe it was a reverse mad cow disease.

The prophet Samuel, speaking the will of God, said to Saul:

> *Why then did you not obey the voice of the Lord? Why did you swoop down on the spoil, and do what was evil in the sight of the Lord?* (1 SAMUEL 15:19)

Massacring men, women, and children does not raise an eyebrow, but keeping a little war booty is "evil." Notice that throughout the Old Testament, "evil" and "wicked" are not moral judgments. Saul is called "evil" because he disobeyed orders.

"I *have* obeyed the voice of the Lord," Saul protested:

> *I have gone on the mission on which the Lord sent me, I have brought Agag the king of Amalek, and I have utterly destroyed the Amalekites. But from the spoil the people took sheep and cattle, the best of the things devoted to destruction, to sacrifice to the Lord your God in Gilgal.* (1 SAMUEL 15:20–21)

He was going to slaughter those lucky animals *later*, not on the battlefield, but on the altar as a sacrifice to God. Saul knew that the Lord continuously craved the killing of the best animals. He slightly bent the rules because he wanted to honor God, thinking that a tiny discretionary decision would make no difference in the big picture.

That defense did not convince Samuel:

> *Has the Lord as great delight in burnt offerings and sacrifices, as in obedience to the voice of the Lord? Surely, to obey is better than sacrifice. . . . Because you have rejected the word of the Lord, he has also rejected you from being king.* (1 SAMUEL 15:22–23)

Sorry Saul. You were a pretty good ethnic cleanser, but not quite up to godly standards. You were B-plus. It's time to call in the A-team. Samuel had said to Saul:

> *You have done foolishly; you have not kept the commandment of the Lord your God, which he commanded you. The Lord would have established your kingdom over Israel forever, but now your kingdom will not continue; the Lord has sought out a man after his own heart; and the Lord has appointed him to be ruler over his people, because you have not kept what the Lord commanded you.* (1 SAMUEL 13:13–14. *This is repeated in the New Testament in* ACTS 13:22.)

So David, "a man after God's own heart," was made king. He became much more popular because he was literally an order of magnitude more violent:

And the women sang to one another as they made merry, "Saul has killed his thousands, and David his ten thousands." Saul was very angry, for this saying displeased him. (1 SAMUEL 18:7–8)

Needless to say, Saul was not merry with the comparison. David was "a man after God's own heart" because he would ruthlessly carry out his superior's lethal wishes to the letter.

That is why the Jews have a Star of David, not a Star of Saul.

It appears that in order to win favor in the eyes of the God of the Old Testament, you have to be an obedient and heartless ethnic cleanser. Otherwise, step aside.

Notice that in many of these examples of ethnic cleansing it is not just the people but their very memory that is wiped out.

"Blot out their name from their places"
DEUTERONOMY 12:2–3 "You must **demolish completely** all the places where the nations whom you are about to dispossess served their gods, on the mountain heights, on the hills, and under every leafy tree. Break down their altars, smash their pillars, burn their sacred poles with fire, and hew down the idols of their gods, and thus **blot out their name from their places**." RSV

"Blot out their name from under heaven"
DEUTERONOMY 7:21–25 "Do not be terrified by them, for the Lord your God, who is among you, is a great and awesome God. The Lord your **God will drive out those nations** before you, little by little. You will not be allowed to eliminate them all at once, or the wild animals will multiply around you. But the Lord your God will deliver them over to you, throwing them into great confusion **until they are destroyed**. He will give their kings into your hand, and you will **wipe out their names from under heaven**. No one will be able to stand up against you; **you will destroy them**. The images of their gods you are to burn in the fire." NIV

Drive them out of the Promised Land
NUMBERS 33:50–53 "In the plains of Moab by the Jordan at Jericho, the Lord spoke to Moses, saying: Speak to the Israelites, and say to them: When you cross over the Jordan into the land of Canaan, you shall **drive out all the inhabitants** of the land from before you, destroy all their figured stones,

destroy all their cast images, and demolish all their high places. You shall **take possession of the land** and settle in it, for I have given you the land to possess." RSV

"Lord Jealous" will drive them out

EXODUS 34:11–13 "Observe what I command you this day. Behold, **I will drive out before you** the Amorites, the Canaanites, the Hittites, the Per'izzites, the Hivites, and the Jeb'usites. Take heed to yourself, lest you make a covenant with the inhabitants of the land whither you go, lest it become a snare in the midst of you. You shall tear down their altars, and break their pillars, and cut down their Ashe'rim (for you shall worship no other god, for the Lord, whose name is Jealous, is a jealous God)." RSV

"Drive out the inhabitants"

2 CHRONICLES 20:6–7 "Lord, the God of our ancestors, are you not the God who is in heaven? You rule over all the kingdoms of the nations. Power and might are in your hand, and no one can withstand you. Our God, did you not **drive out the inhabitants** of this land before your people Israel and give it forever to the descendants of Abraham your friend?" NIV

He clears away many nations

DEUTERONOMY 7:1–2 "When the Lord your God brings you into the land which you are entering to take possession of it, and **clears away many nations before you**, the Hittites, the Gir'gashites, the Amorites, the Canaanites, the Per'izzites, the Hivites, and the Jeb'usites, seven nations greater and mightier than yourselves, and when the Lord your God gives them over to you, and you defeat them; then you must utterly destroy them; you shall make no covenant with them, and show no mercy to them." RSV

Purify the Promised Land

DEUTERONOMY 7:5–6 "But thus shall you deal with them: you shall **break down their altars**, and **dash in pieces their pillars**, and hew down their Ashe'rim, and burn their graven images with fire. For you are a people holy to the Lord your God; the Lord your God has chosen you to be a people for his own possession, out of all the peoples that are on the face of the earth." RSV

"They shall not live in your land"

EXODUS 23:23–24, 33 "My angel will go ahead of you and bring you into the land of the Amorites, Hittites, Perizzites, Canaanites, Hivites and

Jebusites, **and I will wipe them out**. Do not bow down before their gods or worship them or follow their practices. You must **demolish them** and break their sacred stones to pieces. . . . **Do not let them live in your land** or they will cause you to sin against me, because the worship of their gods will certainly be a snare to you." NIV (*This is another example where "sin" is not an issue of morality but of jealousy.*)

Xenophobic cleansing

NEHEMIAH 13:1–3 "On that day they read from the book of Moses in the hearing of the people; and in it was found written that no Ammonite or Moabite should ever enter the assembly of God; for they did not meet the children of Israel with bread and water, but hired Balaam against them to curse them—yet our God turned the curse into a blessing. When the people heard the law, **they separated from Israel all those of foreign descent**." RSV

Towns destroyed

NUMBERS 21:2–3 "And Israel vowed a vow to the Lord, and said, 'If thou wilt indeed give this people into my hand, then I will **utterly destroy their cities**.' And the Lord hearkened to the voice of Israel, and gave over the Canaanites; and they **utterly destroyed them and their cities**; so the name of the place was called Hormah." RSV (*"Hormah" means "destruction."*)

City burned

JOSHUA 8:28 "So Joshua **burned Ai** and made it a permanent heap of ruins, a desolate place to this day." NIV

None were left

JOSHUA 11:21–22 "And Joshua came at that time, and wiped out the Anakim from the hill country, from Hebron, from Debir, from Anab, and from all the hill country of Judah, and from all the hill country of Israel; Joshua utterly destroyed them with their cities. **There was none of the Anakim left in the land of the people of Israel.**" RSV

Midianite cities burned

NUMBERS 31:9–10 "And the people of Israel took captive the women of Mid'ian and their little ones; and they took as booty all their cattle, their flocks, and all their goods. **All their cities in the places where they dwelt, and all their encampments, they burned with fire**." RSV

Town burned and never rebuilt

DEUTERONOMY 13:12–16 "If you hear in one of your cities, which the Lord your God gives you to dwell there, that certain base fellows have gone out among you and have drawn away the inhabitants of the city, saying, 'Let us go and serve other gods,' which you have not known, then you shall inquire and make search and ask diligently; and behold, if it be true and certain that such an abominable thing has been done among you, you shall surely put the inhabitants of that city to the sword, destroying it utterly, all who are in it and its cattle, with the edge of the sword. You shall gather all its spoil into the midst of its open square, and **burn the city** and all its spoil with fire, as a whole burnt offering to the Lord your God; it shall be a heap for ever, **it shall not be built again**." RSV

Tyre will be scraped bare and never rebuilt

EZEKIEL 26:3–14 "This is what the Sovereign Lord says: I am against you, Tyre, and I will bring many nations against you, like the sea casting up its waves. They will destroy the walls of Tyre and pull down her towers; **I will scrape away her rubble and make her a bare rock**. Out in the sea she will become a place to spread fishnets, for I have spoken, declares the Sovereign Lord. . . . I will put an end to your noisy songs, and the music of your harps will be heard no more. I will make you a bare rock, and you will become a place to spread fishnets. **You will never be rebuilt**, for I the Lord have spoken, declares the Sovereign Lord." NIV (*Tyre still exists, by the way. It is the flourishing fourth-largest city in Lebanon.*)

Cities laid waste

LEVITICUS 26:30–31 "And I will destroy your high places, and cut down your incense altars, and cast your dead bodies upon the dead bodies of your idols; and my soul will abhor you. **And I will lay your cities waste**, and will make your sanctuaries desolate, and I will not smell your pleasing odors." RSV

Villages burned

JEREMIAH 49:2 "Therefore, behold, the days are coming, says the Lord, when I will cause the battle cry to be heard against Rabbah of the Ammonites; it shall become a desolate mound, and **its villages shall be burned with fire**; then Israel shall dispossess those who dispossessed him, says the Lord." RSV

"Throw down their altars"

JUDGES 2:2 "And ye shall make no league with the inhabitants of this land; ye shall **throw down their altars**." KJV

Altars smashed to pieces

2 KINGS 11:17–18 "Jehoiada then made a covenant between the Lord and the king and people that they would be the Lord's people. He also made a

covenant between the king and the people. All the people of the land went to the temple of Baal and tore it down. They **smashed the altars** and idols to pieces and killed Mattan the priest of Baal in front of the altars." NIV (*Repeated in* 2 CHRONICLES 23:17)

Altars removed

2 CHRONICLES 14:2–5 "Asa did what was good and right in the eyes of the Lord his God. **He removed the foreign altars** and the high places, **smashed the sacred stones** and cut down the Asherah poles. He commanded Judah to seek the Lord, the God of their ancestors, and to obey his laws and commands. **He removed the high places and incense altars** in every town in Judah, and the kingdom was at peace under him." NIV

Pull down the pagan shrines

2 CHRONICLES 31:1 "Now when all this was finished, all Israel that were present went out to the cities of Judah, and **brake the images** in pieces, and **cut down the groves**, and **threw down the high places and the altars** out of all Judah and Benjamin, in Ephraim also and Manasseh, until they had utterly destroyed them all." KJV

Corpses among the altars

EZEKIEL 6:13–14 "Then shall ye know that I am the Lord, when their **slain men shall be among their idols round about their altars**, upon every high hill, in all the tops of the mountains, and under every green tree, and under every thick oak, the place where they did offer sweet savour to all their idols. So will I stretch out my hand upon them, and make the land desolate, yea, more desolate than the wilderness toward Diblath, in all their habitations: and they shall know that I am the Lord." KJV

Teenage king purges the land

2 CHRONICLES 34:1–7 "Josiah was eight years old when he began to reign, and he reigned in Jerusalem one and thirty years. And he did that which was right in the sight of the Lord, and walked in the ways of David his father, and declined neither to the right hand, nor to the left. For in the eighth year of his reign, while he was yet young, he began to seek after the God of David his father: and in the twelfth year he began to purge Judah and Jerusalem from the high places, and the groves, and the carved images, and the molten images. And they brake down the altars of Baalim in his presence; and the images, that were on high above them, he cut

down; and the groves, and the carved images, and the molten images, he brake in pieces, and made dust of them, and strowed it upon the graves of them that had sacrificed unto them. And he burnt the bones of the priests upon their altars, and cleansed Judah and Jerusalem. And so did he in the cities of Manasseh, and Ephraim, and Simeon, even unto Naphtali, with their mattocks round about. And when he had broken down the altars and the groves, and had beaten the graven images into powder, and cut down all the idols throughout all the land of Israel, he returned to Jerusalem." KJV

9

Misogynistic

"Your desire shall be for your husband, and he shall rule over you."
—Genesis 3:16

The God of the Old Testament was not 100 percent sexist. Here is one example of true gender equality:

You shall eat the flesh of your sons, and you shall eat the flesh of your daughters. (Leviticus 26:29)

Here is another:

My young women and my young men have fallen by the sword; in the day of your anger you have killed them, slaughtering without mercy. (Lamentations 2:21)

When it comes to being eaten or slaughtered, the God of the Old Testament is egalitarian. Other than that, you are better off being born a male. God himself is male, and so are his angels. The Lord Jealous, like the patriarchal men who created him, needed to control women. He could invent no more demeaning insults than to compare a nation or city to a woman—and, to make the insult even nastier, a menstruating woman. And to really top it off, a "whore."

Monetarily, a woman is worth less than a man in the Old Testament, which is especially obvious when the Israelites are buying and selling slaves at God's command. Like slaves, women are property, a vestige of which remains in the anachronistic question, "Who giveth this woman to be married to this man?" in wedding vows still recited in the 21st century. God allows men to have plural wives, but a woman must be married to only one man. The census counts only males. Ancestry is delineated from father to son. The few women who inherit property (if there is no male heir) must marry a male relative to keep it in their father's family. Only males can be priests and approach the altar, while females must wait outside the door. A woman is more unclean after giving birth to a daughter than to a son. Women, not men, must endure a cruel test for infidelity. A woman's promise can be annulled by her father or husband. And so on.

Why all this scorning of women?

The general answer to that question, of course, is male sexism, which we see historically around the world. But the writers of the bible, who were all men, try to provide a religious justification for their denigration of women, and it goes back to the very beginning. Adam was created first, and his sidekick Eve was responsible for the downfall of the human race. Blame the woman.

When God created the idyllic garden for Adam, the landscaping included some magical trees. God told him, "You may freely eat of every tree of the garden; but of the tree of the knowledge of good and evil you shall not eat, for in the day that you eat of it you shall die" (GENESIS 2:16–17). After Eve was pulled out of Adam's side, she was given the same warning, but being a woman, she decided to think for herself. When the serpent told her that God wants humans to remain ignorant— "God knows that when you eat of it your eyes will be opened"—she was curious. Who wouldn't be? She wanted her eyes opened. Eve was the first uppity woman. She took fruit from the forbidden tree and shared some with Adam, who eagerly participated.

> Then the eyes of both were opened, and they knew that they were naked;
> and they sewed fig leaves together and made loincloths for themselves.
> (GENESIS 3:7)

That was the birth of religion, a shameful covering to hide our true human nature and pretend that we don't know what we know.

The all-knowing God, strolling through the garden for an evening constitutional, sensed that something was wrong:

> They heard the sound of the Lord God walking in the garden at the time
> of the evening breeze, and the man and his wife hid themselves from the
> presence of the Lord God among the trees of the garden. But the Lord God
> called to the man, and said to him, "Where are you?" He said, "I heard the
> sound of you in the garden, and I was afraid, because I was naked; and I hid
> myself." He said, "Who told you that you were naked? Have you eaten from
> the tree of which I commanded you not to eat?" The man said, "The woman
> whom you gave to be with me, she gave me fruit from the tree, and I ate."

Then the Lord God said to the woman, "What is this that you have done?"
The woman said, "The serpent tricked me, and I ate." (GENESIS 3:8–13)

Notice that he interrogates the man first (and never mind that an omniscient God has to ask for information in the first place). After the once-ambulatory serpent was condemned to a legless future, Eve was cursed with labor pains:

I will greatly increase your pangs in childbearing; in pain you shall bring
forth children, yet your desire shall be for your husband, and he shall rule
over you. (GENESIS 3:16)

There it is. That is the source of women's inequality in the Middle East, the Western world, and every country infected with biblical belief. In the New Testament, Paul (or someone pretending to be Paul) pounces on this pretext for patriarchy:

Let a woman learn in silence with full submission. I permit no woman to
teach or to have authority over a man; she is to keep silent. For Adam was
formed first, then Eve; and Adam was not deceived, but the woman was
deceived and became a transgressor. (1 TIMOTHY 2:11–14)

Women are second-class. Because of Eve's insubordination, she was forced to become dependent on a man. From then on, all women are inferior, so the bible says, and it's their own fault.

The man was created first. Woman was made from the man

GENESIS 2:20–23 "And Adam gave names to all cattle, and to the fowl of the air, and to every beast of the field; but for Adam there was not found an help meet for him. And the Lord God caused a deep sleep to fall upon Adam, and he slept: and he took one of his ribs, and closed up the flesh instead thereof; **And the rib, which the Lord God had taken from man, made he a woman,** and brought her unto the man. And Adam said, This is now bone of my bones, and flesh of my flesh: she shall be called Woman, because she was taken out of Man." KJV (*Notice the biological reversal: woman comes out of man instead of the other way around.*)

Men reproduce. Women are rarely mentioned as ancestors

GENESIS 5:1–32 "This is the written account of **Adam's family line** . . . "[who] . . . **had a son** in his own likeness, in his own image; and he named him Seth . . . [who] . . . **became the father of Enosh** . . . [who] . . . **became the father of Kenan** . . . [who] . . . **became the father of Mahalalel** . . . [who] . . . **became the father of Jared** . . . [who] . . . **became the father of Enoch** . . . [who] . . . **became the father of Methuselah** . . . [who] . . . **became** the father of Lamech . . . [who] . . . **had a son**. He named him Noah . . . [who] . . . **became the father of Shem, Ham and Japheth**." NIV

The national poll counted only males

NUMBERS 1:1–2 "The Lord spoke to Moses in the wilderness of Sinai, in the tent of meeting, on the first day of the second month, in the second year after they had come out of the land of Egypt, saying, 'Take a census of all the congregation of the people of Israel, by families, by fathers' houses, according to the number of names, **every male**, head by head.'" RSV

Women don't count

NUMBERS 3:15, 28 "'Number the sons of Levi, by fathers' houses and by families; **every male** from a month old and upward you shall number.' . . . According to the number of **all the males**, from a month old and upward, there were eight thousand six hundred, attending to the duties of the sanctuary." RSV

God's covenant is with men only

GENESIS 17:9–14 "And God said to Abraham, 'As for you, you shall keep my covenant, you and your descendants after you throughout their generations. **This is my covenant**, which you shall keep, between me and you and your descendants after you: **Every male among you shall be circumcised**. . . . So shall my covenant be in your flesh an everlasting covenant. Any uncircumcised male who is not circumcised in the flesh of his foreskin shall be cut off from his people; he has broken my covenant.'" RSV

Men only

EXODUS 23:17 "Three times in the year shall **all your males** appear before the Lord God." RSV (*Repeated in* EXODUS 34:23.)

Females stay outside

EXODUS 38:8 "And he made the laver of bronze and its base of bronze, from the mirrors of the ministering women who ministered at the door of the tent of meeting." RSV

Only males can be priests

LEVITICUS 6:14–18 "These are the regulations for the grain offering: **Aaron's sons** are to bring it before the Lord, in front of the altar. . . . **Aaron and his sons** shall eat the rest of it, but it is to be eaten without yeast in the sanctuary area; they are to eat it in the courtyard of the tent of meeting. . . . **Any male descendant of Aaron** may eat it. For all generations to come it is **his** perpetual share of the food offerings presented to the Lord. Whatever touches them will become holy." NIV

If a priest's daughter sleeps around, burn her

LEVITICUS 21:9 "And the daughter of any priest, if she profanes herself by playing the harlot, profanes her father; **she shall be burned with fire.**" RSV (*What about the sons who sleep around?*)

God has sons, never daughters

GENESIS 6:1–2 "When men began to multiply on the face of the ground, and daughters were born to them, the **sons of God** saw that the daughters of men were fair; and they took to wife such of them as they chose." RSV

Noah's Ark. Female animals are "mates," or property of males

GENESIS 7:2 "Take with you seven pairs of all clean animals, **the male and his mate**; and a pair of the animals that are not clean, **the male and his mate.**" RSV

In the Ten Commandments, wives are considered the property of males

EXODUS 20:17 "Thou shalt not covet thy neighbour's house, thou shalt not covet **thy neighbour's wife,** nor his manservant, nor his maidservant, nor his ox, nor his ass, nor any thing that is thy neighbour's." KJV (*The Commandments are addressed to males. This is repeated in* DEUTERONOMY 5:21.)

Wives are swappable property

JEREMIAH 8:9–10 "Since they have rejected the word of the Lord, what kind of wisdom do they have? Therefore I will **give their wives to other men** and their fields to new owners." NIV

A daughter is property of the father, to be sold as a slave or given as a wife

EXODUS 21:7–9 "**When a man sells his daughter as a slave**, she shall not go out as the male slaves do. If she does not please her master, who has designated her for himself, then he shall let her be redeemed; he shall have no right to sell her to a foreign people, since he has dealt faithlessly with her. If he designates her for his son, he shall deal with her as with a daughter." RSV (*This is in the chapter immediately after the Ten Commandments.*)

Female as property. If a man rapes a single woman, he has to pay her father and marry her

DEUTERONOMY 22:28–29 "If a man meets a virgin who is not betrothed, and seizes her and lies with her, and they are found, then the man who lay with her shall give to the father of the young woman fifty shekels of silver, and **she shall be his wife, because he has violated her;** he may not put her away all his days." RSV (*You broke it, you buy it.*)

A daughter/niece is given as a reward for violence

JUDGES 1:12–13 "And Caleb said, 'He who attacks Kir'iath-se'pher and takes it, I will give him Achsah my daughter as wife.' And Oth'ni-el the son of Kenaz, Caleb's younger brother, took it; and **he gave him Achsah his daughter as wife**." RSV

A woman is acquired in a real estate transaction

RUTH 4:5 "Then Bo'az said, 'The day you buy the field from the hand of Na'omi, **you are also buying Ruth** the Moabitess, the widow of the dead, in order to restore the name of the dead to his inheritance.'" RSV

David purchased his wife with 200 foreskins

1 SAMUEL 18:27 "David arose and went, along with his men, and killed two hundred of the Philistines; and David brought their foreskins, which were given in full number to the king, that he might become the king's son-in-law. And **Saul gave him his daughter Michal for a wife**." RSV

"Do as you please with my virgin daughters"

GENESIS 19:6–8 "Lot went out of the door to the men, shut the door after him, and said, 'I beg you, my brothers, do not act so wickedly. Behold, I have two daughters who have not known man; let me bring them out to you, and **do to them as you please**; only do nothing to these men, for they have come under the shelter of my roof.'" RSV (*Although Lot spoke these words, he was favored by God. There is no biblical condemnation of this horrible act, even from God's angels—both male—who were watching.*)

Kill female witches (not male)

EXODUS 22:18 "Thou shalt not suffer a witch to live." KJV (*The NRSV has "female sorcerers." This one verse has resulted in the deaths of many thousands of women through history.*)

God wants your son, not your daughter

EXODUS 22:29–31 "You shall not delay to offer from the fullness of your harvest and from the outflow of your presses. **The first-born of your sons** you shall give to me. You shall do likewise with your oxen and with your sheep: seven days it shall be with its dam; on the eighth day you shall give it to me. You shall be **men** consecrated to me." RSV

Rulers sacrifice male animals . . .

LEVITICUS 4:22–23 "When a ruler sins, doing unwittingly any one of all the things which the Lord his God has commanded not to be done, and is guilty, if the sin which he has committed is made known to him, he shall bring as his offering a goat, **a male without blemish**." RSV

. . . but commoners sacrifice female animals

LEVITICUS 4:27–28 "If any one of the common people sins unwittingly in doing any one of the things which the Lord has commanded not to be done, and is guilty, when the sin which he has committed is made known to him he shall bring for his offering a goat, **a female without blemish**, for his sin which he has committed." RSV

A mother is doubly "unclean" if she has a daughter

LEVITICUS 12:1–5 "The Lord said to Moses, 'Say to the people of Israel, If a woman conceives, and bears a **male child**, then she shall be **unclean seven days**; as at the time of her menstruation, she shall be unclean. And on the eighth day the flesh of his foreskin shall be circumcised. Then she shall continue for **thirty-three days** in the blood of her purifying; she shall not touch any hallowed thing, nor come into the sanctuary, until the days of her purifying are completed. But if she bears a **female child**, then she shall be **unclean two weeks**, as in her menstruation; and she shall continue in the blood of her purifying for **sixty-six days**.'" RSV

Females have lower monetary value

LEVITICUS 27:1–7 "The Lord said to Moses, 'Say to the people of Israel, When a man makes a special vow of persons to the Lord at your valuation, then your **valuation of a male** from twenty years old up to sixty years old shall be **fifty shekels** of silver, according to the shekel of the sanctuary. If the person is a **female**, your valuation shall be **thirty shekels**. If the person is from five years old up to twenty years old, your valuation shall be for a **male twenty shekels**, and for a **female ten shekels**. If the person is from a month old up to five years old, your valuation shall be for a **male five shekels** of silver, and for a **female** your valuation shall be **three shekels** of silver. And if the person is sixty years old and upward, then your valuation for a **male** shall be **fifteen shekels**, and for a **female ten shekels**.'" RSV (*Notice that the adult female/male ratio was 3/5, the same as the early American Constitutional "Three-Fifths Compromise" over the value of slaves.*)

Menstruation is an "infirmity" requiring a "sin offering"

LEVITICUS 15:19, 29–30 "When a woman has a discharge of blood which is her regular discharge from her body, she shall be in her impurity for seven days, and whoever touches her shall be unclean until the evening. . . . And on the eighth day she shall take two turtledoves or two young pigeons, and bring them to the priest, to the door of the tent of meeting. And the priest shall offer one for a **sin offering** and the other for a burnt offering; and **the priest shall make atonement for her before the Lord for her unclean discharge**." RSV

Wives suspected of infidelity must endure a cruel test

NUMBERS 5:15–31 "Then the man shall bring his wife to the priest, and bring the offering required of her . . . a cereal offering of remembrance, bringing iniquity to remembrance. And the priest shall bring her near, and set her before the Lord; and the priest shall take holy water in an earthen vessel, and take some of the dust that is on the floor of the tabernacle and put it into the water. And the priest shall set the woman before the Lord, and unbind the hair of the woman's head. . . . And when he has made her drink the water, then, if she has defiled herself and has acted unfaithfully against her husband, **the water that brings the curse shall enter into her and cause bitter pain**, and her body shall swell, and her thigh shall fall away, and the woman shall become an execration among her people. But if the woman has not defiled herself and is clean, then she shall be free and shall conceive children. This is the law in cases of jealousy. **The man shall be free from iniquity, but the woman shall bear her iniquity.**" RSV (*Philandering husbands endure no such test.*)

Inheritance goes through male relatives, unless a daughter is the only survivor . . .

NUMBERS 27:8–11 "If a man dies, and has no son, then you shall cause his inheritance to pass to his daughter. And if he has no daughter, then you shall give his inheritance to his brothers. And if he has no brothers, then you shall give his inheritance to his father's brothers. And if his father has no brothers, then you shall give his inheritance to his kinsman that is next to him of his family, and he shall possess it. And it shall be to the people of Israel a statute and ordinance, as the Lord commanded Moses." RSV (*Notice that the mother/wife has no say in the matter. This is about male property. See also* DEUTERONOMY 21:16—*inheritance through sons, not daughters.*)

. . . but the daughter can only pass her inheritance on to males

NUMBERS 36:8–12 [Moses speaking] "'And every daughter who possesses an inheritance in any tribe of the people of Israel shall be wife to one of the family of the tribe of her father, so that every one of the people of Israel may possess **the inheritance of his fathers**. So no inheritance shall be transferred from one tribe to another; for each of the tribes of the people of Israel shall cleave to its own inheritance.' The daughters of Zelo'phehad did as the Lord commanded Moses; for Mahlah, Tirzah, Hoglah, Milcah, and Noah, the daughters of Zelo'phehad, were married to sons of their father's brothers. They were married into the families of the sons of Manas'seh the son of Joseph, and **their inheritance remained in the tribe of the family of their father**." RSV

God allows polygamy, for men only

GENESIS 4:19 "And Lamech took **two wives**; the name of the one was Adah, and the name of the other Zillah." RSV

More polygamy

GENESIS 26:34 "When Esau was forty years old, he took to wife Judith the daughter of Be-e'ri the Hittite, and Bas'emath the daughter of Elon the Hittite." RSV

GENESIS 28:9 "Esau went to Ish'mael and took to wife, **besides the wives he had**, Ma'halath the daughter of Ish'mael Abraham's son, the sister of Neba'ioth." RSV

Gideon had many wives and a mistress

JUDGES 8:30–31 "Now Gideon had seventy sons, his own offspring, for he had **many wives**. And his **concubine** who was in Shechem also bore him a son, and he called his name Abim'elech." RSV (*Remember this next time you see a "family values" Gideon Bible in your hotel room.*)

God murdered a husband in order to increase David's harem . . .

1 SAMUEL 25:2–44 "A certain man in Maon, who had property there at Carmel, was very wealthy. . . . His name was Nabal and his wife's name was Abigail. She was an intelligent and beautiful woman, but her husband was surly and mean in his dealings—he was a Calebite. . . . David said to his men, 'Each of you strap on your sword!' . . . About ten days later, **the Lord struck Nabal and he died. . . . Then David sent word to Abigail, asking her to become his wife. . . .** Abigail quickly got on a donkey and, attended by her five female servants, went with David's messengers and became his wife. David had also married Ahinoam of Jezreel, and they both were his wives. But Saul had given his daughter Michal, David's wife, to Paltiel son of Laish, who was from Gallim." NIV

. . . but he needed more . . .

2 SAMUEL 5:13 "After he left Hebron, David took **more concubines and wives** in Jerusalem, and more sons and daughters were born to him." NIV

. . . then David's wives were taken and raped outdoors, to punish him

2 SAMUEL 12:11 "This is what the Lord says: 'Out of your own household I am going to bring calamity on you. Before your very eyes **I will take your wives** and give them to one who is close to you, and **he will sleep with your wives** in broad daylight.'" NIV

David's son raped his mistresses . . .

2 SAMUEL 16:21–22 "Ahithophel answered, 'Sleep with your father's concubines whom he left to take care of the palace. Then all Israel will hear that you have made yourself obnoxious to your father, and the hands of everyone with you will be more resolute.' So they pitched a tent for Absalom on the roof, and **he slept with his father's concubines in the sight of all Israel**." NIV

. . . then David punished the mistresses by locking them up forever

2 SAMUEL 20:3 "And David came to his house at Jerusalem; and the king took the ten concubines whom he had left to care for the house, and put them in a house under guard, and provided for them, but did not go in to them. So **they were shut up until the day of their death**, living as if in widowhood." RSV

Men can make vows, but a woman's vow can be annulled by her father or husband

NUMBERS 30:1–8, 16 "This is what the Lord commands: When a man makes a vow to the Lord or takes an oath to obligate himself by a pledge, he must not break his word but must do everything he said. When a young woman still living in her father's household makes a vow to the Lord or obligates herself by a pledge and . . . her father forbids her when he hears about it, **none of her vows or the pledges by which she obligated herself will stand**; the Lord will release her because her father has forbidden her. If she marries after she makes a vow or after her lips utter a rash promise by which she obligates herself and . . . her husband forbids her when he hears about it, **he nullifies the vow that obligates her.** . . . These are the regulations the Lord gave Moses concerning relationships between a man and his wife, and between a father and his young daughter still living at home." NIV

Your firstborn son is favored in the will, even if he is from a hated wife

DEUTERONOMY 21:15–17 "If a man has two wives, the one loved and the other disliked, and they have borne him children, both the loved and the disliked, and if the first-born son is hers that is disliked, then on the day when he assigns his possessions as an inheritance to his sons, he may not treat the son of the loved as the first-born in preference to the son of the disliked, who is the first-born, but he shall acknowledge the first-born, the son of the disliked, by giving him a double portion of all that he has, **for he is the first issue of his strength**; the right of the first-born is his." RSV

A woman who is not a virgin on her wedding night shall be stoned to death

DEUTERONOMY 22:20–21 "But if the thing is true, that the tokens of virginity were not found in the young woman, then they shall bring out the young woman to the door of her father's house, and **the men of her city shall stone her to death** with stones, because she has wrought folly in Israel by playing the harlot in her father's house; so you shall purge the evil from the midst of you." RSV (*Damaged property must be discarded.*)

A man can simply divorce his wife if he doesn't like her . . .

DEUTERONOMY 24:1 "When a man takes a wife and marries her, if then she finds no favor in his eyes because he has found some indecency in her, and he writes her a bill of divorce and puts it in her hand and **sends her out of his house** . . ." RSV

. . . but they can't be remarried. She is defiled and abhorrent

DEUTERONOMY 24:1–4 ". . . she departs out of his house, and if she goes and becomes another man's wife, and the latter husband dislikes her and writes her a bill of divorce and puts it in her hand and sends her out of his house, or if the latter husband dies, who took her to be his wife, then her former husband, who sent her away, **may not take her again to be his wife, after she has been defiled**; for that is an abomination before the Lord, and you shall not bring guilt upon the land which the Lord your God gives you for an inheritance." RSV

A woman has to marry her dead husband's brother

DEUTERONOMY 25:5–6 "If brothers dwell together, and one of them dies and has no son, the wife of the dead shall not be married outside the family to a stranger; **her husband's brother shall go in to her**, and take her as his wife, and perform the duty of a husband's brother to her. And the first son whom she bears shall succeed to the name of his brother who is dead, that his name may not be blotted out of Israel." RSV (*This is all about patriarchy and inheritance, not love or family values.*)

God killed a man who did not impregnate his brother's wife

GENESIS 38:8–10 "Then Judah said to Onan, 'Go in to your brother's wife, and perform the duty of a brother-in-law to her, and raise up offspring for your brother.' But Onan knew that the offspring would not be his; so when he went in to his brother's wife **he spilled the semen on the ground**, lest he should give offspring to his brother. And what he did was displeasing in the sight of the Lord, and **he slew him also**." RSV (*This is the origin of the word "onanism."*)

Virgins were considered war booty

NUMBERS 31:17–18 "Now therefore, kill every male among the little ones, and kill every woman who has known man by lying with him. But **all the young girls** who have not known man by lying with him, **keep alive for yourselves**." RSV

Virgins were last in the list of war booty

NUMBERS 31:25–35 "And the Lord spake unto Moses, saying, Take the sum of the prey that was taken, both of man and of beast. . . . And Moses and Eleazar the priest did as the Lord commanded Moses. And the booty, being the rest of the prey which the men of war had caught, was six hundred thousand and seventy thousand and five thousand sheep, And threescore and twelve thousand beeves, And threescore and one thousand asses, And thirty and two thousand persons in all, of women that had not known man by lying with him." KJV

Take one or two girls as war booty

JUDGES 5:30 "Have they not divided the prey; **to every man a damsel or two**?" KJV (*This is part of a hymn of praise to God.*)

Murderous raiding party to abduct wives for one of the tribes of Israel . . .

JUDGES 21:10–14 "And the congregation sent thither twelve thousand men of the valiantest, and commanded them, saying, Go and smite the inhabitants of Jabeshgilead with the edge of the sword, with the women and the children. And this is the thing that ye shall do, Ye shall utterly destroy every male, and every woman that hath lain by man. And they found among the inhabitants of Jabeshgilead **four hundred young virgins**, that had known no man by lying with any male: and they brought them unto the camp to Shiloh, which is in the land of Canaan. . . . And Benjamin came again at that time; and **they gave them wives** which they had saved alive of the women of Jabeshgilead. . . ." KJV

. . . but there weren't enough women, so they grabbed some dancers

JUDGES 21:14–23 ". . . and yet so they sufficed them not. . . . Therefore they commanded the children of Benjamin, saying, Go and lie in wait in the vineyards; And see, and, behold, if the daughters of Shiloh come out to dance in dances, then come ye out of the vineyards, and **catch you every man his wife** of the daughters of Shiloh, and go to the land of Benjamin. . . . And the children of Benjamin did so, and **took them wives**, according to their number, of them that danced, whom they caught: and they went and returned unto their inheritance, and repaired the cities, and dwelt in them." KJV

You can have sex with a captured slave (whom you orphaned), but if the sex is bad, you can't sell her

DEUTERONOMY 21:10–14 "When thou goest forth to war against thine enemies, and the Lord thy God hath delivered them into thine hands, and thou hast taken them captive, And seest among the captives a beautiful woman, and hast a desire unto her, that thou wouldest have her to thy wife; Then thou shalt bring her home to thine house, and she shall shave her head, and pare her nails; And she shall put the raiment of her captivity from off her, and shall remain in thine house, and bewail her father and her mother a full month: and after that thou shalt go in unto her, and be her husband, and she shall be thy wife. And it shall be, **if thou have no delight in her, then thou shalt let her go whither she will; but thou shalt not sell her at all for money**, thou shalt not make merchandise of her, because thou hast humbled her." KJV (*Used sex slaves are worthless.*)

Cut off a woman's hand if she touches the penis of her husband's enemy

DEUTERONOMY 25:11–12 "If two men are fighting and the wife of one of them comes to rescue her husband from his assailant, and she reaches out and seizes him by his private parts, you shall **cut off her hand. Show her no pity**." NIV

Woman is intrinsically unclean

JOB 14:1–4 [Job speaking] "Man that is born of a woman is of few days and full of trouble. He cometh forth like a flower, and is cut down: he fleeth also as a shadow, and continueth not. And doth thou open thine eyes upon such an one, and bringest me into judgment with thee? **Who can bring a clean thing out of an unclean?** not one." KJV

JOB 15:14 [Eliphaz speaking] "What is man, that he should be clean? and **he which is born of a woman**, that he should be righteous?" KJV

JOB 25:4 [Bildad speaking] "How then can man be justified with God? or how can he be clean that is **born of a woman**?" KJV (*Perhaps these verses can't be attributed directly to God. However, they were spoken as if they were the truth, in a book supposedly inspired by God.*)

Sex with a woman is "unholy"

1 SAMUEL 21:4–5 "And the priest answered David, and said, There is no common bread under mine hand, but there is hallowed bread; **if the young men have kept themselves at least from women**. And David answered the priest, and said unto him, **Of a truth women have been kept from us** about these three days, since I came out, and the vessels of the young men are

holy, and the bread is in a manner common, yea, though it were sanctified this day in the vessel." KJV

A woman who seduces a male is considered evil

Proverbs 7:27 "Her house is the way to hell, going down to the chambers of death." KJV (*See* Proverbs 7:6–26 *for the whole story.*)

Haughty women will be sexually assaulted by the Lord

Isaiah 3:16–17 "Moreover Adonai [Lord] says: 'Because Tziyon's [Zion] women are so proud, walking with their heads in the air and throwing seductive glances, moving with mincing steps and jingling their anklets— Adonai will strike the crown of the heads of Tziyon's women with sores, and **Adonai will expose their private parts**.'" CJB (*See Chapter 17 for more on this verse.*)

Rape as punishment for disobedience

Jeremiah 13:22, 26 "And if you ask yourself, 'Why have these things happened to me?' it is because of your many sins that your skirts are pulled up and **you have been violated**. . . . **I myself will lift your skirts** above your face, and your privates will be exposed." CJB (*See Chapter 17 for more on this verse.*)

Woman compared to a pig's snout

Proverbs 11:22 "As a jewel of gold in a swine's snout, so is a fair woman which is without discretion." KJV (*What about a handsome **man** without discretion?*)

Women rule over the wicked

Isaiah 3:11–12 "Woe unto the wicked! it shall be ill with him: for the reward of his hands shall be given him. As for my people, children are their oppressors, and **women rule over them**. O my people, they which lead thee cause thee to err, and destroy the way of thy paths." KJV

It is a sign of weakness to be like women

Isaiah 19:16 "In that day shall Egypt be **like unto women**: and it shall be afraid and fear because of the shaking of the hand of the Lord of hosts, which he shaketh over it." KJV (*While the Hebrew word here is "women"— "nashim"—the NIV changes it to "weaklings."*)

Defeated warriors are called "women"

Jeremiah 51:30 "The mighty men of Babylon have forborn to fight, they have remained in their holds: their might hath failed; **they became as women**: they have burned her dwelling places; her bars are broken." KJV

Defeated troops are called "women"

NAHUM 3:13 "Look at your troops! **They behave like women!** Your country's gates are wide open to your foes; fire has consumed their bars." CJB

Egypt will tremble with fear, like women

ISAIAH 19:16 "In that day shall Egypt be **like unto women**: and it shall be afraid and fear because of the shaking of the hand of the Lord of hosts, which he shaketh over it." KJV

Straying Israel compared to a whore

JEREMIAH 3:1, 20 "If a man divorces his wife and she goes from him and becomes another man's wife, will he return to her? Would not that land be greatly polluted? **You have played the harlot** (NRSV: "whore") with many lovers; and would you return to me? says the Lord. . . . Surely, as a **faithless wife** leaves her husband, so have you been faithless to me, O house of Israel, says the Lord." RSV (*Why not compare Israel to an unfaithful husband?*)

Evil Israel compared to a menstruating woman

EZEKIEL 36:16–17 "Again the word of the Lord came to me: 'Son of man, when the people of Israel were living in their own land, they defiled it by their conduct and their actions. Their conduct was **like a woman's monthly uncleanness** in my sight.'" NIV

Faithless Jerusalem compared to a whore

EZEKIEL 16:15 "But thou didst trust in thine own beauty, and playedst the **harlot** (NRSV: "whore") because of thy renown, and pouredst out thy fornications on every one that passed by." KJV (*Read the entire 16th chapter of Ezekiel to see the whoredom card piled on.*)

Jerusalem judged as an adulterous woman

EZEKIEL 16:38–40 "I will sentence you to the punishment of **women who commit adultery** and who shed blood; I will bring on you the blood vengeance of my wrath and jealous anger. Then I will deliver you into the hands of your lovers, and they will tear down your mounds and destroy your lofty shrines. **They will strip you of your clothes** and take your fine jewelry and **leave you stark naked**. They will bring a mob against you, who will stone you and **hack you to pieces** with their swords." NIV (*Why not say, "I will sentence you as men who commit adultery"?*)

Errant Israel compared to a whore whose breasts must be torn off

EZEKIEL 23:28–34 "For this is what the Sovereign Lord says: I am about to deliver you into the hands of those you hate. . . . They will leave you **stark**

naked, and the **shame of your prostitution will be exposed** . . . and you will **tear your breasts**. I have spoken, declares the Sovereign Lord." NIV

Jerusalem's filthiness was "in her skirts"

LAMENTATIONS 1:8–9 "Jerusalem hath grievously sinned; therefore she is removed: all that honored her despise her, because they have seen her nakedness: yea, she sigheth, and turneth backward. **Her filthiness is in her skirts**; she remembereth not her last end; therefore she came down wonderfully: she had no comforter." KJV

Israel is a whore and a prostitute

HOSEA 9:1 "Rejoice not, O Israel! Exult not like the peoples; for you have **played the harlot**, forsaking your God. You have loved a **harlot's hire** upon all threshing floors." RSV

Ninevah compared to a prostitute

NAHUM 3:4–6 "And all for the countless **harlotries of the harlot**, graceful and of deadly charms, who **betrays nations with her harlotries**, and peoples with her charms. Behold, I am against you, says the Lord of hosts, and **will lift up your skirts over your face**; and I will let **nations look on your nakedness** and kingdoms on your shame. I will throw filth at you and treat you with contempt, and make you a gazingstock." RSV

Samaria and Jerusalem are compared to two sexually loose sisters, who are mutilated

EZEKIEL 23:1–49 "The word of the Lord came to me: 'Son of man, there were two women, daughters of the same mother. They became **prostitutes** in Egypt, **engaging in prostitution** from their youth. In that land their breasts were fondled and their virgin bosoms caressed. . . . Oholah is Samaria, and Oholibah is Jerusalem. Oholah engaged in **prostitution** while she was still mine. . . . Therefore I delivered her into the hands of her lovers, the Assyrians, for whom she lusted. **They stripped her naked.** . . . Her sister Oholibah saw this, yet in **her lust and prostitution** she was more depraved than her sister. . . . Therefore, Oholibah, this is what the Sovereign Lord says: I will stir up your lovers against you, those you turned away from in disgust. . . . **They will cut off your noses and your ears**, and those of you who are left will fall by the sword. . . . They will also **strip you of your clothes** and take your fine jewelry. . . . They will leave you **stark naked**, and the **shame of your prostitution** will be exposed. . . . Therefore this is what the Sovereign Lord says: Since you have forgotten me and turned your back on me, you must bear the consequences of your **lewdness and prostitution**. . . .

The mob will stone them and cut them down with their swords; they will kill their sons and daughters and burn down their houses. So I will put an end to lewdness in the land, **that all women may take warning** and not imitate you. . . . Then you will know that I am the Sovereign Lord." NIV

When Elizabeth Cady Stanton said that "The Bible and the Church have been the greatest stumbling blocks in the way of women's emancipation," she was obviously referring to the misogynistic God of the Old Testament.

Homophobic

"You shall not lie with a male as with a woman; it is an abomination."
—LEVITICUS 18:22

One of the reasons we know the God of the Old Testament is a fictional character is because some of the stories about him are overly contrived and fantastic. There can hardly be a more fabricated tale than the story of Sodom in Genesis 19.

Sodom and Gomorrah were described as large cities. They had kings. If they had actually existed and had been destroyed by "fire and brimstone" from the sky, archaeologists should have found good evidence by now. Why did the Old Testament writers invent such a weird fable about those towns?

The story of Sodom is actually Part Two of a three-part saga, and to see the plot in context, we have to zoom the camera out a half-day's walk from the city. Backing up to the 18th chapter of Genesis, Part One begins with the implausible account of Abraham physically meeting God face-to-face. (Let's ignore the fact that God said "you cannot see my face; for no one shall see me and live," EXODUS 33:20.) Abraham and his wife Sarah were very old, well past childbearing age. Sarah was in the tent that day and Abraham was cooling off in the shade of some trees when he looked up and saw three men standing near him. He immediately recognized one of them as "the Lord." The other two were angels. He brought some food to the men, and as they were eating God casually remarked, "I'll be back later, and your wife will conceive a son." Great lunch conversation.

Sarah overheard this and laughed: "After I have grown old, and my husband is old, shall I have pleasure? . . . Shall I indeed bear a child, now that I am old?" (GENESIS 18:12–13).

God rebuked her: "Is anything too wonderful for the Lord? At the set time I will return to you, in due season, and Sarah shall have a son" (GENESIS 18:14).

A very old woman having a son is as unlikely as a virgin birth. It is certainly "wonderful" (translate: "miracle") if you can get a female pregnant outside of her time of sexual activity. The Lord announced that he was going to establish an entire godly nation through Sarah and Abraham's offspring. Right there, that was the birth of the three Abrahamic religions: Judaism, Christianity, and Islam (after Abraham jumped the gun and had sex with his wife's handmaid to produce Ishmael, the putative father of the Arabs and eventually Muslims).

But creating three major world faiths was not the main purpose of their trip. God and the angels were actually heading toward the city of Sodom on a scouting mission to see if the place was as "wicked" as God had heard: "How great is the outcry against Sodom and Gomorrah and how very grave their sin! I must go down and see whether they have done altogether according to the outcry that has come to me; and if not, I will know" (GENESIS 18:20–21).

The writer does not explain why the omniscient Lord would not have known this fact in the first place.

Tramping the dusty roads like ordinary hikers, the angel-men headed out for Sin City. God hung back a bit, giving the worried Abraham a chance to confront him about the apparent lack of justice in destroying an entire population. He knew that his nephew Lot and family were currently living in Sodom. "Shall not the Judge of all the earth do what is just?" he asked. Good question. The inhabitants of Sodom couldn't *all* be bad! God relented and promised to spare the city if they found fifty good people in town. Abraham bravely pressed further, and eventually haggled God down to ten.

Moving to Part Two, the next chapter, the angels arrived at Sodom around evening, tired and hungry. At the gate of the city, they conveniently spotted Lot, who invited them into his house for supper. Angels need to eat. So their first experience with the town was very nice. Maybe it was not such a bad place after all.

But before they went to bed—yes, angels need to sleep—things got weird. The men of Sodom, all of them, young and old, surrounded the house and yelled to Lot: "Where are the men who came to you tonight? Bring them out to us, so that we may know them" (GENESIS 19:5).

Lot stepped outside, shut the door behind him, and said, "I beg you, my brothers, do not act so wickedly" (GENESIS 19:7).

Why did he say that? What was their wickedness? What did they mean when they demanded to "know" the two men? Was it curiosity? Municipal hospitality?

Lot knew exactly what the mob wanted. In the Old Testament, the word "know" was used for sexual intercourse, such as "Adam knew his wife again, and she bore a son" (GENESIS 4:25). The male inhabitants of Sodom were demanding to have sex with the two exotic handsome men (can angels be anything less than gorgeous?) whom they must have ogled while they were heading to his house. What Lot said next is truly shocking, and it shows that he indeed understood what "know" meant: "Look, I have two daughters who have not known a man; let me bring them out to you, and do to them as you please; only do nothing to these men, for they have come under the shelter of my roof" (GENESIS 19:7–8).

Rape my virgin daughters, not my guests. That was genuine hospitality.

But the libidinous gang didn't want the girls. "Stand back," they shouted as they tried to break down the door. The angels must have been listening from the inside. Angels are not omniscient. Before the crowd could storm into the house, the angels "reached out their hands and brought Lot into the house with them, and shut the door. And they struck with blindness the men who were at the door of the house, both small and great, so that they were unable to find the door" (GENESIS 19:10–11).

The threat was neutralized by a miracle, praise God.

But what were the girls thinking? After hearing what their father had said, they might be forgiven if they had screamed: "Throw Dad back out there!" Lot, described as a good and righteous man, had offered his young daughters to be gang-raped. This is evidence that goodness and wickedness in the bible have nothing to do with morality.

The angels had all the proof they needed. Sodom (not Lot) was wicked and doomed. They told Lot to quickly pack and get out of town, "for we are about to destroy this place, because the outcry against its people has become great before the Lord, and the Lord has sent us to destroy it." The fiancés of Lot's daughters didn't want to leave, so the next morning the angels grabbed Lot and his small family (fewer than ten people) by the hand and said: "Flee for your life; do not look back or stop anywhere in the Plain; flee to the hills, or else you will be consumed" (GENESIS 19:17).

Like the climactic explosive scene in an action movie, they rushed out of Sodom with the blazing spectacle erupting behind them: "Then the Lord rained on Sodom and Gomorrah sulfur and fire from the Lord out of heaven; and he overthrew those cities, and all the Plain, and all the inhabitants of the cities, and what grew on the ground" (GENESIS 19:24).

The writers don't tell us why the city of Gomorrah was punished for the inhospitality of its neighbor. Lot's wife, being a silly woman, couldn't resist a glance back at the life she was leaving, "and she became a pillar of salt."

Pan back to Abraham, who is watching all this from a distance: "Abraham went early in the morning to the place where he had stood before the Lord; and he looked down toward Sodom and Gomorrah and toward all the land of the Plain and saw the smoke of the land going up like the smoke of a furnace" (GENESIS 19:27–28).

He should have argued the God of justice down to four. Can the story get any more outrageous? Keep reading.

*　*　*

The saga continues with Part Three. Lot had no sons, remember. Now that his prospective sons-in-law were blinded and roasted and his wife had become a geological feature, how would he have any heirs? After the three survivors escaped to the mountains, the daughters—the same girls who had been offered to be raped—came up with a plan to help their desperate dad. The oldest girl said, "Our father is old, and there is not a man on earth to come in to us after the manner of all the world. Come, let us make our father drink wine, and we will lie with him, so that we may preserve offspring through our father" (GENESIS 19:31–32).

After experiencing such epic trauma, the destruction of her home, the death of her mother and the burning of her fiancé, is there any woman in the world whose first concern would be that her dad has no heirs? This tale was clearly written by men.

Amazingly, the daughters carried out their incestuous plan. The older sister "went in and lay with her father." Lot was too smashed to know about it. The next morning, she said to her little sister, "Look, I lay last night with my father; let us make him drink wine tonight also; then you go in and lie with him, so that we may preserve offspring through our father" (GENESIS 19:34).

So the little sister did the same thing, with Lot none the wiser. "Thus both the daughters of Lot became pregnant by their father" (GENESIS 19:36). Each virgin, knowing exactly what to do with their drunk dad, got pregnant on the first attempt.

So we can see in context that the saga of Sodom is bracketed by the stories of two patriarchal males, Abraham and his nephew Lot, needing to have heirs. By hook or crook—by a godly miracle or God-approved incest—men must have offspring. The fire-and-brimstone episode is the centerpiece of a broader macho agenda. Since the Sodomites rejected Lot's daughters, this indicates that the writers intended the fictional mob to be "wicked" sex-crazed homosexuals. The "wickedness" was not the sexual act between men; it was the refusal to provide offspring for the patriarch. This biblical tale is a warning for those who are so "deviant" that they will not procreate.

In addition to the story of Sodom, the God of the Old Testament makes two clear pronouncements against male homosexuality:

Gays are bad

LEVITICUS 18:22 "You shall not lie with a male as with a woman; **it is an abomination.**" RSV

Gays should be killed

LEVITICUS 20:13 "If a man lies with a male as with a woman, both of them have committed an abomination; **they shall be put to death**; their blood is upon them." RSV

That is fierce language. That one hateful verse is responsible for centuries of violence against homosexuals.

The Old Testament also condemns "male prostitutes," but it is not clear that they were necessarily homosexual. For example: "There were also male temple prostitutes in the land. They committed all the abominations of the nations that the Lord drove out before the people of Israel" (1 KINGS 14:24). It seems unlikely that women in those days would be free enough to visit public gigolos, especially in a place of worship, so those temple prostitutes were likely gay men. However, those passages may be denouncing only prostitution, not the sexuality of the prostitute.

Stretching the literal text, as well as the historical, literary, and contextual meaning, some homosexual Christians and liberal theologians insist that the sin of Sodom was not sexual orientation; rather, it was a lack of hospitality. Well, it was certainly that. But do you scorch a metropolis simply because the townsfolk could have been a bit more welcoming?

Some defenders of scripture point out that since lesbianism is not condemned or even mentioned in the Old Testament, God can't really be homophobic. But this ignores the fact that it was sexist males who wrote the bible. Their main concern was property and inheritance, accomplished by controlling women. (See Chapter 9.) Lesbians wouldn't matter, since the happiness of women was never important. All women were breeding machines, and forcing lesbians to have sex with men would be "natural." (I wonder if any woman was ever happy in those days.) On the other hand, male homosexual acts detract from that overall plan. In the context of patriarchal inheritance, they are not "natural."

Other gay believers point out that the word "abomination" in the Leviticus texts did not mean "immoral." It meant only "ritual uncleanness." Those verses were part of the so-called "Holiness Code" of the Pentateuch, so the "sin" was only religious, not a sin-of-itself, they say. There were many things that were considered "unclean" in a ritual context that are not immoral. Eating pork, for example. Or not taking your hat off when entering a church. There is nothing intrinsically wrong with wearing a hat. But I don't see how this applies to homosexuality. God didn't say "You shall not lie with a male as with a woman *in the tabernacle.*" (That would have been something to see.) All homosexual acts were forbidden, everywhere. Besides, if homosexuality is *only* an abomination, or uncleanness, the best you can say about God is that he is merely "ritually homophobic." That would be like saying Martin Luther was only "ritually antisemitic," so he wasn't so bad.

Biblically, any offense to God, ritual or not, was considered a sin. Today we don't execute people for keeping their hats on in church, or for loving whom they choose to love, but if you committed such an abomination in Old Testament times, your blood would be upon you.

If gay Christians want to affirm their identities and challenge the culture of hatred—as they should—they can't do it by defending or excusing a blinkered patriarchal deity. They should denounce the barbaric mindset of the God of the Old Testament, like they do with every other faithful bigot they meet.

11

Racist

"The Lord your God has chosen you out of all the peoples on earth to be his people, his treasured possession."
—DEUTERONOMY 7:6

In the 25th chapter of Numbers, we are told the grisly story of a cold-blooded God-approved murder of a mixed-race couple. One of the groups living south of the "promised land" was the Midianites, people allegedly descended from Abraham through Midian, the son of one of his other wives (GENESIS 25:1–2). Since they were not through Sarah, the primordial mother of the Israelites, the Midianites were considered outsiders, not chosen, not treasured. Their main defect was that they worshipped other gods, not the Lord Jealous. However, they were so closely related to the Israelites by ancestry and geography that there was unavoidable intercourse, in all meanings of that word. That sort of thing happens all through history, and although from an evolutionary perspective such mixing provides variation that is good for the species, it is very bad for patriarchy, inheritance, territory, religious orthodoxy, and "racial purity."

According to the story, some Israelite men were being seduced by Midianite women south of the border, and not just sexually. After marrying the women, many of the husbands started practicing the religion of their wives. So, of course, "the Lord's anger was kindled against Israel." It seems the main theme of the Old Testament is sex, literally and metaphorically. The Lord Jealous is quick to react like a rejected lover. And what does any love-spurned guy do? God said to Moses:

Take all the chiefs of the people, and impale them in the sun before the
Lord, in order that the fierce anger of the Lord may turn away from Israel.
*(*NUMBERS 25:4*)*

That's right. You can't allow the ones you chose their own free choice to stay or leave. If they mix with the wrong people, the "fierce anger of the Lord" must make an example by torturing them in public.

It gets worse. Moses said to the judges of Israel:

Each of you shall kill any of your people who have yoked themselves to the
*Baal of Peor [the Midianite god]. (*NUMBERS 25:5*)*

That is religious cleansing. National pest control. It would be like saying, "Kill all British who have married Arabs and adopted Islam."

But love is strong. In spite of the public executions and threat of death, one Israelite man still couldn't resist his kissing cousin:

Just then one of the Israelites came and brought a Midianite woman into his
family, in the sight of Moses and in the sight of the whole congregation of the
*Israelites. (*NUMBERS 25:6*)*

What brazen rebellion! That was too much. One of the righteous priests, the furious grandson of the high priest Aaron, had had enough of this abominable miscegenation.

When Phinehas son of Eleazar, son of Aaron the priest, saw it, he got up and
left the congregation. Taking a spear in his hand, he went after the Israelite
man into the tent, and pierced the two of them, the Israelite and the woman,
*through the belly. (*NUMBERS 25:7–8*)*

The man's name was Zimri, and the woman's name was Cozbi. A loving family was murdered by a bigoted priest with the angry blessing of God.

Suppose a Christian American man married a Canadian Buddhist woman and converted to her religion. If a priest broke into their house and slaughtered both of them, for that reason alone, would that not be a hate-crime of the first degree? Not according to the God of the Old Testament. For preserving the purity of the nation, the priest's bloody racism would be rewarded and praised. Look how the Lord Jealous reacted to Pinehas's brutal stabbing:

So the plague was stopped among the people of Israel. Nevertheless those
that died by the plague were twenty-four thousand. The Lord spoke to Moses,
saying: "Phinehas son of Eleazar, son of Aaron the priest, has turned back my
wrath from the Israelites by manifesting such zeal among them on my behalf
that in my jealousy I did not consume the Israelites. Therefore say, 'I hereby
grant him my covenant of peace. It shall be for him and for his descendants
after him a covenant of perpetual priesthood, because he was zealous for his
*God, and made atonement for the Israelites.' " (*NUMBERS 25:8–13*)*

Pinehas was rewarded for hateful homicide. The righteous racist was given a "perpetual priesthood" because he was zealous for God. The wise creator god of the universe put his stamp of approval on the savage murder of a loving couple. Since the race had now been purified by an honor killing, his anger was calmed and he stopped his slaughter after only 24,000 deaths. To further demonstrate his love and compassion, God immediately said to Moses, "Harass the Midianites, and defeat them" (NUMBERS 25:17).

We can't call the God of the Old Testament a racist bigot. We have to call him a bloodthirsty racist bigot.

Racism is not just about skin color. Here is how the United Nations describes it:

> The term "racial discrimination" shall mean any distinction, exclusion, restriction, or preference based on race, color, descent, or national or ethnic origin that has the purpose or effect of nullifying or impairing the recognition, enjoyment or exercise, on an equal footing, of human rights and fundamental freedoms in the political, economic, social, cultural or any other field of public life. (UN International Convention on the Elimination of All of Racial Discrimination, New York, 7 March 1966)

Racism includes prejudice against "national or ethnic origin," such as the diverse tribes of the Canaanites living within the "holy land" and other groups bordering the targeted territory of the so-called "chosen people" during Old Testament times. The God of the Old Testament is therefore a racist, since he denigrates all ethnic groups except the privileged people whom he considers his "treasured possession."

> When the Lord your God brings you into the land that you are about to enter and occupy, and he clears away many nations before you—the Hittites, the Girgashites, the Amorites, the Canaanites, the Perizzites, the Hivites, and the Jebusites, seven nations mightier and more numerous than you—and when the Lord your God gives them over to you and you defeat them, then **you must utterly destroy them**. Make no covenant with them and show them no mercy. **Do not intermarry** with them, giving your daughters to their sons or taking their daughters for your sons, for that would turn away your children from following me, to serve other gods. Then the anger of the Lord would be kindled against you, and he would destroy you quickly. But this is how you must deal with them: break down their altars, smash their pillars, hew down their sacred poles, and burn their idols with fire. For you are a people holy to the Lord your God; **the Lord your God has chosen you out of all the peoples on earth to be his people, his treasured possession**. (DEUTERONOMY 7:1–6)

The Jews were the "superior race." Can there be a stronger example of prejudice, discrimination, ethnic cleansing, genocide, and racial superiority? It is one thing to be proud of your ancestry, ethnicity, and culture. It is something else entirely to elevate it above "all the peoples on earth."

Some of these additional examples of biblical racism overlap with Ethnic Cleanser and Genocidal. See also Chapters 8 and 13.

Interracial marriage is a "great evil"

NEHEMIAH 13:23–30 "In those days also saw I Jews that had married wives of Ashdod, of Ammon, and of Moab: And their children spake half in the speech of Ashdod, and could not speak in the Jews' language, but according to the language of each people. And I contended with them, and cursed them, and smote certain of them, and plucked off their hair, and made them swear by God, saying, **Ye shall not give your daughters unto their sons, nor take their daughters unto your sons, or for yourselves**. . . . Shall we then hearken unto you to do all this great evil, to transgress against our God in **marrying strange wives**? . . . Remember them, O my God, because they have defiled the priesthood, and the covenant of the priesthood, and of the Levites. **Thus cleansed I them from all strangers**." KJV

The descendants of one of Noah's grandsons are cursed to be slaves to the others

GENESIS 9:24–27 "And Noah awoke from his wine, and knew what his younger son had done unto him. And he said, **Cursed be Canaan; a servant of servants shall he be unto his brethren**. And he said, Blessed be the Lord God of Shem; and **Canaan shall be his servant**. God shall enlarge Japheth, and he shall dwell in the tents of Shem; and **Canaan shall be his servant**." KJV (*Many bible believers have interpreted* GENESIS 9:18–27 *as showing the origin of the "three races" of humanity.*)

Racism and territorialism. "They shall not live in your land"

EXODUS 23:23–33 "For mine Angel shall go before thee, and bring thee in unto the Amorites, and the Hittites, and the Perizzites, and the Canaanites, the Hivites, and the Jebusites: and **I will cut them off**. Thou shalt not bow down to their gods, nor serve them, nor do after their works: but **thou shalt utterly overthrow them**, and quite break down their images. And ye shall serve the Lord your God. . . . I will send my fear before thee, and will destroy all the people to whom thou shalt come, and I will make all thine enemies turn their backs unto thee. And I will send hornets before thee, which shall drive out the Hivite, the Canaanite, and the Hittite, from before thee. . . . **And I will set thy bounds** [NRSV: "borders"] **from the Red sea even unto the sea of the Philistines, and from the desert unto the river**: for I will deliver the inhabitants of the land into your hand; and thou shalt drive them out before thee. Thou shalt make no covenant with them, nor with their gods. **They shall not dwell in thy land**, lest they make thee sin against me: for if thou serve their gods, it will surely be a snare unto thee." KJV

Shun the Ammonites and Moabites

DEUTERONOMY 23:3–6 "**An Ammonite or Moabite shall not enter into the congregation of the Lord**; even to their tenth generation shall they not enter into the congregation of the Lord for ever: Because they met you not with bread and with water in the way, when ye came forth out of Egypt. . . . Nevertheless the Lord thy God would not hearken unto Balaam; but the Lord thy God turned the curse into a blessing unto thee, because the Lord thy God loved thee. **Thou shalt not seek their peace nor their prosperity all thy days for ever**." KJV

Kick out all foreigners

NEHEMIAH 13:3 "When they had heard the law, that they separated from Israel all the **mixed multitude** [NRSV: "those of foreign descent]." KJV

Forty-two thousand people killed because of their accent

JUDGES 12:4–6 "Then Jephthah gathered together all the men of Gilead, and fought with Ephraim . . . when those Ephraimites which were escaped said, Let me go over; that the men of Gilead said unto him, Art thou an Ephraimite? If he said, Nay; Then said they unto him, Say now Shibboleth: and he said Sibboleth: **for he could not frame to pronounce it right**. Then they took him, and slew him at the passages of Jordan: and there fell at that time of the Ephraimites forty and two thousand." KJV (*This is the origin of the word "shibboleth," which originally meant stalk of corn or grain.*)

Slaves can be acquired from neighboring nations and resident aliens

LEVITICUS 25:44–46 "As for your male and female slaves whom you may have: **you may buy male and female slaves from among the nations that are round about you**. You may also buy from among **the strangers** [NRSV: "aliens"] who sojourn with you and their families that are with you, who have been born in your land; and **they may be your property**. You may bequeath them to your sons after you, to inherit as a possession for ever; you may make slaves of them, but over your brethren the people of Israel you shall not rule, one over another, with harshness." RSV (*You can be harsh with your slaves, if they are not Israelites.*)

Infanticidal

"Their eyes will not pity the children."
—Isaiah 13:18

Tʜere doesn't seem to be a word for the general killing of children. Infanticide is the killing of a very young child—the British Infanticide Act of 1938 deems it the killing of any child "under the age of twelve months." Neonaticide is the killing of newborns, especially less than a day old. Filicide is the killing of one's own child of any age, even a grown child. Homicide is the killing of any human being, and murdering kids is certainly homicidal. But what do we call the killing of children between the ages of one year and adulthood?

The words translated "infant" and "child" in the Old Testament were imprecise. For example, where the KJV has "infant and suckling" (from *yanaq*, "to suck"), the NRSV translates it "child and infant" (1 Samuel 15:3). Did that distinction make much difference to the Amalekites who were being slaughtered by God's chosen people? As the Hebrew warrior was hacking off the head of a three-year-old, I doubt that he paused to say to the parents, "By the way, this is technically not infanticide. Praise God."

A reader might object that God sending wild bears to attack 42 "small boys" in 2 Kings was not attempted infanticide. They were not toddlers. Then what should we call it?

When the Lord Jealous says "you will eat the fruit of your womb, the flesh of your own sons and daughters" (Deuteronomy 28:53), he doesn't specify the age of the kids. We have to assume this includes tender infants. Since the biblical authors rarely give us exact ages, let's allow "infanticide" to cover young children of any age. If you are uncomfortable with this grouping, you are welcome to make a new chapter called "Childicidal." (Or make up your own word. Puericidal? Minoricidal? Juvenilicidal?)

There are many places, however, where the God of the Old Testament was clearly infanticidal by the strictest definition.

In the early 6th century B.C.E., Jerusalem was invaded and conquered by the Babylonians. Many of the Jews were carried captive and exiled to Babylon, where they lived along the banks of the Tigris and Euphrates rivers, homesick for Zion, the holy city of their promised land.

> *By the rivers of Babylon—there we sat down and there we wept when*
> *we remembered Zion. On the willows there we hung up our harps.*
> *(PSALM 137:1–2)*

God's exiled chosen people were very sad, understandably, though I don't see what difference it makes what tyrant you live under. Anyway, what the psalmist says next is shocking:

> *O daughter Babylon, you devastator! Happy shall they be who pay you back*
> *what you have done to us!* **Happy shall they be who take your little ones and**
> **dash them against the rock!** *(PSALM 137:8–9)*

Can there be a more terrible sentence ever spoken in fiction or history? The God of the Old Testament is telling his people to *enjoy* torturing and murdering babies. This hymn was meant to be intoned during worship. "Sing Hallelujah! Dash babies against the rock!" God wasn't simply acknowledging that we might need to cause regrettable collateral damage during wartime—he said we should be glad to do it. Who but a psychopath would ever form such a thought? The word translated "happy" (*'esher,* or *ashere*) in PSALM 137:9 is the same word in PSALM 144:15, "Happy is the people whose God is the LORD," and PROVERBS 3:13, "Happy are those who find wisdom, and those who get understanding." Some translations render it "blessed." Smashing babies was meant to be a joyous event.

The word "little ones" in that verse is *olal* in the Hebrew. The NIV translates it as "infants" there, and the KJV translates *olal* variously as "babe," "infant," "child," and "little one." This curse against innocent babies is clearly approved by God since it appears without comment in the so-called Good Book. Some argue that PSALM 137:9 is just the psalmist talking, not God, but if we accept that argument, the whole Old Testament should be torn up and discarded, including the famous 23rd Psalm. Not a bad idea.

The command to be happy killing babies is consistent with God's character and actions elsewhere, as we see in other chapters in this book. Here, we will focus on the murderous anger of the Lord Jealous as it is directed at helpless children.

Infants dashed to pieces

ISAIAH 13:11–18 "I will punish the world for its evil. . . . Whoever is found will be thrust through, and whoever is caught will fall by the sword. **Their infants will be dashed in pieces** before their eyes; their houses will be plundered and their wives ravished. . . . Their bows will slaughter the young men; they will have no mercy on the fruit of the womb; **their eyes will not pity children.**" RSV

Kill man, woman, child, and infant

1 SAMUEL 15:2–3 "Thus saith the Lord of hosts, I remember that which Amalek did to Israel. . . . Now go and smite Amalek, and utterly destroy all that they have, and spare them not; **but slay both man and woman, infant and suckling**, ox and sheep, camel and ass." KJV

Infants put to the sword

1 SAMUEL 22:19 "And Nob, the city of the priests, smote he with the edge of the sword, both men and women, **children and sucklings** [NRSV: "infants"], and oxen, and asses, and sheep, with the edge of the sword." KJV (*King Saul did this at God's command.*)

Infants faint in the street

LAMENTATIONS 2:1–11 "How hath the Lord covered [NRSV: "humiliated"] the daughter of Zion with a cloud in his anger. . . . Mine eyes do fail with tears, my bowels are troubled, my liver is poured upon the earth, for the destruction of the daughter of my people; because **the children and the sucklings** [NRSV: "infants and babes"] swoon in the streets of the city." KJV

Starve the infants and children

LAMENTATIONS 4:4 "The tongue of the **sucking child** [NRSV: "infant"] cleaveth to the roof of his mouth for thirst: the **young children ask bread, and no man breaketh it unto them.**" KJV

Infants dashed in pieces

NAHUM 3:10 "Yet was she carried away, she went into captivity: her **young children** [NRSV: "infants"] also were dashed in pieces at the top of all the streets." KJV (*God is speaking favorably of the destruction of Tyre.*)

Little children dashed in pieces

HOSEA 13:16 "Samaria shall become desolate; for she hath rebelled against her God: they shall fall by the sword: **their infants shall be dashed in pieces**, and their women with child shall be ripped up." KJV

Kill all the little boys (but not the virgin girls)

NUMBERS 31:17 "Now therefore **kill every male among the little ones**, and kill every woman that hath known man by lying with him." KJV

Destroy children and parents together

JEREMIAH 13:14 "And I will dash them one against another, even the **fathers and the sons** [NRSV: "parents and children"] together, saith the Lord: I will not pity, nor spare, nor have mercy, but destroy them." KJV

Kill your whole family: children, wife, brother

DEUTERONOMY 13:6–11 "If thy brother, the son of thy mother, or **thy son, or thy daughter**, or the wife of thy bosom, or thy friend, which is as thine own soul, entice thee secretly, saying, Let us go and serve other gods. . . . But **thou shalt surely kill him**. . . . And thou shalt stone him with stones, that he die; because he hath sought to thrust thee away from the Lord thy God, which brought thee out of the land of Egypt, from the house of bondage. And all Israel shall hear, and fear, and shall do no more any such wickedness as this is among you." KJV

You will eat your children

DEUTERONOMY 28:53 "And thou shalt eat the fruit of thine own body, **the flesh of thy sons and of thy daughters**, which the Lord thy God hath given thee." KJV

"Parents shall eat their children"

EZEKIEL 5:8–10 "Therefore thus saith the Lord God; Behold, I, even I, am against thee, and will execute judgments in the midst of thee in the sight of the nations. And I will do in thee that which I have not done, and whereunto I will not do any more the like, because of all thine abominations. Therefore **the fathers shall eat the sons** [NRSV: "parents shall eat their children"] in the midst of thee, and the sons shall eat their fathers; and I will execute judgments in thee, and the whole remnant of thee will I scatter into all the winds." KJV

Eat the flesh of sons and daughters

JEREMIAH 19:3–9 "Thus saith the Lord of hosts, the God of Israel; Behold, I will bring evil upon this place, the which whosoever heareth, his ears shall tingle. . . . And **I will cause them to eat the flesh of their sons and the**

flesh of their daughters, and they shall eat every one the flesh of his friend in the siege." KJV

Utterly destroy children

DEUTERONOMY 3:3–6 "So the Lord our God delivered into our hands Og also, the king of Bashan, and all his people: and we smote him until none was left to him remaining . . . **utterly destroying the men, women, and children**, of every city." KJV

At God's command, Moses killed all the children

DEUTERONOMY 2:31–34 "And the Lord said unto me, Behold, I have begun to give Sihon and his land before thee: begin to possess, that thou mayest inherit his land. . . . And the Lord our God delivered him before us; and we smote him, and his sons, and all his people. And we took all his cities at that time, and **utterly destroyed the men, and the women, and the little ones**, of every city, we left none to remain." KJV

Children attacked by bears for teasing God's prophet

2 KINGS 2:23–24 "And he [Elisha] went up from thence unto Bethel: and as he was going up by the way, there came forth **little children** out of the city, and mocked him, and said unto him, Go up, thou bald head; go up, thou bald head. And he turned back, and looked on them, and cursed them in the name of the Lord. And there came forth two she bears out of the wood, and **tare forty and two children of them**." KJV

God kills all firstborn children

EXODUS 12:29 "And it came to pass, that at midnight the Lord **smote all the firstborn** in the land of Egypt, from the firstborn of Pharaoh that sat on his throne unto the firstborn of the captive that was in the dungeon; and all the firstborn of cattle." KJV

Your children will become orphans

EXODUS 22:24 "And my wrath shall wax hot, and I will kill you with the sword; and your wives shall be widows, and **your children fatherless** [NRSV: "orphans"]." KJV

"I will slay the fruit of their womb"

HOSEA 9:11–16 "As for Ephraim, their glory shall fly away like a bird, **from the birth, and from the womb, and from the conception**. Though they bring up their children, yet will I bereave them, that there shall not be a man left: yea, woe also to them when I depart from them! Ephraim, as I saw Tyrus, is planted in a pleasant place: but **Ephraim shall bring forth his children to the murderer**. Give them, O Lord: what wilt thou give? **give them a**

miscarrying womb and dry breasts. All their wickedness is in Gilgal: for there I hated them: for the wickedness of their doings I will drive them out of mine house, I will love them no more: all their princes are revolters. Ephraim is smitten, their root is dried up, they shall bear no fruit: yea, though they bring forth, **yet will I slay even the beloved fruit of their womb**." KJV

Kill all the little children

EZEKIEL 9:4–6 "And the Lord said unto him, Go through the midst of the city, through the midst of Jerusalem, and set a mark upon the foreheads of the men that sigh and that cry for all the abominations that be done in the midst thereof. And to the others he said in mine hearing, Go ye after him through the city, and smite: let not your eye spare, neither have ye pity: Slay utterly old and young, both maids, **and little children**, and women: but come not near any man upon whom is the mark." KJV

"Wild beasts shall rob you of your children"

LEVITICUS 26:21–22 "And if ye walk contrary unto me, and will not hearken unto me; I will bring seven times more plagues upon you according to your sins. I will also send wild beasts among you, which shall **rob you of your children**, and destroy your cattle, and make you few in number; and your high ways shall be desolate." KJV

Bathsheba's innocent child killed

2 SAMUEL 12:13–18 "And David said unto Nathan, I have sinned against the Lord. And Nathan said unto David, The Lord also hath put away thy sin; thou shalt not die. Howbeit, because by this deed thou hast given great occasion to the enemies of the Lord to blaspheme, **the child also that is born unto thee shall surely die**. And Nathan departed unto his house. **And the Lord struck the child that Uriah's wife bare unto David**, and it was very sick. David therefore besought God for the child; and David fasted, and went in, and lay all night upon the earth. And the elders of his house arose, and went to him, to raise him up from the earth: but he would not, neither did he eat bread with them. And it came to pass on the seventh day, that **the child died**." KJV

"God Who Made The Earth" is a hymn for children:

> God, Who made the earth,
> The air, the sky, the sea,
> Who gave the light its birth,
> He cares for me.

When in Heav'n's bright land
I all His loved ones see,
I'll sing with that blest band,
"God cared for me."

How many children targeted in those Old Testament passages above could sing "God cared for me"? If the Babylonian infants could have spoken, they might have changed some of the words:

When in Hell's dark land
I all His damned ones see,
I'll sing with that curst band,
"God cared not for me."

13

(Genocidal)

"You must not let anything that breathes remain alive.
You shall annihilate them."
—DEUTERONOMY 20:16–17

The crime of genocide is not judged by numbers. There is no such thing as a "lesser genocide," morally speaking. Numerically larger genocides cause more practical harm, but a smaller genocide is just as despicable. By body count alone, the Holocaust was a greater tragedy than the Rwandan genocide—about six times worse—but the contemptible crime against humanity was identical. The perpetrators shared the same cruel intention: wipe them all out.

Noting that all genocides are morally equivalent in their purpose, we still might ask what was the numerically largest genocide in history. The European Holocaust, with estimates ranging between four and seventeen million (depending who is counting and whom you count), is certainly the most painfully wrenching example in recent history. If we take the reasonable historical consensus of six million Jews killed by the Catholic and Lutheran German military, that was two thirds of the nine million Jews living in those countries, or 67 percent of that demographic. The "American Indian Holocaust" following the arrival of Europeans, committed by many Catholic and Protestant actors over centuries, was harder to count. If we add European diseases to the massacres, an estimated 80 to 90 percent of the population of the Americas was annihilated over that period, perhaps totaling more than 50 million lives by many acts of genocide.

But by far the largest single act of genocide, in numbers and percentage, is related in the 6th and 7th chapters of the book of Genesis. The story is fictional, and you would think good Jews and Christians would want it to be. If it really happened, it would make the Lord Jealous the most horrific genocidal monster of history. The population of the earth at that time is estimated at about 20 million humans, and he hated all of them. The omniscient and infallible God of the Old Testament was "grieved," admitting he'd made a mistake in creating the damnable human race. So, being an intelligent designer, he decided to shut down his experiment by killing them all and reboot with a tiny remnant:

> And the Lord was sorry that he had made humankind on the earth, and it grieved him to his heart. So the Lord said, "I will blot out from the earth the human beings I have created—people together with animals and creeping things and birds of the air, for I am sorry that I have made them." But Noah found favor in the sight of the Lord. (Genesis 6:6–8)

Let's not ask why kittens, butterflies, and ducklings needed to be punished. Fuming that "I have determined to make an end of all flesh," God told the blameless Noah to build a floating wooden box large enough to hold his family plus two (Genesis 6:19), or fourteen (Genesis 7:2–3), of every kind of land animal and bird on the planet. The buoyant container was 300 cubits long, about the length of two 747 airplanes, with three decks. A few weeks past Noah's 600th birthday, "all the fountains of the great deep burst forth, and the windows of the heavens were opened." After the family of eight climbed into the crate, with hundreds of thousands of animal species (times two or fourteen), "the rain fell on the earth forty days and forty nights." The rising water, at the rate of a foot every two minutes, lifted the ark fifteen cubits higher than Mount Everest, exterminating everything that could drown.

> He blotted out every living thing that was on the face of the ground, human beings and animals and creeping things and birds of the air; they were blotted out from the earth. Only Noah was left, and those that were with him in the ark. (Genesis 7:23)

Noah's flood was a swift and gruesome genocide of 20 million people. That was 99.99996 percent of the entire human race. Picture the children clinging to their desperately struggling parents. As you watch them succumb to the waves, you can join them as they sing praise to God:

> All things bright and beautiful,
> All creatures great and small,
> All things wise and wonderful,
> The Lord God drowned them all.

The God of the Old Testament committed, commanded, and condoned many more human annihilations. Their totals were smaller in number than the flood, but they were no lesser genocides.

The Promised Land conquered by merciless genocide

DEUTERONOMY 7:1–2 "When the Lord thy God shall bring thee into the land whither thou goest to possess it, and hath cast out many nations before thee, the Hittites, and the Girgashites, and the Amorites, and the Canaanites, and the Perizzites, and the Hivites, and the Jebusites, seven nations greater and mightier than thou; And when the Lord thy God shall deliver them before thee; **thou shalt smite them, and utterly destroy them**; thou shalt make no covenant with them, nor shew mercy unto them." KJV

Dear God, please let us slaughter them all

NUMBERS 21:2–3 "And Israel vowed a vow unto the Lord, and said, If thou wilt indeed deliver this people into my hand, then I will utterly destroy their cities. And the Lord hearkened to the voice of Israel, and delivered up the Canaanites; and **they utterly destroyed them and their cities**: and he called the name of the place Hormah." KJV (*"Hormah" means "destruction."*)

If they don't surrender, annihilate them

DEUTERONOMY 20:10–19 "When you march up to attack a city, make its people an offer of peace. If they accept and open their gates, all the people in it shall be subject to forced labor and shall work for you. If they refuse to make peace and they engage you in battle, lay siege to that city. When the Lord your God delivers it into your hand, put to the sword all the men in it. As for the women, the children, the livestock and everything else in the city, you may take these as plunder for yourselves. And you may use the plunder the Lord your God gives you from your enemies. This is how you are to treat all the cities that are at a distance from you and do not belong to the nations nearby. However, in the cities of the nations the Lord your God is giving you as an inheritance, **do not leave alive anything that breathes. Completely destroy them**—the Hittites, Amorites, Canaanites, Perizzites, Hivites and Jebusites—as the Lord your God has commanded you. . . . When you lay siege to a city for a long time, fighting against it to capture it, do not destroy its trees by putting an ax to them, because you can eat their fruit. Do not cut them down. Are the trees people, that you should besiege them?" NIV (*Kill all the people but not the poor trees!*)

Peaceful people massacred so a tribe of Israel can have a place to live

JUDGES 18:1–28 "And in those days the tribe of the Danites was seeking a place of their own where they might settle, because they had not yet come into an inheritance among the tribes of Israel. . . . Then they said to him, 'Please inquire of God to learn whether our journey will be successful.'

The priest answered them, 'Go in peace. Your journey has the Lord's approval.' . . . Then they took what Micah had made, and his priest, and went on to Laish, against **a people at peace and secure. They attacked them with the sword and burned down their city**. . . . The Danites rebuilt the city and settled there." NIV

Not a single survivor

DEUTERONOMY 2:32–34 "And the Lord our God delivered him before us; and we smote him, and his sons, and all his people. And we took all his cities at that time, and **utterly destroyed** the men, and the women, and the little ones, of every city, **we left none to remain**." KJV

The Lord delivered them for utter destruction

DEUTERONOMY 3:3–6 "So the Lord our God delivered into our hands Og also, the king of Bashan, and all his people: and **we smote him until none was left to him remaining**. And we took all his cities at that time, there was not a city which we took not from them, threescore cities, all the region of Argob, the kingdom of Og in Bashan. All these cities were fenced with high walls, gates, and bars; beside unwalled towns a great many. And **we utterly destroyed them**, as we did unto Sihon king of Heshbon, utterly destroying the men, women, and children, of every city." KJV

Amalekites cursed

DEUTERONOMY 25:17–19 "Remember what Amalek did unto thee by the way, when ye were come forth out of Egypt. . . . Therefore it shall be, when the Lord thy God hath given thee rest from all thine enemies round about, in the land which the Lord thy God giveth thee for an inheritance to possess it, that **thou shalt blot out the remembrance of Amalek** from under heaven; thou shalt not forget it." KJV

Amalekites attacked

I SAMUEL 15:2–3 "Thus saith the Lord of hosts, I remember that which Amalek did to Israel, how he laid wait for him in the way, when he came up from Egypt. Now go and smite Amalek, and utterly destroy all that they have, and **spare them not; but slay both man and woman, infant and suckling**, ox and sheep, camel and ass." KJV

Amalekites destroyed

I SAMUEL 15:7–8 "And Saul smote the Amalekites from Havilah until thou comest to Shur, that is over against Egypt. And he took Agag the king of the Amalekites alive, and **utterly destroyed all the people** with the edge of the sword." KJV

Near-complete genocide, keeping young virgins as "war booty"

NUMBERS 31:7–40 "They fought against Midian, as the Lord commanded Moses, and killed every man. . . . The Israelites captured the Midianite women and children and took all the Midianite herds, flocks and goods as plunder. . . . Moses was angry with the officers. . . . 'Have you allowed all the women to live?' he asked them. . . . **Now kill all the boys. And kill every woman who has slept with a man, but save for yourselves every girl who has never slept with a man**. . . . So Moses and Eleazar the priest did as the Lord commanded Moses. The plunder remaining from the spoils that the soldiers took was 675,000 sheep, 72,000 cattle, 61,000 donkeys and 32,000 women who had never slept with a man. The half share of those who fought in the battle was . . . 16,000 people, of whom the tribute for the Lord was 32." NIV (*God was less humane than the Israelites. They wanted to keep boys and women alive, but God said "only the virgins." The bible doesn't say what the priests did with their "Lord's tribute" of 32 virgins.*)

Seven genocides in thirteen verses

JOSHUA 10:28–40 "And Joshua took Makke'dah on that day, and smote it and its king with the edge of the sword; **he utterly destroyed every person in it**, he left none remaining. . . . Then Joshua passed on from Makke'dah, and all Israel with him, to Libnah, and fought against Libnah; and the Lord gave it also and its king into the hand of Israel; and he smote it with the edge of the sword, and every person in it; **he left none remaining in it** . . . and the Lord gave Lachish into the hand of Israel, and he took it on the second day, and smote it with the edge of the sword, and **every person in it**, as he had done to Libnah. Then Horam king of Gezer came up to help Lachish; and Joshua smote him and his people, until **he left none remaining**. And Joshua passed on with all Israel from Lachish to Eglon; and they laid siege to it, and assaulted it; and they took it on that day, and smote it with the edge of the sword; and **every person in it he utterly destroyed** that day, as he had done to Lachish. Then Joshua went up with all Israel from Eglon to Hebron; and they assaulted it, and took it, and smote it with the edge of the sword, and its king and its towns, and every person in it; **he left none remaining**, as he had done to Eglon, and **utterly destroyed it with every person in it**. Then Joshua, with all Israel, turned back to Debir and assaulted it, and he took it with its king and all its towns; and they smote them with the edge of the sword, and **utterly destroyed every person** in it; **he left none remaining**. . . . So Joshua defeated the whole land, the hill country and the Negeb and the lowland and the slopes, and all their kings; **he left none remaining, but utterly destroyed all that breathed**, as the Lord God of Israel commanded." RSV

Jericho "utterly destroyed"

JOSHUA 6:21 "And they **utterly destroyed** all that was in the city, both man and woman, young and old, and ox, and sheep, and ass, with the edge of the sword." KJV (*Then they plundered the treasure*, JOSHUA 6:24.)

A lifeless heap of ruins

JOSHUA 8:25–28 "And so it was, that all that fell that day, both of men and women, were twelve thousand, even all the men of Ai. For Joshua drew not his hand back, wherewith he stretched out the spear, until he had **utterly destroyed all the inhabitants of Ai**. Only the cattle and the spoil of that city Israel took for a prey unto themselves, according unto the word of the Lord which he commanded Joshua. And Joshua burnt Ai, and made it an heap for ever, even a desolation unto this day." KJV

"No one was left who breathed"

JOSHUA 11:10–11 "And Joshua at that time turned back, and took Hazor, and smote the king thereof with the sword: for Hazor beforetime was the head of all those kingdoms. And they smote all the souls that were therein with the edge of the sword, **utterly destroying them: there was not any left to breathe**: and he burnt Hazor with fire." KJV

And the other towns "utterly destroyed"

JOSHUA 11:12 "And all the cities of those kings, and all the kings of them, did Joshua take, and smote them with the edge of the sword, and he **utterly destroyed them**, as Moses the servant of the Lord commanded." KJV

Exterminated with "no mercy"

JOSHUA 11:16–20 "So Joshua took all that land. . . . He took all their kings, and smote them, and put them to death. Joshua made war a long time with all those kings. There was not a city that made peace with the people of Israel, except the Hivites, the inhabitants of Gibeon; they took all in battle. For it was the Lord's doing to harden their hearts that they should come against Israel in battle, in order that they should be **utterly destroyed, and should receive no mercy but be exterminated, as the Lord commanded Moses**." RSV

Wiped them out

JOSHUA 11:21–22 "And Joshua came at that time, and **wiped out the Anakim** from the hill country, from Hebron, from Debir, from Anab, and from all the hill country of Judah, and from all the hill country of Israel; Joshua **utterly destroyed them** with their cities. There was none of the Anakim left in the land of the people of Israel." RSV

They left no one alive

I SAMUEL 27:8–9 "And David and his men went up, and invaded the Geshurites, and the Gezrites, and the Amalekites: for those nations were of old the inhabitants of the land, as thou goest to Shur, even unto the land of Egypt. And David smote the land, and **left neither man nor woman alive**, and took away the sheep, and the oxen, and the asses, and the camels, and the apparel, and returned, and came to Achish." KJV (*They took their clothes!*)

They killed everyone except the traitor, destroyed the city and took its name.

JUDGES 1:22–26 "And the house of Joseph, they also went up against Bethel: and the Lord was with them. And the house of Joseph sent to descry Bethel. (Now the name of the city before was Luz.) And the spies saw a man come forth out of the city, and they said unto him, Shew us, we pray thee, the entrance into the city, and we will shew thee mercy. And when he shewed them the entrance into the city, **they smote the city with the edge of the sword; but they let go the man and all his family**. And the man went into the land of the Hittites, and built a city, and called the name thereof Luz: which is the name thereof unto this day." KJV (*"Luz" means either "twisted" or "almond tree."*)

Death to Babylon

JEREMIAH 50:21 "Go up against the land of Meratha'im, and against the inhabitants of Pekod. **Slay, and utterly destroy after them**, says the Lord, and do all that I have commanded you." RSV

Completely destroy the "troublemakers" who worship other gods

DEUTERONOMY 13:12–15 "If you hear it said about one of the towns the Lord your God is giving you to live in that troublemakers have arisen among you and have led the people of their town astray, saying, "Let us go and worship other gods" (gods you have not known), then you must inquire, probe and investigate it thoroughly. And if it is true and it has been proved that this detestable thing has been done among you, you must certainly **put to the sword all who live in that town. You must destroy it completely, both its people and its livestock**." NIV

"Consume all the people"

DEUTERONOMY 7:16 "And thou shalt **consume all the people** which the Lord thy God shall deliver thee; thine eye shall **have no pity upon them**: neither shalt thou serve their gods; for that will be a snare unto thee." KJV

14

ꜰilicidal

"Take your son . . . and offer him there as a burnt offering."
—Genesis 22:2

Ｊn Chapter 10 we saw the "wonderful" miracle God performed in Genesis 18 to provide a child to Abraham and Sarah, promising that "Abraham shall become a great and mighty nation" through his son Isaac. Four chapters later, that precious son is in danger. God forced Abraham to endure a cruel test of his faith by asking him to sacrifice Isaac, "whom you love," as a burnt offering.

> *After these things God tested Abraham. He said to him, "Abraham!" And he said, "Here I am." He said, "Take your son, your only son Isaac, whom you love, and go to the land of Moriah, and offer him there as a burnt offering on one of the mountains that I shall show you." (Genesis 22:1–2)*

Without blinking, Abraham did exactly as God commanded. He had no doubt that the Lord could—and would—demand a child as a sacrifice. Children were property, like sheep and oxen. For some godly reason, the only way to appease the deity is by killing something you own, preferably by spilling its blood and burning its flesh "as a pleasing odor to the Lord." (See Chapter 7.)

> *So Abraham rose early in the morning, saddled his donkey, and took two of his young men with him, and his son Isaac; he cut the wood for the burnt offering, and set out and went to the place in the distance that God had shown him. (Genesis 22:3)*

Since he was old enough to haul the firewood up the mountain (while his Dad carried a knife and no animal), Isaac was likely a pre-teen or teenager. He asked his father why they had not brought an animal for the sacrifice, and Abraham lied to his son, telling him that God would provide a lamb when they got there. (He could not have known something like this would actually happen, otherwise the test was a sham. And if not, then the sacrifice would have been a sham, since he would not be offering his own property. Isaac would have known that. If Abraham remembered— how could he forget?—that God had promised to make a great nation out of Isaac, then he might have guessed that the test was phony. Abraham wasn't *that* stupid. Wink, wink. Let's let God play his games, but we have to go along like we mean it. If anyone was stupid, it was the writer of this fictional tale who assumed his readers would be uncritical. The only way the story makes sense is if Abraham actually thought he was on his way to murder his son.)

The true miracle in this story is that Isaac was an obedient teenager. He didn't bolt from his murderous father.

When they came to the place that God had shown him, Abraham built an altar there and laid the wood in order. He bound his son Isaac, and laid him on the altar, on top of the wood. (GENESIS 22:9)

Isaac was big enough to resist being tied up by his elderly parent, so unless Abraham had knocked him out with a rock, the boy was compliant. He loved his Dad.

Put yourself in this scenario. Picture yourself tying up your child. Try to imagine worshipping a master who demands that you slaughter your son or daughter to gain his approval. Personally, I would prefer the approval of my child over the approval of a lord. In my mind, Abraham failed the test.

Some Christians reply that God didn't ask Abraham to do anything he wouldn't do himself. He offered his only-begotten son Jesus as a final sacrifice to pay for the sins of the world, they say. But why does that make it good? If murdering your own child is the only way to calm your psychopathic anger, then you don't have the courage to calm it by killing yourself. A child is a child! Sane loving parents do not kill their children.

Abraham "passed" the test:

Then Abraham reached out his hand and took the knife to kill his son. But the angel of the Lord called to him from heaven, and said, "Abraham, Abraham!" And he said, "Here I am." He said, "Do not lay your hand on the boy or do anything to him; for now I know that you fear God, since you have not withheld your son, your only son, from me." (GENESIS 22:10–12)

"Now I know that you fear God"? How could the omniscient creator not have known this? Abraham had seen the flames and smoke from the destruction of Sodom, so he was familiar with the furious wrath of God. How could he *not* fear such a strongman? This was like forcing someone to commit a criminal act at gunpoint. Is that the moral of this story? "Cower before me! Ignore your loving parental instincts and kill your only child. Prove that you can do anything I command, or you know what I will do to you!"

The test was over, but they couldn't go home yet. The story ends with God receiving the burnt offering he so desperately craved:

> *And Abraham looked up and saw a ram, caught in a thicket by its horns.*
> *Abraham went and took the ram and offered it up as a burnt offering instead of*
> *his son. So Abraham called that place "The Lord will provide"; as it is said to*
> *this day, "On the mount of the Lord it shall be provided."* (GENESIS 22:13–14)

After what he had just experienced, was the only thing Abraham could think to name the place "The Lord will provide"? Is the moral of this story that God needed an offering so badly that he miraculously provided it for himself? Is the horrific attempted murder of a child merely incidental to worship? If Abraham's tongue had not been tied with fear, he might have called the place "The Lord will torment."

Isaac, by the way, was not Abraham's first son. He had an older son named Ishmael, the purported "father of the Arabs," born through his second wife Hagar, the Egyptian handmaid of his first wife Sarah, at Sarah's request. But the bible, written by Jews, says Isaac was "the son whom you love." The Quran does not name which son Abraham was asked to sacrifice, and many Islamic scholars claim it was Ishmael. The tension between the Jews and the Arabs continues to this day.

The story of Abraham and Isaac overtly condones child sacrifice. It certainly does not condemn it. However, some believers will point out that God never intended Abraham to go through with it. Ignoring the fact that God praised and rewarded Abraham for being willing to slaughter a child, many believers insist that since it didn't actually happen, God cannot be accused of filicide.

Then what do they say about the story of Jephthah's daughter, as told in the 11th chapter of Judges? In this case, the godly sacrifice of a child was carried through, to everyone's satisfaction.

Jephthah was the illegitimate son of a man from Gilead who had had sex with a prostitute. He grew up in his father's house, but was eventually kicked out by his half-brothers, the legal sons: "You shall not inherit anything in our father's house; for you are the son of another woman." Needing to improve his position in life, Jephthah became a mighty warrior, but had higher aspirations. Years later, when the hated Ammonites invaded Israel, the men from Gilead (including the half-brothers who had kicked him out) asked Jephthah: "Come and be our commander, so that we may fight with the Ammonites." Jephthah sensed an opportunity, and negotiated with his former family: "If you bring me home again to fight with the Ammonites, and the Lord gives them over to me, I will be your head." He demanded to be supreme commander. They agreed.

After diplomatic efforts with the Ammonites failed, "the spirit of the Lord came upon Jephthah," and he made a desperate vow to God:

> If you will give the Ammonites into my hand, then whoever comes out
> of the doors of my house to meet me, when I return victorious from the
> Ammonites, shall be the Lord's, to be offered up by me as a burnt offering.
> (Judges 11:30–31)

So that's how to get God to do what you want? Offer him a live body to be sacrificed? "Oh, boy," God must have thought, "this is one deal I can't pass up." And what was Jephthah thinking? He had only one child, and he promised that whoever came out of his house would be offered as a burnt offering. Was his vow simple devotion to God, or ruthless opportunism?

Notice that God didn't say, "No deal, Jephthah! I don't accept child sacrifice." The Old Testament writer related the vow as the most natural thing a holy warrior might propose to the biblical deity. Once you speak it, you are committed. God must have been happy with Jephthah's offer because he "gave the enemy into his hand."

> So Jephthah crossed over to the Ammonites to fight against them; and
> the Lord gave them into his hand. He inflicted a massive defeat on them
> from Aroer to the neighborhood of Minnith, twenty towns, and as far as
> Abel-keramim. So the Ammonites were subdued before the people of Israel.
> (Judges 11:32–33)

General Jephthah won the war and became a national hero. Pennants and parades! God kept his end of the deal. Now it is payback time.

> Then Jephthah came to his home at Mizpah; and there was his daughter
> coming out to meet him with timbrels and with dancing. She was his only
> child; he had no son or daughter except her. (Judges 11:34)

Who was he expecting to come out to greet him as he returned from battle? The family goat? Only his wife or his daughter could come out that door, happy to see him home safe from the war.

> When he saw her, he tore his clothes, and said, "Alas, my daughter! You
> have brought me very low; you have become the cause of great trouble to me.
> For I have opened my mouth to the Lord, and I cannot take back my vow."
> (Judges 11:35)

She was the blame? Wasn't the real cause of the trouble the rash macho vow made between a power-hungry politician and a praise-hungry dictator?

Like Isaac, the nameless daughter was compliant:

*She said to him, "My father, if you have opened your mouth to the Lord, do to me according to what has gone out of your mouth, now that the Lord has given you vengeance against your enemies, the Ammonites." (*JUDGES 11:36*)*

No matter who suffers, no matter how rash or foolhardy, a promise to God must be kept. Even the innocent victims of such reckless bargaining were forced to agree.

If the bible were truly a "Good Book," at this point in the narrative, the loving, compassionate and merciful God of the Old Testament should have stepped in to say: "Forget it, Jephthah. You don't have to kill your daughter. She is precious and beautiful, and a talented dancer. I annul the vow. I wanted those horrible Ammonites defeated anyway."

That would have been a better story, a tale of love and mercy. Instead, after a brief stay of execution, the Lord Jealous demanded his hundred pounds of flesh:

*And she said to her father, "Let this thing be done for me: Grant me two months, so that I may go and wander on the mountains, and bewail my virginity, my companions and I." "Go," he said and sent her away for two months. So she departed, she and her companions, and bewailed her virginity on the mountains. At the end of two months, she returned to her father, who did with her according to the vow he had made. (*JUDGES 11:37–39*)*

Jephthah *did with his daughter* according to the vow. He burned her as a sacrifice of thanksgiving to God.

Was that good? Apparently it was. Like Abraham, Jephthah was rewarded by God for his faithfulness. After slaughtering his daughter, he continued to do well in battle, and then became "a judge in Israel for six years," a high position of respect and approval. The same author had written: "Whenever the Lord raised up judges for them, the Lord was with the judge, and he delivered them from the hand of their enemies all the days of the judge" (JUDGES 2:18). When Jephthah died, he was buried honorably in the hometown that had originally expelled him. Today, he would have died in prison.

Here are a few more examples of the filicidal family values of the God of the Old Testament.

Stubborn son publicly executed

DEUTERONOMY 21:18–21 "If a man have a stubborn and rebellious son, which will not obey the voice of his father, or the voice of his mother, and that, when they have chastened him, will not hearken unto them: Then shall his father and his mother lay hold on him, and bring him out unto the elders of his city, and unto the gate of his place; And they shall say unto the elders of his city, This our son is stubborn and rebellious, he will not obey our voice; he is a glutton, and a drunkard. And **all the men of his city shall stone him with stones, that he die**: so shalt thou put evil away from among you; and all Israel shall hear, and fear." KJV

Daughter burned to death

LEVITICUS 21:9 "And the daughter of any priest, if she profane herself by playing the whore, she profaneth her father: **she shall be burnt with fire.**" KJV

Kill your children who leave the faith

DEUTERONOMY 13:6–10 "If thy brother, the son of thy mother, **or thy son, or thy daughter**, or the wife of thy bosom, or thy friend, which is as thine own soul, entice thee secretly, saying, Let us go and serve other gods. . . . Thou shalt not consent unto him, nor hearken unto him; neither shall thine eye pity him, neither shalt thou spare, neither shalt thou conceal him: **But thou shalt surely kill him**; thine hand shall be first upon him to put him to death, and afterwards the hand of all the people. And **thou shalt stone him with stones, that he die**; because he hath sought to thrust thee away from the Lord thy God." KJV (*This is broader than just filicide, a complete intolerance toward other religions.*)

Eat your own children

LEVITICUS 26:27–29 "And if ye will not for all this hearken unto me, but walk contrary unto me; Then I will walk contrary unto you also in fury; and I, even I, will chastise you seven times for your sins. **And ye shall eat the flesh of your sons, and the flesh of your daughters shall ye eat.**" KJV

"You will eat the fruit of your womb"

DEUTERONOMY 28:53 "And thou shalt eat the fruit of thine own body, **the flesh of thy sons and of thy daughters,** which the Lord thy God hath given thee, in the siege, and in the straitness, wherewith thine enemies shall distress thee." KJV

Grisly curse for disobedience

DEUTERONOMY 28:56–57 "The most tender and delicately bred woman among you, who would not venture to set the sole of her foot upon the ground because she is so delicate and tender, will grudge to the husband of her bosom, to her son and to her daughter, **her afterbirth** that comes out from between her feet and **her children** whom she bears, because **she will eat them secretly,** for want of all things, in the siege and in the distress with which your enemy shall distress you in your towns." RSV

God will make you eat your kids and neighbors

JEREMIAH 19:9 "And I will cause them to **eat the flesh of their sons and the flesh of their daughters,** and they shall eat every one the flesh of his friend in the siege and straitness, wherewith their enemies, and they that seek their lives, shall straiten them." KJV

Reciprocal cannibalism

EZEKIEL 5:9–10 "And I will do in thee that which I have not done, and whereunto I will not do any more the like, because of all thine abominations. Therefore **the fathers shall eat the sons** in the midst of thee, and **the sons shall eat their fathers;** and I will execute judgments in thee, and the whole remnant of thee will I scatter into all the winds." KJV

Children boiled

LAMENTATIONS 4:10 "The hands of compassionate women have **boiled their own children;** they became their food in the destruction of the daughter of my people." RSV

"Offer your firstborn to me"

EXODUS 22:29–30 "You shall not delay to offer from the fulness of your harvest and from the outflow of your presses. **The first-born of your sons you shall give to me.** You shall do likewise with your oxen and with your sheep: seven days it shall be with its dam; on the eighth day you shall give it to me." RSV (*Although this doesn't explicitly say to kill sons, they are offered to God just like the animals. It couldn't simply be devotion to the priesthood, since that function was covered by the Levites.*)

False prophets stabbed by their fathers and mothers

ZECHARIAH 13:2–3 "And it shall come to pass in that day, saith the Lord of hosts, that I will cut off the names of the idols out of the land, and they shall no more be remembered: and also I will cause the prophets and the unclean spirit to pass out of the land. And it shall come to pass, that when any shall yet prophesy, then his father and his mother that begat him shall say unto him, Thou shalt not live; for thou speakest lies in the name of the Lord: and **his father and his mother that begat him shall thrust him through when he prophesieth.**" KJV

15

𝔓estilential

"I will heap disasters upon them."
—DEUTERONOMY 32:23

One of the most beloved passages in the bible, quoted frequently by Christians, is in the book of 2nd Chronicles:

If my people, which are called by my name, shall humble themselves,
and pray, and seek my face, and turn from their wicked ways; then will
I hear from heaven, and will forgive their sin, and will heal their land.
(2 CHRONICLES 7:14, KJV)

Hundreds of ministries around the world have adopted that optimistic verse as a call to personal, national, and global repentance. The National Day of Prayer Task Force, founded by the evangelical Christians Shirley and James Dobson, utilizes 2 CHRONICLES 7:14 in many of the proclamations they compose and send to mayors, governors, and the U.S. President for the National Day of Prayer on the first Thursday of every May. While President Eisenhower was taking the oath of office during his first inauguration in 1953, his left hand was placed on a bible open to 2 CHRONICLES 7:14, at the urging of evangelist Billy Graham.

That verse sounds very majestic, but what does "heal their land" mean? Christians always tell us that if we want to understand a biblical text, we must take it in context. So let's do that. By including the entire sentence from which that clause is extracted, we can see exactly what God was talking about when he said he would "heal their land." Here are the words immediately preceding 2 CHRONICLES 7:14:

If I shut up heaven that there be no rain, or if I command the locusts to devour
the land, or if I send pestilence among my people; . . . (2 CHRONICLES 7:13, KJV)

Now we see what is meant by "heal their land." God is telling the Israelites how they could be healed *of himself*. The drought, locusts, and pestilence the nation was experiencing were brought on by the Lord Jealous, who was punishing his chosen people for loving someone else. 2 Chronicles 7:13 is a conditional clause, not a complete sentence, and there is no period at the end, so 7:14 is the continuation. But most Christians start 7:14 with a capitalized "If," taking it out of context. They should quote the entire sentence:

> *When I shut up the heavens so that there is no rain, or command the locust to devour the land, or send pestilence among my people, if my people who are called by my name humble themselves, pray, seek my face, and turn from their wicked ways, then I will hear from heaven, and will forgive their sin and heal their land. (2 Chronicles 7:13–14, NRSV)*

Now it is easy to see that this was a local love spat: I will stop tormenting you if you will humbly apologize for cheating on me. It's your own fault. I'll make it rain again if you come back to me and apologize. Don't make me hurt you more than I have to. I am pestilential because I love you!

Pestilence is deadly epidemic disease. The Bubonic Plague (the Black Death) was called "The Great Pestilence" or "The Great Plague" in the 14th century. As one of his preferred forms of punishment, the God of the Old Testament spread epidemic diseases liberally. This included infecting people and animals as well as poisoning the land.

Consuming Pestilence

Deuteronomy 32:23–24 "I will heap calamities on them and spend my arrows against them. I will send wasting famine against them, consuming **pestilence** and deadly plague; I will send against them the fangs of wild beasts, the venom of vipers that glide in the dust." NIV

The 5th Plague: pestilence

Exodus 9:1–6 "Thus says the Lord, the God of the Hebrews: 'Let my people go, so that they may worship me. For if you refuse to let them go and still hold them, the hand of **the Lord will strike with a deadly pestilence your livestock in the field**: the horses, the donkeys, the camels, the herds, and the flocks. But the Lord will make a distinction between the livestock of Israel and the livestock of Egypt, so that nothing shall die of all that belongs to the Israelites.' The Lord set a time, saying, 'Tomorrow the Lord will do this thing in the land.' And on the next day the Lord did so; **all the livestock of the Egyptians died**, but of the livestock of the Israelites not one died.

Pharaoh inquired and found that not one of the livestock of the Israelites was dead." NRSV

The 6th Plague: boils

EXODUS 9:8–10 "And the Lord said to Moses and Aaron, 'Take handfuls of ashes from the kiln, and let Moses throw them toward heaven in the sight of Pharaoh. And it shall become fine dust over all the land of Egypt, and become **boils breaking out in sores** on man and beast throughout all the land of Egypt.' So they took ashes from the kiln, and stood before Pharaoh, and Moses threw them toward heaven, and it became **boils breaking out in sores on man and beast**." RSV

God threatens Egypt with pestilence

EXODUS 9:15–16 "For by now I could have put forth my hand and struck you and your people with **pestilence**, and you would have been cut off from the earth; but for this purpose have I let you live, to show you my power, so that my name may be declared throughout all the earth." RSV

Egyptians not spared from death

PSALM 78:50 "He made a path for his anger; he did not spare them from death, but gave their lives over to the **plague**." RSV

Avoiding pestilence is a reason to worship

EXODUS 5:3 "Then they said, 'The God of the Hebrews has met with us; let us go, we pray, a three days' journey into the wilderness, and sacrifice to the Lord our God, lest he fall upon us with **pestilence** or with the sword.'" RSV

A plague on the people

EXODUS 32:35 "And the Lord sent a **plague** upon the people, because they made the calf which Aaron made." RSV

Plagues, sword, pestilence, terror, fever, consumption

LEVITICUS 26:14–35 "But if you will not obey me, and do not observe all these commandments, if you spurn my statutes, and abhor my ordinances, so that you will not observe all my commandments, and you break my covenant, I in turn will do this to you: I will bring **terror** on you; **consumption** and **fever** that **waste** the eyes and cause life to pine away. You shall sow your seed in vain, for your enemies shall eat it. . . . If in spite of these punishments you have not turned back to me, but continue hostile to me, then I too will continue hostile to you: I myself will strike you sevenfold for your sins. I will bring the **sword** against you, executing vengeance for the covenant; and if you withdraw within your cities, I will send **pestilence** among you, and you shall be delivered into enemy hands. . . . I will **devastate** the land, so that your enemies who come to settle in it shall be appalled at it. And you I will scatter among the nations, and I will unsheathe the **sword** against you; **your land shall be a desolation**, and your cities a waste. Then the land shall enjoy its sabbath years as long as it lies **desolate**, while you are in the land of your enemies; then the land shall rest, and enjoy its sabbath years. As long as it lies desolate, it shall have the rest it did not have on your sabbaths when you were living on it." NRSV (*Notice that if the Israelites do not honor the Sabbath by resting on that day, God will make the land desolate, "then the land will rest and enjoy its sabbath years." God will destroy the crops so that he can be honored, no matter what!*)

Plague hits before you can swallow

NUMBERS 11:33 "While the meat was yet between their teeth, before it was consumed, the anger of the Lord was kindled against the people, and the Lord smote the people with a **very great plague**." RSV

Bearers of bad news killed by plague

NUMBERS 14:36–37 "And the men whom Moses sent to spy out the land, and who returned and made all the congregation to murmur against him by bringing up an evil report against the land, the men who brought up an evil report of the land, died by **plague** before the Lord." RSV

Pestilence kills 70,000

2 SAMUEL 24:15 "So the Lord sent a **pestilence** upon Israel from the morning until the appointed time; and there died of the people from Dan to Beer-sheba seventy thousand men." RSV

Pestilence kills another 70,000

1 CHRONICLES 21:14 "So the Lord sent a **pestilence** upon Israel; and there fell seventy thousand men of Israel." RSV (*These numbers are obvious exaggerations.*)

Pestilence within the cities

LEVITICUS 26:25 "And I will bring a sword upon you, that shall avenge the quarrel of my covenant: and when ye are gathered together within your cities, I will send the **pestilence** among you; and ye shall be delivered into the hand of the enemy." KJV

Pestilence in the streets

EZEKIEL 28:22–23 "And say, Thus saith the Lord God; Behold, I am against thee, O Zidon; and I will be glorified in the midst of thee: and they shall know that I am the Lord, when I shall have executed judgments in her, and shall be sanctified in her. For I will send into her **pestilence**, and blood

into her streets; and the wounded shall be judged in the midst of her by the
sword upon her on every side; and they shall know that I am the Lord." KJV

National pestilence

NUMBERS 14:12 "I will smite them with the **pestilence**, and disinherit
them, and will make of thee a greater nation and mightier than they." KJV

Plague on the heathens

ZECHARIAH 14:18 "And if the family of Egypt go not up, and come not,
that have no rain; there shall be the **plague, wherewith the Lord will smite
the heathen** [NRSV: "nations"] that come not up to keep the feast of
tabernacles." KJV

Plague of diarrhea is all in the family

2 CHRONICLES 21:14–15 "Behold, with a **great plague** will the Lord smite
thy people, and thy children, and thy wives, and all thy goods: And thou
shalt have great sickness by **disease of thy bowels**, until thy bowels fall out
by reason of the sickness day by day." KJV

Personal pestilence

2 CHRONICLES 21:18–19 "And after all this the Lord smote him in his
bowels with an **incurable disease**. And it came to pass, that in process
of time, after the end of two years, his bowels fell out by reason of his
sickness: so he died of sore diseases [NRSV: "great agony"]." KJV

Plague of God's wrath

NUMBERS 16:46 "And Moses said unto Aaron, Take a censer, and put fire
therein from off the altar, and put on incense, and go quickly unto the
congregation, and make an atonement for them: for there is wrath gone out
from the Lord; **the plague is begun**." KJV

Soil devastated by brimstone and salt

DEUTERONOMY 29:22–23 "So that the generation to come of your children
that shall rise up after you, and the stranger that shall come from a far land,
shall say, when they see the **plagues** of that land, and the **sicknesses** which the
Lord hath laid upon it; And that the whole land thereof is **brimstone** [NRSV:
"sulfur"], and **salt**, and **burning**, that it is not sown, nor beareth, nor any grass
groweth therein, like the overthrow of Sodom, and Gomorrah, Admah, and
Zeboim, which the Lord overthrew in his anger, and in his wrath." KJV

The land has become a waste

JEREMIAH 25:36–38 "Hark, the cry of the shepherds, and the wail of the
lords of the flock! For **the Lord is despoiling their pasture**, and the peaceful

folds are devastated, because of the fierce anger of the Lord. Like a lion he has left his covert, for **their land has become a waste** because of the sword of the oppressor, and because of his fierce anger." RSV

Great pestilence

JEREMIAH 21:6 "And I will smite the inhabitants of this city, both man and beast: they shall die of a **great pestilence**." KJV

Israel struck with a "wasting disease"

PSALM 106:14–15 "But they had a wanton craving in the wilderness, and put God to the test in the desert; he gave them what they asked, but sent a **wasting disease** among them." RSV

Terrified with tumors

1 SAMUEL 5:6 "The hand of the Lord was heavy upon the people of Ashdod, and he terrified and **afflicted them with tumors** [JUB: "hemorrhoids"], both Ashdod and its territory." RSV

Philistines struck with plague and tumors

1 SAMUEL 5:9–12 "The hand of the Lord was against the city, causing a very great panic, and he afflicted the men of the city, both young and old, so that **tumors broke out** upon them. . . . For there was a deathly panic throughout the whole city. The hand of God was very heavy there; the men who did not die were **stricken with tumors**, and the cry of the city went up to heaven." RSV

The Lord makes warriors ill

ISAIAH 10:16 "Therefore the Lord, the Lord of hosts, will send **wasting sickness** among his stout warriors, and under his glory a burning will be kindled, like the burning of fire." RSV

Stinky pestilence

AMOS 4:10 "I sent among you a **pestilence** after the manner of Egypt; I slew your young men with the sword; I carried away your horses; and I made the stench of your camp go up into your nostrils; yet you did not return to me, says the Lord." RSV

Pestilence and burning coals

HABAKKUK 3:3–6 "His glory covered the heavens, and the earth was full of his praise. And his brightness was as the light; he had horns coming out of his hand: and there was the hiding of his power. Before him went the **pestilence**, and burning coals went forth at his feet. He stood, and measured the earth: he beheld, and drove asunder the nations; and the everlasting mountains were scattered, the perpetual hills did bow." KJV

Deadly diseases

JEREMIAH 16:3–4 "For thus says the Lord concerning the sons and daughters who are born in this place, and concerning the mothers who bore them and the fathers who begot them in this land: **They shall die of deadly diseases.** They shall not be lamented, nor shall they be buried; they shall be as dung on the surface of the ground. They shall perish by the sword and by famine, and their dead bodies shall be food for the birds of the air and for the beasts of the earth." RSV

Flesh, eyes, and tongue rot away

ZECHARIAH 14:12 "And this shall be the **plague** wherewith the Lord will smite all the people that have fought against Jerusalem; **Their flesh shall consume away** while they stand upon their feet, and **their eyes shall consume away** in their holes, and **their tongue shall consume** away in their mouth." KJV

Don't forget the animals

ZECHARIAH 14:15 "And so shall be the **plague** of the horse, of the mule, of the camel, and of the ass, and of all the beasts that shall be in these tents, as this **plague.**" KJV

Now let's watch the prophets Ezekiel and Jeremiah unleash more than a dozen passages containing the Triple Threat: sword, famine, and pestilence. Ezekiel explains how the Triple Threat is apportioned:

Wherefore, as I live, saith the Lord God; Surely, because thou hast defiled my sanctuary with all thy detestable things, and with all thine abominations, therefore will I also diminish thee; neither shall mine eye spare, neither will I have any pity. A third part of thee shall die with the **pestilence,** *and with* **famine** *shall they be consumed in the midst of thee: and a third part shall fall by the* **sword** *round about thee; and I will scatter a third part into all the winds, and I will draw out a sword after them.* (EZEKIEL 5:11–12, KJV)

Then he explains where each of the three Triple Threats is to occur:

Thus says the Lord God: Clap your hands and stamp your foot, and say, Alas for all the vile abominations of the house of Israel! For they shall fall by the **sword,** *by* **famine,** *and by* **pestilence.** *Those far off shall die of* **pestilence;** *those nearby shall fall by the* **sword;** *and any who are left and are spared shall die of* **famine.** *Thus I will spend my fury upon them.* (EZEKIEL 6:11–12)

The **sword** *is outside,* **pestilence** *and* **famine** *are inside; those in the field die by the sword; those in the city—***famine** *and* **pestilence** *devour them.* (EZEKIEL 7:15)

A few chapters later, Ezekiel says God will spare a few survivors from the Triple Threat, not out of mercy, but as a need for witnesses:

> But I will let a few of them escape from the **sword**, from **famine** and **pestilence**, so that they may tell of all their abominations among the nations where they go; then they shall know that I am the Lord. (Ezekiel 12:16)

Jeremiah is something of a broken record on the Triple Threat theme.

Unforgiving pestilence

Jeremiah 14:11–12 "Then said the Lord unto me, Pray not for this people for their good. When they fast, I will not hear their cry; and when they offer burnt offering and an oblation, I will not accept them: but I will consume them by the **sword**, and by the **famine**, and by the **pestilence**." KJV

Pestilence is the way of death

Jeremiah 21:8–9 "And unto this people thou shalt say, Thus saith the Lord; Behold, I set before you the way of life, and the way of death. He that abideth in this city shall die by the **sword**, and by the **famine**, and by the **pestilence**." KJV

Utterly destroyed by pestilence

Jeremiah 24:10 "And I will send the **sword**, the **famine**, and the **pestilence**, among them, till they be consumed from off the land that I gave unto them and to their fathers." KJV

Complete destruction by pestilence

Jeremiah 27:8 "And it shall come to pass, that the nation and kingdom which will not serve the same Nebuchadnezzar the king of Babylon, and that will not put their neck under the yoke of the king of Babylon, that nation will I punish, saith the Lord, with the **sword**, and with the **famine**, and with the **pestilence**, until I have consumed them by his hand." KJV

Pestilence let loose

Jeremiah 29:17–19 "Thus saith the Lord of hosts; Behold, I will send upon them the **sword**, the **famine**, and the **pestilence**, and will make them like vile figs, that cannot be eaten, they are so evil. And I will persecute them with the **sword**, with the **famine**, and with the **pestilence**, and will deliver them to be removed to all the kingdoms of the earth, to be a curse, and an astonishment, and an hissing, and a reproach, among all the nations whither I have driven them: Because they have not hearkened to my words, saith the Lord." KJV

City conquered by the triple threat

Jeremiah 32:36 "And now therefore thus saith the Lord, the God of Israel, concerning this city, whereof ye say, It shall be delivered into the hand of the king of Babylon by the **sword**, and by the **famine**, and by the **pestilence**." KJV

"A liberty to pestilence"

JEREMIAH 34:17 "Therefore thus saith the Lord; Ye have not hearkened unto me, in proclaiming liberty, every one to his brother, and every man to his neighbour: behold, I proclaim a liberty for you, saith the Lord, to the **sword**, to the **pestilence**, and to the **famine**." KJV

Get out of town, or die by pestilence

JEREMIAH 38:2 "Thus saith the Lord, He that remaineth in this city shall die by the **sword**, by the **famine**, and by the **pestilence**: but he that goeth forth to the Chaldeans shall live; for he shall have his life for a prey, and shall live." KJV

Stay out of Egypt, or die by pestilence

JEREMIAH 42:17 "So shall it be with all the men that set their faces to go into Egypt to sojourn there; they shall die by the **sword**, by the **famine**, and by the **pestilence**: and none of them shall remain or escape from the evil that I will bring upon them." KJV (*God admits that his pestilence is "evil." The word "evil" in the Hebrew here is "rah."*)

Egyptian residents punished with pestilence

JEREMIAH 44:13 "For I will punish them that dwell in the land of Egypt, as I have punished Jerusalem, by the **sword**, by the **famine**, and by the **pestilence**." KJV

Just when you thought it couldn't get any worse, God makes it a Quadruple Threat. Here come the wild animals!

"My four deadly acts of judgment"

EZEKIEL 14:12–21 "The word of the Lord came to me: Mortal, when a land sins against me by acting faithlessly, and I stretch out my hand against it, and break its staff of bread and send **famine** upon it, and cut off from it human beings and animals. . . . If I send **wild animals** through the land to ravage it, so that it is made desolate, and no one may pass through because of the animals. . . . Or if I bring a **sword** upon that land and say, 'Let a sword pass through the land,' and I cut off human beings and animals from it; . . . Or if I send a **pestilence** into that land, and pour out my wrath upon it with blood, to cut off humans and animals from it; . . . For thus says the Lord God: How much more when I send upon Jerusalem **my four deadly acts of judgment, sword, famine, wild animals, and pestilence**, to cut off humans and animals from it!" NRSV

"Bitter pestilence" and "teeth of beasts"

DEUTERONOMY 32:23–25 "I will heap **mischiefs** upon them; I will spend mine **arrows** upon them. They shall be burnt with **hunger**, and devoured with burning **heat**, and with **bitter destruction** [NRSV: "pestilence"]: I will also send the **teeth of beasts** upon them, with the **poison** of serpents of the dust. The **sword** without, and terror within, shall destroy both the young man and the virgin, the suckling also with the man of gray hairs." KJV

Pestilence, evil arrows of famine, and evil beasts

EZEKIEL 5:15–17 "So it shall be a reproach and a taunt, an instruction and an astonishment unto the nations that are round about thee, when I shall execute judgments in thee in anger and in fury and in furious rebukes. I the Lord have spoken it. When I shall send upon them the **evil arrows of famine**, which shall be for their destruction, and which I will send to destroy you: and I will increase the **famine** upon you, and will break your staff of bread: So will I send upon you **famine** and **evil beasts**, and they shall bereave thee: and **pestilence** and blood shall pass through thee; and I will bring the **sword** upon thee. I the Lord have spoken it." KJV

Beasts outside, pestilence inside

EZEKIEL 33:27 "Say thou thus unto them, Thus saith the Lord God; As I live, surely they that are in the wastes shall fall by the **sword**, and him that is in the open field will I give to the **beasts** to be devoured, and they that be in the forts and in the caves shall die of the **pestilence**." KJV

Fiery serpents

NUMBERS 21:6 "And the Lord sent **fiery serpents** [NRSV: "poisonous serpents"] among the people, and they bit the people; and much people of Israel died." KJV

Here is a passage in Ezekiel that exemplifies many of the traits in Dawkins's list: jealous and proud of it, bloodthirsty, pestilential, megalomaniacal, and a bully.

For in my **jealousy** *and in the fire of my* **wrath** *have I spoken, Surely in that day there shall be a great shaking in the land of Israel; So that the fishes of the sea, and the fowls of the heaven, and the beasts of the field, and all creeping things that creep upon the earth, and all the men that are upon the face of the earth, shall* **shake at my presence**, *and the mountains shall be thrown down, and the steep places shall fall, and every wall shall fall to the ground. And I will call for a* **sword** *against him throughout all my mountains, saith the Lord God: every man's sword shall be against his brother. And I will plead against him with* **pestilence** *and with* **blood**; *and I will rain upon him, and upon his bands, and upon the many people that are with him, an overflowing rain, and great* **hailstones, fire,** *and* **brimstone**. *Thus will* **I magnify myself**, *and sanctify myself; and I will be known in the eyes of many nations, and* **they shall know that I am the Lord**. (EZEKIEL 38:19–23, KJV)*

Notice the sentence "I will plead against him with pestilence." God here is "reasoning" with violence.

"I'm gonna make him an offer he can't refuse," says the Godfather.

Let's end with a scathing passage of fifty-four continuous verses of pestilential curses screamed from the mouth of the Lord Jealous that would have impressed even Jonathan Edwards. See if you can read it all the way through. Pestilence appears near the top, but notice how creative the God of the Old Testament could get with his fiendish threats.

Pestilence, mildew, tumors, scab and itch! Ulcers, blindness, and "plagues wonderful!"

DEUTERONOMY 28:15–68 "But it shall come to pass, if thou wilt not hearken unto the voice of the Lord thy God, to observe to do all his commandments and his statutes which I command thee this day; that all these **curses** shall come upon thee, and overtake thee:

"**Cursed** shalt thou be in the city, and cursed shalt thou be in the field.

"**Cursed** shall be thy basket and thy store.

"**Cursed** shall be the fruit of thy body, and the fruit of thy land, the increase of thy kine, and the flocks of thy sheep.

"**Cursed** shalt thou be when thou comest in, and cursed shalt thou be when thou goest out.

"The Lord shall send upon thee **cursing**, vexation, and rebuke, in all that thou settest thine hand unto for to do, until thou be destroyed, and until thou perish quickly; because of the wickedness of thy doings, whereby thou hast forsaken me.

"The Lord shall make the **pestilence** cleave unto thee, until he have consumed thee from off the land, whither thou goest to possess it.

"The Lord shall smite thee with a **consumption**, and with a **fever**, and with an **inflammation**, and with an extreme **burning**, and with the **sword**, and with **blasting**, and with **mildew**; and they shall pursue thee until thou perish. And thy heaven that is over thy head shall be brass, and the earth that is under thee shall be iron.

"The Lord shall make the rain of thy land powder and dust: from heaven shall it come down upon thee, until thou be destroyed. The Lord shall cause thee to be smitten before thine enemies: thou shalt go out one way against them, and flee seven ways before them: and shalt be removed into all the kingdoms of the earth. And thy carcase shall be meat unto all fowls of the air, and unto the beasts of the earth, and no man shall fray them away.

"The Lord will smite thee with the **botch** [NRSV: "boils"] of Egypt, and with the **emerods** [NRSV: "tumors"], and with the **scab**, and with the **itch**, whereof thou canst not be healed. The Lord shall smite thee with **madness**, and **blindness**, and astonishment of heart: And thou shalt grope at noonday, as the blind gropeth in darkness, and thou shalt not prosper in thy ways: and thou shalt be only oppressed and spoiled evermore, and no man shall save thee.

"Thou shalt betroth a wife, and another man shall lie with her: thou shalt build an house, and thou shalt not dwell therein: thou shalt plant a vineyard, and shalt not gather the grapes thereof. Thine ox shall be **slain** before thine eyes, and thou shalt not eat thereof: thine ass shall be violently taken away from before thy face, and shall not be restored to thee: thy sheep shall be given unto thine enemies, and thou shalt have none to rescue them. Thy sons and thy daughters shall be given unto another people, and thine eyes shall look, and fail with longing for them all the day long; and there shall be no might in thine hand.

"The fruit of thy land, and all thy labours, shall a nation which thou knowest not eat up; and thou shalt be only **oppressed** and **crushed** alway: So that thou shalt be mad for the sight of thine eyes which thou shalt see.

"The Lord shall **smite** thee in the knees, and in the legs, with a sore **botch** that cannot be healed, from the sole of thy foot unto the top of thy head.

"The Lord shall bring thee, and thy king which thou shalt set over thee, unto a nation which neither thou nor thy fathers have known; and there shalt thou serve other gods, wood and stone. And thou shalt become an astonishment, a proverb, and a byword, among all nations whither the Lord shall lead thee.

"Thou shalt carry much seed out into the field, and shalt gather but little in; for the **locust** shall consume it. Thou shalt plant vineyards, and dress them, but shalt neither drink of the wine, nor gather the grapes; for the **worms** shall eat them. Thou shalt have olive trees throughout all thy coasts, but thou shalt not anoint thyself with the oil; for thine olive shall cast his fruit.

"Thou shalt beget sons and daughters, but thou shalt not enjoy them; for they shall go into **captivity**. All thy trees and fruit of thy land shall the **locust** consume.

"The stranger that is within thee shall get up above thee very high; and thou shalt come down very low. He shall lend to thee, and thou shalt not lend to him: he shall be the head, and thou shalt be the tail.

"Moreover all these **curses** shall come upon thee, and shall pursue thee, and overtake thee, till thou be destroyed; because thou hearkenedst not unto the voice of the Lord thy God, to keep his commandments and his statutes which he commanded thee: And they shall be upon thee for a sign and for a wonder, and upon thy seed for ever. Because thou servedst not the Lord thy God with joyfulness, and with gladness of heart, for the abundance of all things;

"Therefore shalt thou **serve thine enemies** which the Lord shall send against thee, in **hunger**, and in **thirst**, and in **nakedness**, and in want of all things: and he shall put a **yoke of iron** upon thy neck, until he have destroyed thee.

"The Lord shall bring a nation against thee from far, from the end of the earth, as swift as the eagle flieth; a nation whose tongue thou shalt not understand; A nation of fierce countenance, which shall not regard the person of the old, nor shew favour to the young: And he shall eat the fruit of thy cattle, and the fruit of thy land, until thou be destroyed: which also shall not leave thee either corn, wine, or oil, or the increase of thy kine, or flocks of thy sheep, until he have destroyed thee. And he shall besiege thee in all thy gates, until thy high and fenced walls come down, wherein thou trustedst, throughout all thy land: and he shall besiege thee in all thy gates throughout all thy land, which the Lord thy God hath given thee.

"And thou shalt eat the fruit of thine own body, the flesh of thy sons and of thy daughters, which the Lord thy God hath given thee, in the siege, and in the straitness, wherewith thine enemies shall distress thee: So that the man that is tender among you, and very delicate, his eye shall be evil toward his brother, and toward the wife of his bosom, and toward the remnant of his children which he shall leave: So that he will not give to any of them of the flesh of his children whom he shall eat: because he hath nothing left him in the siege, and in the straitness, wherewith thine enemies shall distress thee in all thy gates.

"The tender and delicate woman among you, which would not adventure to set the sole of her foot upon the ground for delicateness and tenderness, her eye shall be evil toward the husband of her bosom, and toward her son, and toward her daughter, And toward her young one that cometh out from between her feet, and toward her children which she shall bear: for she shall eat them for want of all things secretly in the siege and straitness, wherewith thine enemy shall distress thee in thy gates.

"If thou wilt not observe to do all the words of this law that are written in this book, that thou mayest fear this glorious and fearful name, The Lord Thy God; Then the Lord will make thy **plagues wonderful**, and the **plagues** of thy seed, even **great plagues**, and of long continuance, and **sore sicknesses**, and of long continuance.

"Moreover he will bring upon thee all the **diseases** of Egypt, which thou wast afraid of; and they shall cleave unto thee. Also every **sickness**, and every **plague**, which is not written in the book of this law, them will the Lord bring upon thee, until thou be destroyed.

"And ye shall be left few in number, whereas ye were as the stars of heaven for multitude; because thou wouldest not obey the voice of the Lord thy God. And it shall come to pass, that as the Lord rejoiced over you to do you good, and to multiply you; so the Lord will rejoice over you to **destroy you,** and to bring you to nought; and ye shall be plucked from off the land whither thou goest to possess it.

"And the Lord shall scatter thee among all people, from the one end of the earth even unto the other; and there thou shalt serve other gods, which neither thou nor thy fathers have known, even wood and stone. And among these nations shalt thou **find no ease**, neither shall the sole of thy foot have rest: but the Lord shall give thee there a **trembling heart**, and **failing of eyes**, and **sorrow of mind**: And thy life shall hang in doubt before thee; and thou shalt fear day and night, and shalt have none assurance of thy life: In the morning thou shalt say, Would God it were even! and at even thou shalt say, Would God it were morning! for the fear of thine heart wherewith thou shalt fear, and for the sight of thine eyes which thou shalt see.

"And the Lord shall bring thee into Egypt again with ships, by the way whereof I spake unto thee, Thou shalt see it no more again: and there ye shall be **sold unto your enemies** for bondmen and bondwomen, and no man shall buy you." KJV

For the 2014 National Day of Prayer, a special prayer was composed and recited by Anne Graham Lotz, the daughter of the Rev. Billy Graham. Skipping (as usual) the part about God bringing drought, locusts, and pestilence, she intoned: "We have turned away from You. Yet You have promised in 2 Chronicles 7, that if we—a people identified with You—would humble ourselves, pray, seek Your face, and turn from our wicked ways, then You would hear our prayer, forgive our sin, and heal our land."

The verse she misquoted was merely a local scheme for God to save his chosen people from his own pestilential self. It is not appropriate for modern evangelical purposes. Read it again, the sanitized and deliberately misleading version theocrats like to quote:

If my people, which are called by my name, shall humble themselves,
and pray, and seek my face, and turn from their wicked ways; then will
I hear from heaven, and will forgive their sin, and will heal their land.
(2 Chronicles 7:14, KJV)

"If my people" was referring to God's chosen people, the Israelites, not to any other country in the world, or any other time of history. He had latched on to *them*, like an obsessed lover who will go to any lengths to conquer and own the object of his fixation.

"Which are called by my name" refers to the name of the nation of Israel. "Israel" ends with "El," one of the names of God. "Isra-el" means "struggled with God." America is certainly not "called by God's name." America was named after the Italian explorer Amerigo, one of the Vespucci brothers from Florence. The name "United States of America" was chosen by the anti-Christian deist Thomas Paine. No other country—not Scotland, Ireland (named after a pagan fertility goddess), England, France, Australia, the Philippines, South Africa, Indonesia, Cameroon, Brazil, New Zealand, you name it—is called by the name of El or Yahweh. Trinidad is named after the Christian trinity, though "trinity" appears nowhere in the bible, and it is not a name. The closest might be El Salvador—"Salvador" means "Savior," but "El" in this case just means "The."

"Turn from their wicked ways" is not a plea to act morally. The people were deemed "wicked" simply because they chose to worship other gods, which made the Lord Jealous angry, not because they had committed any actual harm. To evangelicals, "turn from their wicked ways" means "turn back to God." This runs contrary to the American First Amendment, as well as the charter of rights of most secular democracies and the United Nations, which recognize and respect religious freedom, including the freedom to dissent from God or religion. According to the god El, it is not just atheism that is "wicked." (See PSALM 14.) All religions that do not "seek his face" are evil.

"Then will I hear from heaven" is a curious phrase for a God to speak. From whom is the creator of the universe expecting to hear? The author tells us that God spoke these words to King Solomon in the middle of the night. (So how does he know about it?) It is possible the author was confused about who was speaking, bumbling the idea that "If my [God's] people pray, then I [Solomon] will hear from heaven, and I [God] will heal their land." Let's be charitable—we can't blame God or Solomon for the sloppy writing of one of their chroniclers.

Amazingly, many modern believers think the Old Testament is all about *them*. Notice that Anne Graham Lotz twisted the meaning of the verse in an attempt to bring it into our modern world. Besides changing "heal their land" to "heal our land," she changed "people which are called by my name" to "a people identified with You." The United States was never "identified with" the God of the Old Testament. Modern evangelical Christians may wish to identify themselves with Israel's God, but that does not mean the rest of us must respect or humble ourselves before their pestilential Lord.

16

Megalomaniacal

"So I will display my greatness and my holiness and
make myself known in the eyes of many nations.
Then they shall know that I am the Lord."
—Ezekiel 38:23

The Lord Jealous had a bit of a problem: he wanted people to be impressed with his greatness, but they were not allowed to look at him. We saw in Chapter 1 that the crowd was barred from coming up Mount Sinai to see God face to face when he delivered his Ten Commandments. All they witnessed was a clouded, quaking, burning peak. The stage was roped off. Only Moses was allowed access to a personal performance. Or so he said. Like Mount Sinai, the Ark of the Covenant (which God supposedly inhabited) was also hidden and blanketed. Moses and the high priest were permitted a peek once a year. So how could the people know how majestic the Lord was if they never saw him? How can you say God is great if all you have is the word of the preachers? The obvious answer is that God is a fiction and the authors had to invent reasons why nobody could see him.

To get around this problem, the writer of the story decided to let God relax his rule and throw a once-in-a-lifetime backstage party for seventy-four lucky people who got to meet him in person.

*Then Moses and Aaron, Nadab, and Abihu, and seventy of the elders of Israel
went up, and **they saw the God of Israel**. Under his feet there was something
like a pavement of sapphire stone, like the very heaven for clearness. God
did not lay his hand on the chief men of the people of Israel; also they beheld
God, and they ate and drank. (*Exodus 24:9–11*)

Seventy-two people besides Moses and Aaron got to see God and not die. What
an honor! The Lord cordially restrained himself from killing them ("did not lay his
hand" on them) while they dined in his fearful presence. While they were eating and
drinking, God stepped off his sparkling gem-like platform and called Moses to the
peak to collect the decalogue stones:

*The Lord said to Moses, "Come up to me on the mountain, and wait there;
and I will give you the tablets of stone, with the law and the commandment,
which I have written for their instruction." So Moses set out with his assistant
Joshua, and Moses went up into the mountain of God. To the elders he had
said, "Wait here for us, until we come to you again; for Aaron and Hur are
with you; whoever has a dispute may go to them." (*Exodus 24:12–14*)

I can picture those seventy-two elders partying while Moses left to pick up the
goods. "Wow, that was awesome! We got to meet God in person!" They must have
been drinking a lot because Moses anticipated they would get into a fight. I wonder
if they actually saw God, or if they only saw Moses double through blasted eyes and
thought one of them was God. In the end, none of them witnessed the Command
Performance itself.

*Then Moses went up on the mountain, and the cloud covered the mountain.
The glory of the Lord settled on Mount Sinai, and the cloud covered it for
six days; on the seventh day he called to Moses out of the cloud. Now the
appearance of the glory of the Lord was like a devouring fire on the top of the
mountain in the sight of the people of Israel. Moses entered the cloud, and
went up on the mountain. Moses was on the mountain for forty days and
forty nights. (*Exodus 24:15–18*)

None of the common folk, not even the seventy elders, got to see God's full majesty. All they saw was "the glory of the Lord like a devouring fire on the top of the
mountain." This is worse than mere megalomania. This is saying "Lower your eyes.
I'm so great that you can't even look at me!"

Megalomania does not have a precise medical definition. In the old days, it was called
a "narcissistic personality disorder," and that seems to fit the God of the Old Testament
perfectly." Look at me, me, me! I am wonderful! Nobody is more powerful!" Here
is some more henotheistic chest-thumping:

"There is no god besides me"

DEUTERONOMY 32:39 "See now that I, even I, am he, and **there is no god beside me**; I kill and I make alive; I wound and I heal; and there is none that can deliver out of my hand." RSV (*This is not monotheism. The KJV says "there is no god with me" and other translations say "there is no god beside me." It means no other god is alongside Yahweh.*)

Those other gods are not as great

PSALM 95:3 "For **the Lord is a great God**, and a great King above all gods." RSV

He is more fearful than all gods

I CHRONICLES 16:25 "For **great** is the Lord, and greatly to be praised: he also is to be feared above all gods." KJV

More majestic than the other gods

EXODUS 15:11 "Who is like you, O Lord, among the gods? Who is like you, **majestic** in holiness, **awesome** in **splendor**, doing wonders?"

Feared above other gods

PSALM 96:4 "For the Lord is **great**, and greatly to be praised: he is to be **feared above all gods**." KJV

More mighty and awesome than the other gods

DEUTERONOMY 10:17, 20 "For the Lord your God is God of gods and Lord of lords, **the great God, mighty and awesome**. . . . Fear the Lord your God and serve him." NIV

"The King of glory"

PSALM 24:7–10 "Lift up your heads, O ye gates; and be ye lift up, ye everlasting doors; and the **King of glory** shall come in. Who is this King of glory? The Lord **strong and mighty**, the Lord **mighty in battle**. Lift up your heads, O ye gates; even lift them up, ye everlasting doors; and the **King of glory** shall come in. Who is this **King of glory**? The Lord of hosts, he is the **King of glory**." KJV

The Old Testament is crammed with ego-stroking proclamations, attention-seeking and show-off displays of God's self-proclaimed majesty.

A great and awesome God

DEUTERONOMY 7:21 "Do not be terrified by them, for the Lord your God, who is among you, is a **great and awesome God**." NIV (*This sounds like "The great and powerful Oz."*)

Greatness of his excellency

Exodus 15:7 "And in **the greatness of thine excellency** thou hast overthrown them that rose up against thee: thou sentest forth thy wrath, which consumed them as stubble." KJV

"Acknowledge my might"

Isaiah 33:10–12 "Now will I rise, saith the Lord; now will I be **exalted**; now will **I lift up myself**. Ye shall conceive chaff, ye shall bring forth stubble: your breath, as fire, shall devour you. And the people shall be as the burnings of lime: as thorns cut up shall they be burned in the fire. Hear, ye that are far off, what I have done; and, ye that are near, **acknowledge my might**." KJV

The terrible God who loves only those who obey him

Nehemiah 1:5 "And said, I beseech thee, O Lord God of heaven, the **great and terrible God**, that keepeth covenant and mercy for them that love him and observe his commandments." KJV (*And with nobody else.*)

"The earth will shake at my presence"

Ezekiel 38:19–20 "For in my jealousy and in the fire of my wrath have I spoken, Surely in that day there shall be a great shaking in the land of Israel; So that the fishes of the sea, and the fowls of the heaven, and the beasts of the field, and all creeping things that creep upon the earth, and **all the men that are upon the face of the earth, shall shake at my presence**." KJV

"I will magnify myself"

Ezekiel 38:22–23 "And I will plead against him [Gog] with pestilence and with blood; and I will rain upon him, and upon his bands, and upon the many people that are with him, an overflowing rain, and great hailstones, fire, and brimstone. **Thus will I magnify myself**, and sanctify myself; and **I will be known in the eyes of many nations, and they shall know that I am the Lord**." KJV (*The whole point of the violence is for God to be noticed.*)

The plagues were to "gain glory for myself"

Exodus 14:4, 17–18 "And I will harden Pharaoh's heart, and he will pursue them. But **I will gain glory for myself** through Pharaoh and all his army, and the Egyptians will know that I am the Lord. . . . I will harden the hearts of the Egyptians so that they will go in after them. And I will **gain glory** through Pharaoh and all his army, through his chariots and his horsemen. The Egyptians will know that I am the Lord when I **gain glory** through Pharaoh, his chariots and his horsemen." NIV

The unapproachable glory of the Lord

Exodus 40:35 "And Moses was not able to enter into the tent of the congregation, because the cloud abode thereon, and **the glory of the Lord** filled the tabernacle." KJV

His unapproachable glory filled the house
2 CHRONICLES 7:2 "And the priests could not enter into the house of the Lord, because the **glory of the Lord** had filled the Lord's house." KJV

The glory of the Lord appeared
NUMBERS 14:10–11 "And **the glory of the Lord** appeared in the tabernacle of the congregation before all the children of Israel. And the Lord said unto Moses, How long will this people provoke me? and how long will it be ere they believe me, for all the signs which I have shewed among them?" KJV

Look at me, I am glorious
NUMBERS 16:19 "And the **glory of the Lord** appeared unto all the congregation." KJV

"The earth will be filled with my glory"
NUMBERS 14:21–23 "But as truly as I live, all the earth shall be filled with **the glory of the Lord**. Because all those men which have seen my **glory**, and my miracles, which I did in Egypt and in the wilderness, and have tempted me now these ten times, and have not hearkened to my voice; Surely they shall not see the land which I sware unto their fathers, neither shall any of them that provoked me see it." KJV

Show us your greatness
DEUTERONOMY 3:24 "O Lord God, thou hast begun to shew thy servant **thy greatness**, and thy **mighty hand**: for what God is there in heaven or in earth, that can do according to thy works, and according to thy might?" KJV

We saw his greatness and didn't die!
DEUTERONOMY 5:24 "Behold, the Lord our God hath shewed us his **glory** and his **greatness**, and we have heard his voice out of the midst of the fire: we have seen this day that God doth talk with man, and he liveth." KJV

Acknowledge his greatness
DEUTERONOMY 11:2 "And know ye this day: for I speak not with your children which have not known, and which have not seen the chastisement of the Lord your God, his **greatness**, his **mighty hand**, and his stretched out arm." KJV

Proclaim his greatness
DEUTERONOMY 32:3 "Because I will publish the name of the Lord: ascribe ye **greatness** unto our God." KJV

Make known his glory

Psalm 145:11–13 "They shall speak of the **glory** of thy kingdom, and talk of thy **power**; To make known to the sons of men his **mighty acts**, and the **glorious majesty** of his kingdom. Thy kingdom is an everlasting kingdom, and thy **dominion** endureth throughout all generations." KJV

Declare his glory

1 Chronicles 16:24: "Declare his **glory** among the heathen; his **marvellous works** among all nations." KJV

Broadcast his glory and power

Psalm 145:11 "They shall speak of the **glory of thy kingdom**, and talk of thy power." KJV

Sing of his great glory

Psalm 138:5 "Yea, they shall sing in the ways of the Lord: for **great is the glory** of the Lord." KJV

His glory revealed

Isaiah 40:5 "And the **glory of the Lord** shall be revealed, and all flesh shall see it together: for the mouth of the Lord hath spoken it." KJV

Everybody say "Glory"

Psalm 29:9 "The voice of the Lord makes the oaks to whirl, and strips the forests bare; and in his temple all cry, '**Glory!**'" RSV

International glory

Psalm 96:3 "**Declare his glory** among the nations, his marvelous works among all the peoples!" RSV

Greatness exalted above all

1 Chronicles 29:11 "Thine, O Lord is the **greatness**, and the **power**, and the **glory**, and the **victory**, and the **majesty**: for all that is in the heaven and in the earth is thine; thine is the kingdom, O Lord, and **thou art exalted** as head above all." KJV

How excellent is his name!

Psalm 8:1 "O Lord, our Lord, how **excellent** is thy name in all the earth! who hast set thy **glory** above the heavens." KJV

Great and terrible name

Psalm 99:3 "Let them praise thy **great and terrible** name! Holy is he!" RSV

The glory of his name

Psalm 29:2 "Give unto the Lord the **glory** due unto his name; worship the Lord in the beauty of holiness." KJV

My "glorious and fearful name"

DEUTERONOMY 28:58–59 "If thou wilt not observe to do all the words of this law that are written in this book, that thou mayest fear this **glorious and fearful name**, The Lord Thy God; Then the Lord will make thy plagues wonderful, and the plagues of thy seed, even great plagues, and of long continuance, and sore sicknesses, and of long continuance." KJV

Bless and worship his glorious name

NEHEMIAH 9:5–6 "Stand up and bless the Lord your God for ever and ever: and blessed be thy **glorious name**, which is **exalted** above all blessing and praise. Thou, even thou, art Lord alone; thou hast made heaven, the heaven of heavens, with all their host, the earth, and all things that are therein, the seas, and all that is therein, and thou preservest them all; and the host of heaven worshippeth thee." KJV

Fear the name of the Lord

PSALM 102:15 "The nations will **fear the name of the Lord**, and all the kings of the earth thy **glory**." RSV

He made a glorious name for himself

ISAIAH 63:14–15 "So didst thou lead thy people, to make thyself **a glorious name**. Look down from heaven, and behold from the habitation of thy holiness and of thy **glory**." KJV

Great is the Lord

PSALM 48:1 "**Great is the Lord**, and greatly to be praised in the city of our God, in the mountain of his holiness." KJV

A lofty throne

ISAIAH 6:1: "In the year that king Uzziah died I saw also the Lord sitting upon a **throne, high and lifted up**, and his train filled the temple." KJV

A glorious throne

JEREMIAH 17:12–13 "A **glorious high throne** from the beginning is the place of our sanctuary. O Lord, the hope of Israel, all that forsake thee shall be ashamed." KJV

The earth is full of his glory

ISAIAH 6:3 "And one cried unto another, and said, Holy, holy, holy, is the Lord of hosts: **the whole earth is full of his glory**." KJV

The whole earth filled with his glory

PSALM 72:18–19 "Blessed be the Lord God, the God of Israel, who only doeth wondrous things. And blessed be his **glorious name** for ever: and let the **whole earth be filled with his glory**; Amen, and Amen." KJV

Glory above all the earth, say it twice

PSALM 57:5, 11 "Be thou exalted, O God, above the heavens; let thy **glory** be above all the earth. . . . Be thou exalted, O God, above the heavens: let thy **glory** be above all the earth." KJV

Glory above the heavens

PSALM 113:4 "The Lord is high above all nations, and his **glory** above the heavens." KJV

His glory is above earth and heaven

PSALM 148:13 "Let them praise the name of the Lord: for his name alone is excellent; his **glory is above the earth and heaven**." KJV

The universe proclaims his glory

PSALM 19:1 "The heavens declare **the glory of God**; and the firmament sheweth his handywork." KJV

Exalted above the heavens

PSALM 108:5 "Be thou **exalted**, O God, above the heavens: and thy **glory** above all the earth." KJV

Strength and power exalted

PSALM 21:13 "Be thou **exalted**, Lord, in thine own **strength**: so will we sing and praise thy **power**." KJV

Glory forever

PSALM 72:19 "And blessed be his **glorious name** for ever: and let the whole earth be filled with his **glory**; Amen, and Amen." KJV

Unsearchable greatness

PSALM 145:3 "**Great is the Lord, and greatly to be praised**; and his greatness is unsearchable." KJV

Excellent greatness

PSALM 150:2 "Praise him for his mighty acts: praise him according to his **excellent greatness**." KJV

Hide from the fear of his majesty

ISAIAH 2:10 "Enter into the rock, and hide thee in the dust, for fear of the Lord, and for the **glory of his majesty**." KJV

Hide from the terror of his glory

ISAIAH 2:19 "And they shall go into the holes of the rocks, and into the caves of the earth, **for fear** [NRSV; "terror"] **of the Lord, and for the glory of his majesty**." KJV

God deceived, defiled, and horrified to prove he is in control

EZEKIEL 20:25–26 "Wherefore I gave them also statutes that were **not good**, and judgments whereby they should not live; And I **polluted** them in their own gifts, in that they caused to pass through the fire all that openeth the womb, that I might make them desolate, to the end **that they might know that I am the Lord**." KJV

Greater than the moon and sun

ISAIAH 24:23 "Then the moon shall be confounded, and the sun ashamed, when the Lord of hosts shall reign in mount Zion, and in Jerusalem, and before his ancients **gloriously**." KJV

Greater than the sun and moon

ISAIAH 60:19 "The sun shall be no more thy light by day; neither for brightness shall the moon give light unto thee: but the Lord shall be unto thee an everlasting light, and **thy God thy glory**." KJV

Glory like the oceans

HABAKKUK 2:14 "For the earth shall be filled with the knowledge of the **glory of the Lord,** as the waters cover the sea." KJV

More majestic than the waves

PSALM 93:1–5 "The Lord reigns; he is robed in **majesty**; the Lord is robed, he is girded with **strength**. Yea, the world is established; it shall never be moved; thy throne is established from of old; thou art from everlasting. The floods have lifted up, O Lord, the floods have lifted up their voice, the floods lift up their roaring. **Mightier** than the thunders of many waters, **mightier** than the waves of the sea, the Lord on high is **mighty**! Thy decrees are very sure; holiness befits thy house, O Lord, for evermore." RSV

"See my glory. Worship me"

ISAIAH 66:18, 23 "I will gather all nations and tongues; and they shall come, and **see my glory**. . . . from one new moon to another, and from one sabbath to another, **shall all flesh come to worship before me**, saith the Lord." KJV

Gushing glory

EZEKIEL 43:2 "And, behold, the **glory of the God of Israel** came from the way of the east: and his voice was like a noise of many waters: and the earth shined with his **glory**." KJV

International glory

EZEKIEL 39:21 "And I will set my **glory among the nations**; and all the nations shall see my judgment which I have executed, and my hand which I have laid on them." RSV

International greatness

EZEKIEL 38:23 "So I will show **my greatness** and my holiness and make myself known in the eyes of many nations. Then they will know that I am the Lord." RSV

God is mighty

JOB 36:5 "Behold, **God is mighty**, and despiseth not any: he is mighty in strength and wisdom." KJV

"I can do anything"

JEREMIAH 32:27 "Behold, I am the Lord, the God of all flesh: **is there any thing too hard for me?**" KJV

God brags about his powers

JOB, CHAPTERS 38–41 "I laid the foundations of the earth" • clouds • oceans • winds • sunrise • rain • stars • lightning • lions • goats • unicorns • peacock feathers • horses • hawks • eagles • thunder • behemoth • leviathan. (*The entire Chapter 41 is about how terrible the leviathan is, which God made.*)

A powerful hand

JOSHUA 4:24 "For the Lord your God dried up the Jordan . . . so that all the peoples of the earth might know that the hand of the Lord is **powerful** and so that you might always fear the Lord your God." NIV

A powerful voice

PSALM 29:4 "The voice of the Lord is **powerful**; the voice of the Lord is full of **majesty**." KJV

Awesome anger!

PSALM 76:7 "But you indeed are **awesome**! Who can stand before you when once your anger is roused?" NRSV

Bring gifts to the terrible one

PSALM 76:11–12 "Vow, and pay unto the Lord your God: let all that be round about him bring presents unto **him that ought to be feared**. He shall cut off the spirit of princes: he is **terrible** to the kings of the earth." KJV

Greatly to be praised

PSALM 48:1 "**Great is the Lord, and greatly to be praised** in the city of our God, in the mountain of his holiness." KJV

The mighty one speaks

PSALM 50:1 "**The Mighty One**, God, the Lord, speaks and summons the earth from the rising of the sun to where it sets." NIV

Super teacher

JOB 36:22 "God is **exalted** in his power. Who is a teacher like him? Who has prescribed his ways for him, or said to him, 'You have done wrong'?" NIV

He saved people for *his sake, not theirs*

PSALM 106:8 "Nevertheless he saved them for his name's sake, that he might make his **mighty power** to be known." KJV

Glorious splendor, majesty, wondrous, might, awesome, greatness

PSALM 145:5–6 "I will speak of the glorious **honour** of thy **majesty**, and of thy **wondrous works**. And men shall speak of the might of thy **terrible** acts: and I will declare thy **greatness**." KJV

Power and majesty

PSALM 68:34 "Ascribe **power** to God, whose **majesty** is over Israel, and his **power** is in the skies." RSV

The power of his anger

PSALM 90:11 "Who knoweth the **power** of thine anger? even according to thy fear, so is thy wrath." KJV

The eyes of his glory

ISAIAH 3:8 "For Jerusalem is ruined, and Judah is fallen: because their tongue and their doings are against the Lord, to provoke **the eyes of his glory**." KJV

Magnify his glorious law

ISAIAH 42:21 "The Lord was pleased, for his righteousness' sake, to **magnify** his law and make it **glorious**." RSV

Great, mighty and awesome

NEHEMIAH 9:32 "Now therefore, our God, the great God, **mighty and awesome**." NIV

More glorious than the mountains

PSALM 76:1–4 In Judah is God known: his name is great in Israel. . . . Thou art more **glorious** and **excellent** than the mountains of prey." KJV

"Everyone will know I am mighty"

ISAIAH 49:26 "Then all mankind will know that I, the Lord, am your Savior, your Redeemer, the **Mighty One** of Jacob." NIV

Great and mighty God

JEREMIAH 32:18–19 "The **Great**, the **Mighty God**, the Lord of hosts, is his name, **Great** in counsel, and **mighty** in work." KJV

Greatness, power, glory, victory, majesty, honor, might

1 CHRONICLES 29:11–13 "Thine, O Lord is the **greatness**, and the **power**, and the **glory**, and the **victory**, and the **majesty**: for all that is in the heaven and in the earth is thine; thine is the kingdom, O Lord, and thou art **exalted** as head above all. Both riches and **honour** come of thee, and thou reignest over all; and in thine hand is **power** and **might**; and in thine hand it is to **make great**, and to **give strength** unto all. Now therefore, our God, we thank thee, and praise thy **glorious** name." KJV

"I let you live so I can show you my power"

EXODUS 9:15–16 "For by now I could have put forth my hand and struck you and your people with pestilence, and you would have been cut off from the earth; but for this purpose have I let you live, **to show you my power, so that my name may be declared throughout all the earth**." RSV

Majestic sneeze

EXODUS 15:6–8 "Thy right hand, O Lord, is become **glorious in power**: thy right hand, O Lord, hath dashed in pieces the enemy. And in the greatness of thine excellency thou hast overthrown them that rose up against thee: thou sentest forth thy wrath, which consumed them as stubble. And **with the blast of thy nostrils** the waters were gathered together, the floods stood upright as an heap, and the depths were congealed in the heart of the sea." KJV

His powerful voice breaks the trees

PSALM 29:3–5 "The voice of the Lord is upon the waters: the **God of glory** thundereth: the Lord is upon many waters. **The voice of the Lord is powerful**; the voice of the Lord is full of **majesty**. The voice of the Lord breaketh the cedars; yea, the Lord breaketh the cedars of Lebanon." KJV

His voice is thunder!

JOB 37:4–5 "After it a voice roareth: he thundereth with the voice of his excellency; and he will not stay them when his voice is heard. **God thundereth marvellously with his voice**; great things doeth he, which we cannot comprehend." KJV

Rays flashed from his hands!

HABAKKUK 3:3–6 "**His glory covered the heavens** and his praise filled the earth. His splendor was like the sunrise; **rays flashed from his hand**, where his power was hidden. Plague went before him; pestilence followed his steps. He stood, and shook the earth; he looked, and made the nations tremble. The ancient mountains crumbled and the age-old hills collapsed—but he marches on forever." NIV (*His power is hidden in his hands—light saber?*)

By now you have noticed that the Ten Commandments are not monotheistic. The first Commandment prohibits having other gods, and the second Commandment states that God is jealous of those other gods:

> *I am the Lord your God, who brought you out of the land of Egypt, out of the house of slavery;* **you shall have no other gods before me***. You shall not make for yourself an idol, whether in the form of anything that is in heaven above, or that is on the earth beneath, or that is in the water under the earth. You shall not bow down to them or worship them;* **for I the Lord your God am a jealous God***. (*EXODUS 20:2–5*)*

You can't be jealous of someone who does not exist. The entire Old Testament is about the Lord Jealous viciously fending off competitive suitors of his chosen sweetheart. The Promised Land was to be their love nest, cleared free of any potential challenges to his dominance and her compliance. Like an alpha male thumping his chest, the God of the Old Testament tries desperately to impress his chosen mate with braggadocio, ruthlessly scaring off and eliminating rivals and threatening her with the same treatment if she does not graciously submit to his love.

The early Israelites indeed believed there were many gods, but imagined that theirs was supreme. This is known as henotheism, or monarchical polytheism. Their god was the "Lord of Lords" and "King of Kings." Like a football player showing off to both impress the cheerleaders and intimidate the competition, the Lord Jealous was a macho boaster. "Look at me! I am the great and terrible Lord!"

It seems to me that a truly great person would not have to brag about it. Truly great people don't need to draw attention to themselves. A truly great person is concerned about the effects of their actions in the real world, not about how they are perceived by underlings. Truly great people are psychologically secure, not dependent on the opinions of others.

God is not great. He is merely megalomaniacal.

17

Sadomasochistic

*"The Lord will afflict with scabs the heads of
the daughters of Zion, and the LORD will
lay bare their secret parts."*
—ISAIAH 3:16–17

Jeremiah, the "weeping prophet," was tasked with explaining to the Israelites why they had suffered defeat, destruction, and exile at the hands of the Babylonians:

> And when your people say, "Why has the Lord our God done all these things to us?" you shall say to them, "As you have forsaken me and served foreign gods in your land, so you shall serve strangers in a land that is not yours."
> (JEREMIAH 5:19)

So it was their own fault: "You have forsaken me." There is no freedom in love, apparently. God's lover had a wandering eye, so it was eye for an eye. The Lord Jealous invited foreigners to attack his chosen people because, like a cheating wife, they had defamed his honor, wounded his pride, and hurt his fragile feelings.

To lay it on thick, Jeremiah pens one of the most shocking passages in the entire Old Testament. Not content with being merely misogynistic and bloodthirsty, the Lord brags that he is also a rapist:

> Hear and give ear; do not be haughty, for the Lord has spoken. . . . And if you say in your heart, "Why have these things come upon me?" it is for the greatness of your iniquity that **your skirts are lifted up, and you are violated** . . .

because you have forgotten me and trusted in lies. **I myself will lift up your skirts over your face,** *and your shame will be seen.* (JEREMIAH 13:15–26)

The phrase "skirts are lifted up" is sexual assault. The word "violate" is rape. If you read only the King James Version, which has the quaint idiom "heels made bare," you might miss the sexual molestation. Some older translations render the literal euphemism "heels violated," but the meaning was sexual. For "skirts lifted up," some English translations have "skirts torn off" (NIV), "stripped" (NLT and CEB), "clothes torn off" (CEV), and "raped" (LB). For "violated," we have "mistreated" (NIV), "abused" (CEV), "destroyed" (LB), and "raped" (NLT). The Good News Translation has the good news that "your clothes have been torn off and you have been raped."

What happens to women during wartime? Historically, it was the Babylonians who committed this atrocity against the Israelites; but biblically, God took the credit: "I myself will lift up your skirts over your face." From the point of view of the biblical authors, the invasion (rape) was not simply territorial expansionism by King Nebuchadnezzar. Jeremiah said that the Lord caused it to happen to his own people as a punishment for their betrayal. Nebuchadnezzar's troops might have done the deed, but the Lord Jealous wanted them to know that they were being raped by God himself.

In the context of the brutality of war, God's sexually harassing remark was a full-frontal threat of sexual violence. Today a man would be fired from his job or slapped with a restraining order for such aggressive words of sexual harassment.

The *American Heritage Dictionary* defines sadomasochism as "The combination of sadism and masochism, in particular the deriving of pleasure, especially sexual gratification, from inflicting or submitting to physical or emotional abuse."

Although sexual gratification is not a requirement for sadomasochism, the God of the Old Testament clearly had a "sexual" relationship with his chosen people. They were a married couple:

> *On that day, says the Lord, you will call me, "My husband," and no longer will you call me, "My Baal." . . . And I will take you for my wife forever; I will take you for my wife in righteousness and in justice, in steadfast love, and in mercy. I will take you for my wife in faithfulness; and you shall know the Lord.* (HOSEA 2:16–20)

Isaiah and Jeremiah agreed:

> *For your Maker is your husband, the Lord of hosts is his name. . . . For the Lord has called you like a wife forsaken and grieved in spirit, like the wife of a man's youth when she is cast off, says your God.* (ISAIAH 54:5–6)

"Return, faithless people," declares the Lord, "for I am your husband."
(JEREMIAH 3:14, NIV)

God told Hosea that he loved the Israelites "as a woman":

Go, love a woman who has a lover and is an adulteress, just as the Lord loves the people of Israel, though they turn to other gods and love raisin cakes.
(HOSEA 3:1)

I'm not sure how the raisin cakes fit in, but the Lord Jealous certainly deems infidelity to be more than simply being an infidel. Some theologians call this a "mystical marriage" between God and his people, whom he considered his bride:

Thus says the Lord: I remember the devotion of your youth, your love as a bride, how you followed me in the wilderness. (JEREMIAH 2:2)

For as a young man marries a young woman, so shall your builder marry you, and as the bridegroom rejoices over the bride, so shall your God rejoice over you. (ISAIAH 62:5)

When his wife commits adultery, the Lord Jealous becomes an outraged husband:

For they have committed adultery, and blood is on their hands; with their idols they have committed adultery. (EZEKIEL 23:37)

For the land commits great whoredom by forsaking the Lord. (HOSEA 1:2)

If a man divorces his wife and she goes from him and becomes another man's wife, will he return to her? Would not such a land be greatly polluted? You have played the whore with many lovers; and would you return to me? says the Lord. (JEREMIAH 3:1)

The God of the Old Testament was obsessed with sexual imagery in his denunciations:

*I am against you, says the Lord of hosts, and **will lift up your skirts over your face**; and I will let nations look on your nakedness and kingdoms on your shame.* (NAHUM 3:5)

*Jerusalem sinned grievously, so she has become a mockery; all who honored her despise her, for they have seen her nakedness; she herself groans, and turns her face away. **Her uncleanness was in her skirts**.*
(LAMENTATIONS 1:8–9)

Fictional characters can be sexual creatures. The Old Testament clearly portrays God as a male and his people as a female. How could it be otherwise? The writers were all men.

Many view the erotic Song of Solomon, including what looks like oral sex, as love letters between the Lord and his wife.

*Blow upon my garden that its fragrance may be wafted abroad. Let my beloved come to his garden, and eat its choicest fruits. (*SONG OF SOLOMON 4:16*)*

Here is a graphic sexual passage you never hear from the pulpit:

*Your breasts are like two fawns, like twin fawns of a gazelle. . . . How beautiful you are and how pleasing, my love, with your delights! Your stature is like that of the palm, and your breasts like clusters of fruit. I said, 'I will climb the palm tree; I will take hold of its fruit.' May your breasts be like clusters of grapes on the vine, the fragrance of your breath like apples, and your mouth like the best wine. May the wine go straight to my beloved, flowing gently over lips and teeth. I belong to my beloved, and his desire is for me. NIV (*SONG OF SOLOMON 7:3-10*)*

Imagine teenage boys and girls standing up in church to recite from the bible: "Your breasts are like clusters of fruit. I will climb the palm tree and take hold of its fruit." How many of them could say those words before the congregation without snickering? Although sex is a natural and positive human activity, it is not something you expect to hear during worship services. The couple is lying down ("arm under head," "arm embraces") and the woman is "arouse[d]" and "awaken[ed]":

*If only you were to me like a brother, who was nursed at my mother's breasts! . . . His left arm is under my head and his right arm embraces me. Daughters of Jerusalem, I charge you. Do not arouse or awaken love until it so desires. NIV (*SONG OF SOLOMON 8:1-4*)*

Although the Song of Solomon does not mention God and deals plainly with sexual love, the Jews accepted it into their canon as a metaphor for God's love for his chosen people. Christians, like the Israelites, consider the church to be a bride and believe their father-in-law got a woman pregnant.

This is all allegorical, of course, but believers take it very seriously. We never hear them praying, "Our metaphorical Father which art in heaven." So let's do the same thing and take the fictional God to be a sexual male, as he is described. If God is not really a jealous husband because he is not biologically sexual, then neither is he really a father, since he is not a biological parent.

* * *

Sadomasochism does not have to be sexual, but it does have to involve pain and abuse. In that respect, the Lord Jealous, like an abusive husband, is clearly guilty of brutality. We saw in Chapter 12 how God told his people to enjoy torturing and murdering babies:

> *Happy shall they be who take your little ones and dash them against the rock!* (PSALM 137:9)

If they are happy, then he is happy. Another happy verse is found in the book of Job, where God is described as causing pain in order to garner praise for stopping it:

> *How happy is the one whom God reproves; therefore do not despise the discipline of the Almighty. For he wounds, but he binds up; he strikes, but his hands heal.* (JOB 5:17–18)

God happily causes his lover to suffer and wants her to enjoy it. ("Well meant are the wounds a friend inflicts" [PROVERBS 27:6].) This is like a fireman deliberately starting a blaze in order to claim the credit for putting it out. God beats his wife hard enough to cause bruises, then he smiles and plays the loving husband, saying "Here, sweetheart. Let me put bandages on those wounds. I only did it for your own good."

God injures so that he can heal
HOSEA 6:1 "Come, and let us return unto the Lord: for **he hath torn**, and he will heal us; **he hath smitten**, and he will bind us up." KJV

God's perfect servant exults in the pain he causes
JOB 6:8–10 "O that I might have my request, and that God would grant my desire; that **it would please God to crush me**, that he would let loose his hand and cut me off! This would be my consolation; **I would even exult in pain** unsparing; for I have not denied the words of the Holy One." RSV

God kills and maims
DEUTERONOMY 32:39 "See now that I, even I, am he; there is no god beside me. **I kill and I make alive; I wound and I heal**; and there is none that can deliver out of my hand." RSV

The Lord kills and brings to life
1 SAMUEL 2:6 "**The Lord killeth, and maketh alive**: he bringeth down to the grave, and bringeth up." KJV

God will heal the harm he causes
2 CHRONICLES 7:13–14 "If I . . . **send pestilence among my people**; If my people, which are called by my name, shall humble themselves . . . then

will I hear from heaven, and will forgive their sin, and **will heal their land**." KJV

God desired to cause pain and suffering

ISAIAH 53:10 "Yet it was the Lord's will to **crush** him and **cause him to suffer**." NIV

God punishes with wounds

JEREMIAH 10:18–19 "For thus says the Lord: 'Behold, I am slinging out the inhabitants of the land at this time, and **I will bring distress** on them, that they may feel it.' Woe is me because of my hurt! **My wound is grievous**. But I said, 'Truly this is an **affliction**, and I must bear it.'" RSV

The Lord adds sorrow to pain, then ends it with disaster

JEREMIAH 45:3–5 "You said, 'Woe is me! for **the Lord has added sorrow to my pain**; I am weary with my groaning, and I find no rest.' Thus shall you say to him, Thus says the Lord: Behold, what I have built I am breaking down, and what I have planted I am plucking up—that is, the whole land. And do you seek great things for yourself? Seek them not; for behold, **I am bringing evil upon all flesh**, says the Lord." RSV

The Lord causes evil

AMOS 3:6 "Shall a trumpet be blown in the city, and the people not be **afraid**? shall there be **evil** in a city, and the Lord hath not done it?" KJV (*Have you noticed that "acts of God" are always bad?*)

Sadomasochism is more than simply causing pain and abuse. It is taking pleasure in what you are doing to another person or yourself. We can assume that if God wants to do something, then he is getting something out of it. He loves to cause fear, and loves those who fear him.

God gets pleasure from those who fear him

PSALM 147:11 "The Lord taketh **pleasure** in them that **fear** him, in those that hope in his mercy." KJV

He wants his people to be happy to be afraid of him

PSALM 112:1 "Praise ye the Lord. Blessed is the man that **feareth** the Lord, that **delighteth** greatly in his commandments." KJV (*Notice that fear and delight go hand in hand, a component of sadomasochism.*)

You are happy if you are afraid

PSALM 128:1 "Blessed is every one who **fears** the Lord, who walks in his ways!" RSV

He'll protect you if you fear him

PSALM 33:18–19 "Behold, the eye of the Lord is upon **them that fear him**, upon them that hope in his mercy; To deliver their soul from death, and to keep them alive in famine." KJV (*This is like a protection racket.*)

He wants the whole world to fear him

PSALM 33:8 "Let all the earth **fear the Lord**: let all the inhabitants of the world stand in awe of him." KJV

Walk in fear

DEUTERONOMY 8:6 "Therefore thou shalt keep the commandments of the Lord thy God, to walk in his ways, and to **fear him**." KJV

God wants *only* fear

DEUTERONOMY 10:12 "And now, Israel, what doth the Lord thy God require of thee, but to **fear the Lord thy God**, to walk in all his ways, and to love him, and to serve the Lord thy God with all thy heart and with all thy soul." KJV

You can only be God's friend if you are afraid of him

PSALM 25:14 "The friendship of the Lord is for those who **fear** him, and he makes known to them his covenant." RSV

Teach children how to be afraid

PSALM 34:11 "Come, ye children, hearken unto me: I will teach you the **fear of the Lord**." KJV

God loves those who fear him

PSALM 103:13, 17 "Like as a father pitieth his children, so the Lord pitieth them that **fear him**. . . . But the mercy of the Lord is from everlasting to everlasting upon them that **fear him**, and his righteousness unto children's children." KJV

The people fear him who loves them

PSALM 118:4 "Let them now that **fear** the Lord say, that his mercy endureth for ever." KJV

Some defenders of God claim that "fear" means simply "respect" in this context. It doesn't mean "cower in terror of punishment," they insist. It means "respect your elders," like saying "honor your father because he is wise and loving, but he is also stern and just." I don't see what difference this makes. Since respect is something that must be earned, and since the God of the Old Testament asserts his authority with powerful threats and actual acts of violence, "fear God" boils down to "be frightened of his cruelty," no matter how you look at it.

In any event, the Old Testament most often connects the fear of God with punishment, not earned respect.

Fear and dread

ISAIAH 8:13 "Sanctify the Lord of hosts himself; and **let him be your fear**, and let him be your **dread**." KJV

"God terrifies me"

JOB 23:15–16 "Therefore I am **terrified** at his presence; when I consider, I am in **dread** of him. God has made my heart **faint**; the Almighty has **terrified** me." RSV

Don't hit me, God

JOB 13:21 "Withdraw thine hand far from me: and **let not thy dread make me afraid**." KJV

The prophet Isaiah was famous for preaching the "wrath of God." He named one of his sons Maher-Shalal-Hash-Baz, which means "Spoil quickly, plunder speedily." (*Maher-Shalal-Hash-Baz would make a good name for a raptor, like a peregrine falcon, the speediest attacker on the planet. In the time it takes to call its name, it has already had lunch.*)

Like Jeremiah, Isaiah was also misogynistic and sadomasochistic—or at least that is how he portrayed his God. In his third chapter, Isaiah describes one of the most gruesome sexual assaults in the Old Testament. After complaining that "Jerusalem has stumbled and Judah has fallen, because their speech and their deeds are against the Lord, defying his glorious presence" (ISAIAH 3:8), he unleashes this cruel threat:

The Lord said: Because the daughters of Zion are haughty and walk with outstretched necks, glancing wantonly with their eyes, mincing along as they go, tinkling with their feet; the Lord will afflict with scabs the heads of the daughters of Zion, and **the LORD will lay bare their secret parts**. (ISAIAH 3:16–17)

This is sexual molestation, and it is committed by God himself. "Lay bare their secret parts" is similar to "lift up their skirts." The Hebrew word for "secret parts" is *poth*, which means "hinged opening," or vagina. The KJV and Geneva Bible got it right with the discreet "discover their secret parts," and many versions agree with the NRSV (above), but the NIV tries to cover up the uncovering with "make their scalps bald." Most translations are more honest: "lay bare their nakedness" (OJB), "stripped naked" (AB), "expose their private parts" (CJB), "uncover their private parts" (CEV), "expose their nakedness for all to see" (LB).

Notice that Isaiah 3:17 says "the LORD" will lay bare their secret parts. That is Yahweh, the Lord Jealous, committing this shameful crime. And what was the offense of the "daughters of Zion" that earned such wrath? They were dressing as they pleased, walking proudly, drawing notice for being—horrors!—unsubmissive women!

Imagine the Lord Jealous—or the misogynistic sexually frustrated and emotionally immature Hebrew males who wrote the Old Testament—peering lasciviously at those attractive independent females who were "glancing wantonly with their eyes." Then picture those sweaty "men of God" shrieking their hateful sadomasochistic words at the women, like those insufferable street preachers who invade college campuses to yell "whores!" at the coeds. Ezekiel was just like that:

A cup of horror and desolation is the cup of your sister Samaria; you shall drink it and drain it out, and gnaw its sherds, and tear out your breasts. (EZEKIEL 23:33–34)

Why are these verses in the "Good Book"? Is it civilized or sane to tell a proudly rebellious woman to tear out her breasts with broken pottery?

I used to admire the God of the Old Testament, singing the hymn "Great Is Thy Faithfulness." Why did I do that?

18

Capriciously Malevolent

"I make peace, and create evil:
I the Lord do all these things."
—Isaiah 45:7, KJV

𝕴 don't know why the Book of Job is held in such high regard. It does have some literary value as an example of ancient poetic drama addressing the universal question of why good people suffer. However, its "answer" is no answer at all. It is not only philosophically antiquated and perplexingly irrelevant, but it makes the God of the Old Testament the most malevolent creature in all fiction.

Here is the Book of Job in a nutshell:

GOD: "Job is a good man. I will torture him to see if he stays good."
JOB: "Why is God punishing me?"
JOB'S FRIENDS: "It must be your own fault."
JOB: "I am undeserving, but it's not my fault."
ELIHU: "God is greater than all of us."
GOD: "Yes, I am greater than all of you."
JOB: "You are powerful. I'm sorry."
GOD: "Correct answer. I'll stop torturing you now."

That's it. There is no moral lesson in those forty-two chapters. No answer to suffering. No reasons, no redeeming social value to the graphic violence. The point of the book is simply: "The Lord is powerful. He can make you suffer. Don't ask why. Be faithful. Might makes right. God can do whatever he wants."

* * *

When it comes to the character of God, the Book of Job contains the single most damning verse in the entire Old Testament. We will see it when we get to the second chapter.

The first chapter describes Job as a man who was "blameless and upright, one who feared God and turned away from evil." (Never mind that other biblical authors claim that nobody is blameless: ECCLESIASTES 7:20, ROMANS 3:10–12.) Job was prosperous and happy, with a loving wife, seven sons and three daughters, many slaves and servants, and vast herds of cattle. In later chapters, we learn that he had helped the handicapped, widows, foreigners, and the needy. He apprehended and punished criminals. He was a good man. Faithful in worship, regularly sacrificing to the Lord, Job was "the greatest of all the people of the east."

One day Satan was walking around the earth with some heavenly friends (literally, "sons of God"), and they decided to pop in to see the Lord. As anyone does when they get a visit from the Devil and his pals, God greeted them cordially, and then said to Satan:

> *Have you considered my servant Job? There is no one like him on the earth, a*
> *blameless and upright man who fears God and turns away from evil. (JOB 1:8)*

The Lord was quite proud of his poster boy. Unprompted, he had turned the spotlight on Job as a shining example of a perfect believer, as if to boast: "See, there really are good people who love and worship me." But Satan was skeptical:

> *Does Job fear God for nothing? Have you not put a fence around him and*
> *his house and all that he has, on every side? You have blessed the work*
> *of his hands, and his possessions have increased in the land. But stretch out*
> *your hand now, and touch all that he has, and he will curse you to your face.*
> *(JOB 1:9–11)*

Job was faithful only because life was good, Satan argued. It's easy to praise God when everything is going well. "You are buying his love. Take it all away and then see how faithful he is!"

At this point in the story—if this were a true moral tale—the loving omniscient God would have said: "Get thee behind me, Satan. You cannot tempt the Lord. I know Job's heart. He is a good man, with a beautiful and faithful loving family. I am not going to hurt him—that is insane. I have promised to bless my followers who bless me. So, no deal."

Instead, God says: "You're on!"

> *The Lord said to Satan, "Very well, all that he has is in your power; only do*
> *not stretch out your hand against him!" So Satan went out from the presence*
> *of the Lord. (JOB 1:12)*

The God we are told to trust with our lives said "Very well" to Satan. He took down the protective fence, opened the gate to Job's family, and told his evil adversary: "Have at him. Just don't hurt him personally. Let's watch what happens."

What did he *think* was going to happen? Suppose a murderous child rapist came to your door and said, "You have a beautiful family, but I bet your children only love you because you are taking good care of them. Let me in the house, and I'm sure they won't love you anymore." You confidently open the door, step aside, and say, "Very well. Go on in. My kids will love me no matter what happens." Then you peer through the window to watch what this moral monster does to your precious family.

Who is the criminal?

So Satan went out to do what devils do. While God was watching, Job's oxen and donkeys were stolen and servants were killed. A "fire from heaven" burned up the sheep, and other servants were killed. The camels were carried off, and those servants were killed. Then the surviving servant brought Job the worst news:

> *Your sons and daughters were eating and drinking wine in their eldest*
> *brother's house, and suddenly a great wind came across the desert, struck the*
> *four corners of the house, and it fell on the young people, and they are dead;*
> *I alone have escaped to tell you. (*JOB 1:18–19*)*

All ten of Job's children were murdered by the Big Bad Wolf. What does any normal person do when confronted with such sudden overwhelming tragedy?

> *Then Job arose, tore his robe, shaved his head, and fell on the ground and*
> *worshipped. He said, "Naked I came from my mother's womb, and naked*
> *shall I return there; the Lord gave, and the Lord has taken away; blessed*
> *be the name of the Lord." In all this Job did not sin or charge God with*
> *wrongdoing. (*JOB 1:20–22*)*

Is that how you would react? Would you *worship* your family's assassin? "Blessed be the name of the murderer." If a maniac senselessly killed all of your children, would you not accuse him of any wrongdoing? Would you say, "Oh, well, God gives and he can take away"? The writer obviously thinks this is an important point, which means that he knew that the Lord was capriciously malevolent as he stood back and looked the other way. Murdering people on a bet is morally wrong. We all know that. All of our instincts and ethical judgments scream "Evil!"

But the blameless poster boy bit his tongue and stayed faithful. God must have felt smug and happy.

Now we come to Chapter 2, which contains the most damning verse in the Old Testament. Get ready for this. If you ever thought God might have good reasons for his violence, reasons that transcend human understanding, you will never think it again.

Satan, a sore loser, arranged another meeting. After initial pleasantries, God exulted in his victory:

> The Lord said to Satan, "Have you considered my servant Job? There is no one like him on the earth, a blameless and upright man who fears God and turns away from evil. He still persists in his integrity, although you incited me against him, to destroy him for no reason." (Job 2:3)

There it is, God's incriminating self-indictment: "You incited me against him, to destroy him *for no reason*." The Lord confesses openly that he heartlessly destroyed a loving faithful family for no reason. This is perfectly capricious and malevolent. If the police ask why you let the pedophile predator into your happy home and you reply "No reason. The Devil made me do it," we would consider *you* the moral monster and lock you up for reckless endangerment and homicide.

We would certainly not worship you. Morally healthy people do not admire anyone who is so easily "incited" by the Devil.

The phrase "for no reason" in Job 2:3 doesn't refer to Satan. Satan had a reason: to challenge God's ability to command devotion. It means *God* didn't have a reason. As he explicitly made clear, Job was blameless, so there was no reason to punish him. (It follows that it *might* have been okay to murder his family if he had not been blameless and upright.)

Satan, like a devil, was unimpressed. He thought God was too easy on Job. He was sure Job's faith would fold if he were physically tortured:

> Skin for skin! All that people have they will give to save their lives. But stretch out your hand now and touch his bone and his flesh, and he will curse you to your face. (Job 2:4–5)

Again, a scrap of decency might have been salvaged from this wreck of a moral tale if the Lord had said at that moment, "Enough. I'm tired of this pointless game. We are not going to physically torment my faithful servant." Instead, God upped the ante:

> "Very well, he is in your power; only spare his life." (Job 2:6)

There's that phrase again. He should have said "Go to hell." Instead, he said "Very well." Satan requested permission, and God gave swift authorization to the crime.

> So Satan went out from the presence of the Lord, and inflicted loathsome sores on Job from the sole of his foot to the crown of his head. Job took a potsherd with which to scrape himself, and sat among the ashes. (Job 2:7–8)

Job is at rock bottom, sitting on black ashes, scraping bleeding scabs off his body. His fortune is gone. His children are killed. His life is ruined. He is totally humiliated. What will he do now?

> Then his wife said to him, "Do you still persist in your integrity? Curse God, and die." But he said to her, "You speak as any foolish woman would speak. Shall we receive the good at the hand of God, and not receive the bad?" In all this Job did not sin with his lips. (JOB 2:9–10)

So God proudly won the bet, a second time. Job is amazing! He refuses to "sin with his lips." The Lord destroyed his life, but after all that terrible treatment, Job stubbornly refuses to call God a capriciously malevolent monster.

I don't have that much "integrity." Could *you* admire someone who is so recklessly cruel?

Notice that Job told his wife that humans "receive bad at the hand of God" (KJV: "receive evil"). He knew that God is malevolent. In case you are thinking there might be some way to interpret JOB 2:3 so that God does not *really* come off as a self-confessed killer, read what Job himself said about the attack:

> For he [God] crushes me with a tempest, and multiplies my wounds without cause; he will not let me get my breath, but fills me with bitterness. (JOB 9:17–18)

Job knew it was God, not Satan, who had crushed him "without cause." Satan is an agent of God, unable to act without license. "Who can command and have it done, if the Lord has not ordained it?" (LAMENTATIONS 3:37). In case you might be thinking the Lord is not *really* to blame because he only hired the hit man, notice that Job himself knew exactly what was going on:

> Your hands fashioned and made me; and now you turn and destroy me. (JOB 10:8)

> Know then that God has put me in the wrong, and closed his net around me. . . . He has kindled his wrath against me. (JOB 19:6–11)

> Have pity on me . . . for the hand of God has touched me! (JOB 19:21)

> God has made my heart faint; the Almighty has terrified me. (JOB 23:16)

> For the arrows of the Almighty are in me; my spirit drinks their poison; the terrors of God are arrayed against me. (JOB 6:4)

Job knew who was tormenting him. He called him a terrorist.

We don't know who wrote the Book of Job, but the author agrees with Job that God himself was guilty of the crime. In the final chapter of the book, the Lord rewarded Job's "integrity," restoring his health and wealth and giving him ten more children. (Job did not appear to grieve the death of his original children, only the loss of his belongings. The children were fungible commodities, replaceable property of the patriarch, disposable pawns in a deadly game.) It wasn't just Job who knew that God was the evildoer. In the last paragraph, the writer tells us that friends and relatives came to comfort Job for the "evil" that the Lord had done to him.

> Then there came to him all his brothers and sisters and all who had known him before, and they ate bread with him in his house; they showed him sympathy and comforted him for all the evil that the Lord had brought upon him. (JOB 42:11)

Richard Dawkins could have stated it more forcefully. He calls the God of the Old Testament merely a capriciously malevolent bully when he could have used the stronger words from the bible itself: God is an evil terrorist.

Malevolence is a desire to cause harm. The preceding chapters in this book have already demonstrated the godly inclination toward mischief and mayhem. Genocide and infanticide are obviously malevolent. So are bloodthirsty behavior and pestilential attacks. In the previous chapter we saw how the Lord caused wounds so that he could heal them.

"Evil" is one way to describe malevolence:

> I form the light, and create darkness: I make peace, and **create evil**: I the Lord do all these things. (ISAIAH 45:7, KJV)

That is the famous King James Version, placing the blame for evil squarely on God's character. He not only confesses it, he brags about it. In place of "evil," the NRSV has "woe," the NIV has "disaster," and the ESV and NASB have "calamity." The Hebrew word there is *rah*, which is most often used in the Old Testament for moral evil (such as "the knowledge of good and evil" in Genesis 2 and 3), but which sometimes might be interpreted as "bad" or "harm" in a consequentialist sense. Since morality is measured by intentional harm, committing or creating *rah* is malevolent no matter how the word is translated. Whatever you call it—evil or calamity—God created it, God did it, and it is malevolent.

Here are some other verses that show that God is responsible for *rah* or *rasha* (evil or wicked person), shown in boldface:

God claims credit for good and evil

LAMENTATIONS 3:38 "Out of the mouth of the most High proceedeth not **evil** and good?" KJV

Praise God for evil disasters

AMOS 3:6 "Shall a trumpet be blown in the city, and the people not be afraid? shall there be **evil** in a city, and the Lord hath not done it?" KJV

Who else, but God, unleashes the wicked?

JOB 9:22–24 "He destroyeth the perfect and the wicked. If the scourge slay suddenly, he will laugh at the trial of the innocent. The earth is given into the hand of the **wicked**: he covereth the faces of the judges thereof; if not, where, and who is he?" KJV

God created wicked people so he could cause trouble

PROVERBS 16:4 "The Lord hath made all things for himself: yea, even the **wicked** for the day of **evil**." KJV

If you think the "bad" actions of the God of the Old Testament were deserved punishments by a loving but stern parent—and remember, Job was not being punished for anything—that does not mean they were not evil actions. It just means you are the kind of person who thinks violence is an acceptable form of parental discipline. Like an angry, impulsive, unreasonable, and unimaginative father or husband who repeatedly beats his kids or his wife for the slightest appearance of wrongdoing, God's hateful "punishments" were excessive and malevolent.

The fourteenth chapter of the book of Judges tells another story about losing a bet, and this one reads like something out of a dark action-hero comic book. In order to deceive and kill a few of his enemies, God confessedly set up a bizarre charade.

Like Hercules, the mighty Samson also had a divine birth. His barren mother had been told by an angel of the Lord that she would conceive a child, so his parents knew that Samson was destined for great things for the nation of Israel. That may be why they were surprised at his choice of a mate. When Samson was old enough to start thinking about marriage, a beautiful woman caught his eye. He told his parents:

> I saw a Philistine woman at Timnah; now get her for me as my wife.
> (JUDGES 14:2)

Women were property, remember, so wives had to be purchased, and that was fine with Samson's parents. But a Philistine woman? Remember the warlike Philistines we read about in Chapter 3? They were the hated oppressors of the Israelites. His concerned parents asked him:

> Is there not a woman among your kin, or among all our people, that you must go to take a wife from the uncircumcised Philistines? (JUDGES 14:3)

Not only was the woman an outsider—a Capulet, or a Shark—but her pagan father had unmutilated genitals! They were understandably perplexed.

His father and mother did not know that this was from the Lord; for he was seeking a pretext to act against the Philistines. At that time the Philistines had dominion over Israel. (JUDGES 14:4)

Samson's parents thought their son was just a healthy sexual male making an unwise choice, not knowing that this was all being orchestrated by the Lord Jealous—"this was from the Lord"—as a "pretext" (charade) to slaughter the hated Philistines whose gods were rivals to his chosen people. Mom and Dad were disappointed, but they went along with their blessed child's demand, and traveled to meet the woman and her family.

Then a strange thing happened to Samson on the way to the Philistine town:

When he came to the vineyards of Timnah, suddenly a young lion roared at him. The spirit of the Lord rushed on him, and he tore the lion apart bare-handed as one might tear apart a kid. (JUDGES 14:5–6)

Wow. Mighty Samson kills a lion with his hands. This might look like a contrived sidebar to demonstrate Samson's strength, but nobody witnessed the scene. The bible says "the spirit of the Lord" was actually controlling the event. Curiously, Samson didn't tell anyone about the lion. The first meeting of the families went well; and on the next visit, the tale gets even more weird:

After a while he returned to marry her, and he turned aside to see the carcass of the lion, and there was a swarm of bees in the body of the lion, and honey. He scraped it out into his hands, and went on, eating as he went. When he came to his father and mother, he gave some to them, and they ate it. But he did not tell them that he had taken the honey from the carcass of the lion. (JUDGES 14:8–9)

Yum. Needless to say, this was an imaginatively creative way for God to plan an attack on the Philistines. How would a honeycomb find its way into the decomposing body of a lion? It turns out that this miraculous incident was all a setup for a ridiculous *riddle*. That's right. The Lord of the universe manipulated the lion and the bees in order to provide Samson with a brainteaser that he could use for financial gain by betting the Philistines that they could not solve it.

And God wanted Samson to *lose* the bet.

During the wedding feast, Samson challenged the thirty uneasy Philistine men (they were enemies, remember) who were appointed to be his companions:

Let me now put a riddle to you. If you can explain it to me within the seven days of the feast, and find it out, then I will give you thirty linen garments and thirty festal garments. But if you cannot explain it to me, then you shall give me thirty linen garments and thirty festal garments. (JUDGES 14:12–13)

It was a tempting bet. The payout would have been lucrative for the winner, especially for Samson. The thirty men were given seven days to think about it—more than two hundred days of total brain time—so they agreed to the bet. Here is Samson's riddle:

Out of the eater came something to eat. Out of the strong came something sweet. (JUDGES 14:14)

Nobody knew about the lion and the bees, and on the fourth day of the feast, the thirty men had obviously not come up with the answer. So they approached Samson's nameless wife:

Coax your husband to explain the riddle to us, or we will burn you and your father's house with fire. Have you invited us here to impoverish us? (JUDGES 14:15)

They were the ones who had taken the bet, but now *she* was the one with the problem. She couldn't allow her family to be destroyed, so she begged Samson to tell her the answer. Samson protested that he hadn't even told his parents, so why should he tell her? But she pestered him for the remainder of the feast, crying and nagging, until he finally relented and gave her the answer. She immediately told her people, and just before sundown on the last day, the men came to Samson and said:

What is sweeter than honey? What is stronger than a lion? (JUDGES 14:18)

Samson knew immediately that he had been cheated. Now, God got what he wanted from Samson:

Then the spirit of the Lord rushed on him, and he went down to Ashkelon. He killed thirty men of the town, took their spoil, and gave the festal garments to those who had explained the riddle. In hot anger he went back to his father's house. (JUDGES 14:19)

God caused Samson to kill and rob innocent Philistines—parties who were not even at the party—so that he could pay off a gambling bet! (Notice that when the "spirit of the Lord" comes upon a person, the result is often anger and violence.) The attraction of the foreign woman to Samson, the confusion and acquiescence of the parents, the elaborate wedding plans, the lion, the honeycomb, the bees, the bet, the riddle, the threat to his wife's family—the whole ludicrous plot—was a "pretext" of the Lord Jealous to eliminate a few men who belonged to a tribe that did not worship him.

Why not simply give those thirty unidentified men heart attacks? How could a loving God cause someone to commit such a dreadful deed? (And, as with the story of Job, who is the criminal?) God must have known Samson's wife would betray him, or the scheme would have failed. It was all a cruel joke. The Lord Jealous played fast and reckless with people's lives and feelings so that he could remove from his chosen people a little bit of temptation to mix with those who worship other gods.

If the Israelites were prohibited from mixing with pagan wives, why did God arrange for Samson to marry the Philistine in the first place? It turns out that even the marriage was a sham. In God's eyes, holy matrimony is not sacred. Samson quickly dumped her:

> And Samson's wife was given to his companion, who had been his best man.
> (JUDGES 14:20)

That's how the story ends, with Samson's unwanted property—his nameless wife—being given away to someone else. There is obviously no love here. The new husband got a lucky windfall, a rich man's cast-off belongings. And what did Samson's parents get for their generosity? They got the bill for a wrecked wedding. Can there be any doubt that human beings are dispensable tokens in a treacherous game of jealousy played by a capriciously malevolent deity?

Sometimes God's methods were more direct, though no less capricious, like the time he shot down the Amorites with meteors:

> The Lord said to Joshua, "Do not fear them, for I have handed them over to you; not one of them shall stand before you." So Joshua came upon them suddenly, having marched up all night from Gilgal. And the Lord threw them into a panic before Israel, who inflicted a great slaughter on them at Gibeon. . . . As they fled before Israel, while they were going down the slope of Beth-boron, the Lord threw down huge stones from heaven on them as far as Azekah, and they died. (JOSHUA 10:8–11)

And to make sure the massacre was complete, he caused the earth to stop spinning!

> On the day when the Lord gave the Amorites over to the Israelites, Joshua spoke to the Lord; and he said in the sight of Israel, "Sun, stand still at Gibeon, and Moon, in the valley of Aijalon." And the sun stood still, and the moon stopped, until the nation took vengeance on their enemies.
> (JOSHUA 10:12–13)

God, the supposed creator of life, could have simply caused people to die in their sleep. Instead, he invented all sorts of creatively cruel devices of malevolence.

God creates disabled people

EXODUS 4:11 "And the Lord said unto him, Who hath made man's mouth? or **who maketh the dumb**, or deaf, or the seeing, or the blind? have not I the Lord?" KJV

God gave Israel bad commandments, then punished them for it!

EZEKIEL 20:25–26 "Wherefore I gave them also **statutes that were not good**, and judgments whereby they should not live; And I **polluted them** in their own gifts, in that they caused to pass through the fire all that openeth the womb, that I might make them desolate, to the end that they might know that I am the Lord." KJV

God hardened the hearts of the neighboring kingdoms, then destroyed them for that

JOSHUA 11:20 "For it was of the Lord to **harden their hearts**, that they should come against Israel in battle, that he might destroy them utterly, and that they might have no favour, but that he might destroy them, as the Lord commanded Moses." KJV

God will afflict you with every malady, named and unnamed

DEUTERONOMY 28:61 "Also every sickness, and every plague, which is not written in the book of this law, them will the Lord bring upon thee, until thou be destroyed." KJV

God punishes the widows and orphans of nonbelievers

ISAIAH 9:17 "Therefore the Lord shall have no joy in their young men, neither shall have mercy on their fatherless and widows." KJV

Changing your mind is not capricious. People can and should change their minds for good reasons. God, however, cannot:

*For I the Lord do not change. (*MALACHI 3:6*)*

*God is not a human being, that he should lie, or a mortal, that he should change his mind. Has he promised, and will he not do it? Has he spoken, and will he not fulfill it? (*NUMBERS 23:19*)*

To say that you never change your mind, and then change it anyway, is capricious. Here are a few passages that show that the malevolent God indeed changed his mind.

God promised to destroy his people who worshipped someone else . . .

EXODUS 32:7–10 "Then the Lord said to Moses, 'Go down, because your people, whom you brought up out of Egypt, have become corrupt. They have been quick to turn away from what I commanded them and have made themselves an idol cast in the shape of a calf. They have bowed down to it and sacrificed to it and have said, "These are your gods, Israel, who brought you up out of Egypt." I have seen these people,' the Lord said to Moses, 'and they are a stiff-necked people. Now leave me alone so that my anger may burn against them and that I may destroy them. Then I will make you into a great nation.'" NIV

. . . but then changed his mind

Exodus 32:11–14 "But Moses sought the favor of the Lord his God. 'Lord,' he said, 'why should your anger burn against your people, whom you brought out of Egypt with great power and a mighty hand? Why should the Egyptians say, "It was with evil intent that he brought them out, to kill them in the mountains and to wipe them off the face of the earth"? Turn from your fierce anger; relent and do not bring disaster on your people. Remember your servants Abraham, Isaac and Israel, to whom you swore by your own self: "I will make your descendants as numerous as the stars in the sky and I will give your descendants all this land I promised them, and it will be their inheritance forever."' **Then the Lord relented** and did not bring on his people the disaster he had threatened." NIV (*Notice that Moses is more compassionate and reasonable than God.*)

God restrained himself and changed his mind

Ezekiel 20:21–22 "Notwithstanding the children rebelled against me: they walked not in my statutes, neither kept my judgments to do them, which if a man do, he shall even live in them; they polluted my sabbaths: **then I said, I would pour out my fury upon them**, to accomplish my anger against them in the wilderness. **Nevertheless I withdrew mine hand**, and wrought for my name's sake, that it should not be polluted in the sight of the heathen, in whose sight I brought them forth." KJV (*This was the argument Moses used above, and now God takes credit for it.*)

The Lord backtracked about his announced disaster

Jeremiah 26:19 "Did not Hezekiah fear the Lord and seek his favor? And **did not the Lord relent**, so that he did not bring the disaster he pronounced against them? We are about to bring a terrible disaster on ourselves!" NIV

The Lord regretted his decision

1 Samuel 15:10–11 "Then came the word of the Lord unto Samuel, saying, **It repenteth me that I have set up Saul to be king**: for he is turned back from following me, and hath not performed my commandments." KJV (*This was because Saul was not murderous enough for God's tastes. See Chapter 8.*)

*   *   *

Sometimes an adjective limits a noun, and sometimes it expands it. To call God "capriciously malevolent" does not mitigate the evil; it magnifies it. The God of the Old Testament played with people's lives for something as vainly capricious as a bet with Satan. That makes him more of a devil than the Devil.

Just to be clear, Satan is also a fictional character. Satan and God are flip sides of the same counterfeit coin.

19

Bully

"He destroys both the blameless and the wicked. When disaster brings sudden death, he mocks at the calamity of the innocent."
—Job 9:22-23

We arrive at the noun at the end of Richard Dawkins's list. After moving down that lengthy chain of non-prayer beads representing sixteen nasty adjectives, two pejorative nouns, and one flaky adverb, we finally get to the term being described.

We could stop here. The ultimate noun for the God of the Old Testament could be a blank space for you to fill in:

The God of the Old Testament is arguably the most unpleasant character in all fiction: jealous and proud of it; a petty, unjust, unforgiving control freak; a vindictive, bloodthirsty ethnic cleanser; a misogynistic, homophobic, racist, infanticidal, genocidal, filicidal, pestilential, megalomaniacal, sadomasochistic, capriciously malevolent _____.

What word would you insert here? After reading the previous eighteen chapters documenting Dawkins' detailed directory of dreadful descriptors, would you call him a despot? A dictator? Tyrant? Martinet? Fascist?

Dawkins chose "bully," and that is the best word. "Tyrant" and "dictator" conjure up Genghis Khan and Adolf Hitler, malicious individuals indeed, but they were real people. Using those words to describe the God of the Old Testament would be giving him too much respect. He is a fictional character, after all, more like Cruella de Vil than Ivan the Terrible. "Bully" brings to mind the mean red-faced kid on the playground, a small-time punk who makes himself seem big by putting others down, the braggart rascal who withers when he realizes the adults are watching.

And we are watching.

What was the point of the first nine plagues of Egypt?

Every year during Passover, the Jews hold a festive feast where they celebrate the Tenth Plague. They eat unleavened bread, drink wine, sing, and commemorate the slaughter of tens of thousands of innocent children. The word "Passover" is a translation of the Hebrew *pesach*, which most likely means "he passed over." During the final plague of Egypt, while children were being murdered by the God of the Old Testament through no fault of their own, the children of the Israelites who smeared lamb's blood on their doors were spared. They were passed over. Apparently, searching for that blood mark was the only way God's Angel of Death could tell the difference between the bad innocent children and the good innocent children. Jews all over the world annually rejoice over that non-difference, happy that *they* are the good chosen people.

The story of the plagues is fictional. There is no historical or archaeological evidence of the enslavement of Jews on the Nile River or their exodus to Canaan as a result of God's forcing Pharaoh to "let my people go." But taking the tale at face value, according to EXODUS, CHAPTERS 7–12, the tenth plague, which killed all of the first-born sons of the Egyptians, was the one that did the trick and set the Israelites free. The God of the Old Testament, being omniscient, would have known that the first nine plagues would have had no effect. In fact, he "hardened Pharaoh's heart" so that he would resist them. Why? If the final plague was the clincher, why did God bother with the first nine?

Perhaps a perverse case could be made for the utility of the tenth plague, as unnecessarily cruel and unfair as it was, as a way to unleash the Jews from oppressive slavery. But the first nine plagues were wanton violence for no purpose other than bullying.

The first plague turned the Nile River to blood:

> *Thus says the Lord, "By this you shall know that I am the Lord." See, with the staff that is in my hand I [Moses] will strike the water that is in the Nile, and it shall be turned to blood . . . and all the water in the river was turned into blood, and the fish in the river died. The river stank so that the Egyptians could not drink its water, and there was blood throughout the whole land of Egypt. . . . And all the Egyptians had to dig along the Nile for water to drink, for they could not drink the water of the river. (*EXODUS 7:17–24*)

Notice that this plague was done with the express purpose of showing off: "By this you shall know that I am the Lord."

After that came more grandstanding plagues: the second was an infestation of frogs, the third was gnats, the fourth was a swarm of flies, and the fifth was a disease that killed all their livestock. Each time, Pharaoh refused to let the people go.

The sixth plague was a disease of boils on all the people. They were painful but not deadly. The plagues had exterminated animals but so far had not directly killed any humans. God explained why:

> But this is why I have let you live: to show you my power, and to make my name resound through all the earth. (EXODUS 9:16)

He did not spare their lives out of compassion. He was posturing—"to show you my power"—establishing his superiority over his helpless victims. If everyone had been exterminated, there would have been nobody to impress. Then he threatened to do even worse with plague number seven, an epic hailstorm:

> Tomorrow at this time I will cause the heaviest hail to fall that has ever fallen in Egypt from the day it was founded until now. Send, therefore, and have your livestock and everything that you have in the open field brought to a secure place; every human or animal that is in the open field and is not brought under shelter will die when the hail comes down upon them. (EXODUS 9:18–19)

The writer neglects to tell us how there would have been any livestock to protect since they had already been killed off in the fifth plague. When the hail came down, destroying all the flax and barley, Pharaoh finally relented:

> Enough of God's thunder and hail! I will let you go; you need stay no longer. (EXODUS 9:28)

The Jews were emancipated, hallelujah! But wait. God wasn't finished bullying yet. He couldn't allow Pharaoh to change his mind so quickly.

> Then the Lord said to Moses, "Go to Pharaoh; for **I have hardened his heart** and the heart of his officials, **in order that I may show these signs of mine among them**, and that you may tell your children and grandchildren how I have made fools of the Egyptians and what signs I have done among them— so that you may know that I am the Lord." (EXODUS 10:1–2)

Read that again. God admits that he "hardened Pharaoh's heart" and would not let him change his mind and do the right thing because he still wanted to "show these signs of mine." Like a cat with a mouse, God was toying with human lives so that he could manifest his power. He still had a repertoire to play out, a bag of tricks to display, and he couldn't stop his proud performance prematurely just because Pharaoh had caved in too soon. (God must have had ten fingers, like us, and wanted to make it an impressive round number. Like the Commandments.) He was eager to threaten with the next horrible plague: locusts!

> *Thus says the Lord, the God of the Hebrews, "How long will you refuse to*
> *humble yourself before me? Let my people go, so that they may worship me.*
> *For if you refuse to let my people go, tomorrow I will bring locusts into your*
> *country. They shall cover the surface of the land, so that no one will be able*
> *to see the land. They shall devour the last remnant left you after the hail,*
> *and they shall devour every tree of yours that grows in the field. They shall*
> *fill your houses, and the houses of all your officials and of all the Egyptians—*
> *something that neither your parents nor your grandparents have seen, from*
> *the day they came on earth to this day." (*Exodus 10:3–6*)*

This is unbelievable. God chastised Pharaoh, knowing full well that he had already agreed to let his people go. So Pharaoh agreed again. However, perhaps because his mind had been "hardened," he didn't understand what Moses was asking. When Moses said they wanted to be set free so that they could worship God, Pharaoh focused on the word "worship" rather than "set free." He said to Moses:

> *Go, worship the Lord your God! But which ones are to go? (*Exodus 10:8*)*

And Moses replied:

> *We will go with our young and our old; we will go with our sons and*
> *daughters and with our flocks and herds, because we have the Lord's festival*
> *to celebrate. (*Exodus 10:9*)*

Heart-hardened, Pharaoh smelled a trick and changed his mind again:

> *The Lord indeed will be with you, if ever I let your little ones go with you!*
> *Plainly, you have some evil purpose in mind. No, never! Your men may go*
> *and worship the Lord, for that is what you are asking. (*Exodus 10:10–11*)*

Men only, Pharaoh decided. If the Israelite children were allowed to leave Egypt, then they might *all* escape! This is obviously a kludgy plot device to keep the action going.

So Moses stretched out his magic staff and a huge wind brought the eighth plague:

> *The locusts came upon all the land of Egypt and settled on the whole country*
> *of Egypt, such a dense swarm of locusts as had never been before, nor ever*
> *shall be again. They covered the surface of the whole land, so that the land*
> *was black; and they ate all the plants in the land and all the fruit of the trees*
> *that the hail had left; nothing green was left, no tree, no plant in the field, in*
> *all the land of Egypt. (*Exodus 10:14–15*)*

His country ravaged, Pharaoh now gets it and agrees, once more, to let the people go. All of them. So God caused a huge wind from the west to blow every single locust into the Red Sea. Good aim. Now the Israelites can leave.

But wait. God is enjoying himself too much.

But the Lord hardened Pharaoh's heart, and he would not let the Israelites go. (EXODUS 10:20)

We can't blame Pharaoh for this. God couldn't wait to show us his next trick. The ninth plague covered the land with "dense darkness."

Then the Lord said to Moses, "Stretch out your hand toward heaven so that there may be darkness over the land of Egypt, a darkness that can be felt." So Moses stretched out his hand toward heaven, and there was dense darkness in all the land of Egypt for three days. People could not see one another, and for three days they could not move from where they were; but all the Israelites had light where they lived. (EXODUS 10:21–23)

How could a darkness be so viscous that people could not even move? Didn't they have candles or torches? This was not blindness, because Moses was instructed to stretch his hand "toward heaven" to stop the light. And how could thousands of Israelites have light while the Egyptians did not? Wouldn't their flames have provided *some* ambient illumination to the rest of the country? Did the Israelites have daylight when the Egyptians did not?

We'll have to count the ninth plague as another artificial device to draw out the plot.

So again, for the fourth time, Pharaoh said to Moses, Okay, "Let your people go."

Go, worship the Lord. Only your flocks and your herds shall remain behind. Even your children may go with you. (EXODUS 11:24)

Will Pharaoh never stop acting like Elmer Fudd? Moses replied that they could hardly leave to worship if they didn't have animals to sacrifice. Once again the egg-headed Egyptian makes things worse:

But the Lord hardened Pharaoh's heart, and he was unwilling to let them go. Then Pharaoh said to him, "Get away from me! Take care that you do not see my face again, for on the day you see my face you shall die." Moses said, "Just as you say! I will never see your face again." (EXODUS 10:27–29)

God had one more arrow in his quiver:

The Lord said to Moses, "I will bring one more plague upon Pharaoh and upon Egypt; afterwards he will let you go from here; indeed, when he lets you go, he will drive you away." (EXODUS 11:1)

Moses told the people to make a final sacrifice of a lamb to obtain blood to sprinkle on the doorposts, and to hurry and make travel preparations. There wasn't time for the bread to rise, so they later called it the "feast of unleavened bread."

And when your children ask you, "What do you mean by this observance?" you shall say, "It is the passover sacrifice to the Lord, for he passed over the houses of the Israelites in Egypt, when he struck down the Egyptians but spared our houses." (EXODUS 12:26–27)

That verse is quoted to this day by Jews all over the world as they celebrate the Seder, the Passover meal honoring the savage slaughter of Egypt's firstborn. The hasty departure from Egypt is the origin of the unleavened Matzo flatbread available during Passover week each year. Every time I see one of those flaky crackers, I think "dead babies."

The tenth and final plague took place:

At midnight the Lord struck down all the firstborn in the land of Egypt, from the firstborn of Pharaoh who sat on his throne to the firstborn of the prisoner who was in the dungeon, and all the firstborn of the livestock. Pharaoh arose in the night, he and all his officials and all the Egyptians; and there was a loud cry in Egypt, for there was not a house without someone dead. (EXODUS 12:29–30)

This was God's grand finale. Bullying with infanticide was the righteous magnum force he was waiting to unleash. He must have been so proud of himself.

Remember, not only were the first nine plagues unnecessary, but the last four happened *after* God had gotten what he wanted. The massacre of thousands of innocent children was grossly gratuitous.

The plagues ended, but the drama continued. God's people were free at last, free at last. We all know the sensational story of the Israelites dashing across the parting Red Sea pursued by the Egyptians, but remember that this only happened because God wanted a final flourish:

I will harden Pharaoh's heart, and he will pursue them, so that I will gain glory for myself over Pharaoh and all his army; and the Egyptians shall know that I am the Lord. (EXODUS 14:4)

The purpose of the heart-hardening, violence, drowning, bloodshed, and malevolence, God boasts, is "so that I will gain glory for myself." That is the perfect example of a bully.

Bullying is more than cruelty. It stems from a power imbalance maintained through repeated actions usually accompanied by words of superiority. "You are beneath me, and I will prove it." Bullying is the combination of megalomania and malevolence. You can be malevolent without being a bully, like a person who poisons a water supply. You can be megalomaniacal without being malevolent, like someone with a Napoleon complex, or a God complex. But join the two (Chapters 16, "Megalomaniacal," and 18, "Capriciously Malevolent"), and you have the consummate bully.

Here are a few examples you may recognize from earlier chapters. Notice that they combine violence with words of superiority:

Bullying with flood

EXODUS 15:6–8 "Thy right hand, O Lord, is become **glorious in power**: thy right hand, O Lord, hath dashed in pieces the enemy. And in the greatness of thine excellency thou hast overthrown them that rose up against thee: thou sentest forth thy wrath, which consumed them as stubble. And with the blast of thy nostrils the waters were gathered together, **the floods stood upright as an heap**, and the depths were congealed in the heart of the sea." KJV (*This is referring to the Egyptians drowned in the Red Sea.*)

Bullying with earthquake

EZEKIEL 38:19–20 "For in my jealousy and in the fire of my wrath have I spoken, Surely in that day there shall be a **great shaking in the land** of Israel; So that the fishes of the sea, and the fowls of the heaven, and the beasts of the field, and all creeping things that creep upon the earth, and **all the men that are upon the face of the earth, shall shake at my presence**, and the mountains shall be thrown down, and the steep places shall fall, and every wall shall fall to the ground." KJV

Bullying with rain, hail, fire and brimstone

EZEKIEL 38:22–23 "And I will plead against him with pestilence and with blood; and I will **rain** upon him, and upon his bands, and upon the many people that are with him, an overflowing **rain**, and great **hailstones**, **fire**, and **brimstone**. Thus **will I magnify myself**, and sanctify myself; and I will be known in the eyes of many nations, and they shall know that I am the Lord." KJV

Bullying with sickness

DEUTERONOMY 28:58–59 "If thou wilt not observe to do all the words of this law that are written in this book, that thou mayest **fear this glorious and fearful name, The Lord Thy God**; Then the Lord will make thy **plagues** wonderful, and the plagues of thy seed, even great plagues, and of long continuance, and sore **sicknesses**, and of long continuance." KJV

Bullying with pestilence

EXODUS 9:15–16 "For by now I could have put forth my hand and struck you and your people with **pestilence**, and you would have been cut off from the earth; but for this purpose have **I let you live, to show you my power**, so that my name may be declared throughout all the earth." RSV

Bullying with plague, pestilence, and earthquake

HABAKKUK 3:3–6 "**His glory covered the heavens**, and the earth was full of his praise. And his brightness was as the light; he had horns coming out of his hand: and there was the hiding of his power. Before him went the **pestilence, and burning coals** went forth at his feet. He stood, and measured the earth: he beheld, and drove asunder the nations; and the everlasting **mountains were scattered**, the perpetual hills did bow: his ways are everlasting." KJV

Bullying with pestilence and bloodshed

EZEKIEL 28:22–23 "Thus saith the Lord God; Behold, I am against thee, O Zidon; and **I will be glorified** in the midst of thee: and they shall know that I am the Lord, when I shall have executed judgments in her, and shall be sanctified in her. For I will send into her **pestilence**, and **blood** into her streets; and the wounded shall be judged in the midst of her by the sword upon her on every side; and **they shall know that I am the Lord**." KJV

Bullying with deceiving, defiling, and horrifying

EZEKIEL 20:25–26 "Moreover I gave them **statutes that were not good** and ordinances by which they could not have life; and I **defiled** them through their very gifts in making them offer by fire all their first-born, that I might **horrify** them; I did it **that they might know that I am the Lord**." RSV

Bullying with ultimate censorship

LEVITICUS 24:16 "And he that **blasphemeth the name of the Lord**, he shall surely be put to **death**, and all the congregation shall certainly **stone him**: as well the stranger, as he that is born in the land, when he **blasphemeth** the name of the Lord, shall be put to **death**." KJV (*Blasphemy is insulting God's holiness and greatness.*)

Bullying with corpses and calamity

EZEKIEL 6:5–10 "And I will lay the dead **carcases** of the children of Israel before their idols; and I will scatter your **bones** round about your altars. . . . And the slain shall fall in the midst of you, and ye shall know that I am the

Lord. . . . And **they shall know that I am the Lord**, and that I have not said in vain that I would do this **evil** unto them." KJV

Bullying with terrorism

ISAIAH 2:19 "And men shall enter the caves of the rocks and the holes of the ground, from before the **terror of the Lord**, and from **the glory of his majesty**, when he rises to **terrify the earth**." RSV

Bullying with killing

DEUTERONOMY 32:39 "See now that I, even I, am he, and **there is no god with me: I kill**, and I make alive; **I wound**, and I heal: neither is there any that can deliver out of my hand." KJV

While torturing and humiliating Job (see Chapter 18), the Lord kept browbeating him verbally, boasting about his power and mocking his puny victim:

"I am stronger than you"

JOB 40:6–9 "Then answered the Lord unto Job out of the whirlwind, and said, Gird up thy loins now like a man: I will demand of thee, and declare thou unto me. Wilt thou also disannul my judgment? wilt thou condemn me, that thou mayest be righteous? **Hast thou an arm like God? or canst thou thunder with a voice like him?**" KJV

"Let's see you try to be as majestic and angry as I am!"

JOB 40:10–14 [God sarcastically mocking Job] "Deck thyself now with **majesty** and excellency; and array thyself with glory and beauty. Cast abroad the **rage of thy wrath**: and behold every one that is proud, and abase him. Look on every one that is proud, and bring him low; and tread down the wicked in their place. Hide them in the dust together; and bind their faces in secret. Then will I also confess unto thee that thine own right hand can save thee." KJV

"Ha, ha!" God laughs at his victims

JOB 9:22–23 "He destroyeth the perfect and the wicked. If the scourge slay suddenly, **he will laugh at the trial of the innocent**." KJV

"How dare you disagree with me!"

JOB 40:1–2 "And the Lord said to Job: **Shall a faultfinder contend with the Almighty?** He who argues with God, let him answer it." RSV

If you wash it, God will make it dirty again

JOB 9:30–31 [Job speaking] "If I wash myself with snow, and cleanse my hands with lye, yet thou wilt plunge me into a pit, and my own clothes will abhor me." RSV

"Be still and know that I am God" is a calming verse for many believers. It is the title of some hymns and Christian songs. One of them has the lyrics:

> Be still and know that I am God.
> I am the Lord that healeth thee.
> In thee, O Lord, I put my trust.

On their face, those words sound relaxing, inspiring, and worshipful. Many Christians and Jews feel that to "be still" in the presence of the spirit of God is a way to find inner peace while praying and meditating on the love of the heavenly father. But if we look up the actual biblical passage from which those words originate, we see something completely different. "Be still" is a phrase of bullying!

> Come, behold the works of the Lord; **see what desolations he has brought** on
> the earth. He makes wars cease to the end of the earth; he breaks the bow,
> and shatters the spear; he burns the shields with fire. "**Be still, and know
> that I am God**! I am exalted among the nations, I am exalted in the earth."
> (Psalm 46:8–10)

That is exactly how a bully talks. "Be still," in this passage, is a demand for military surrender and hegemonic superiority. The Hebrew word *rapha* actually means "be weak." It does not mean "Relax and enjoy the calm presence of the spirit"; it means "Shut up and stop fighting." God is telling us in that Psalm to "Say 'Uncle,' you puny weaklings. I am the greatest!"

Even the word "peace" does not mean what most believers think it means. *Shalom* did not mean "inner calm" or "let's be friends." Like "be still," it was also a term of military submission. "Peace," in the Old Testament, meant "pacification." Like the Pax Romana, it was achieved not through reasonable persuasion and respectful cooperation, but through the violent imperial conquest of all neighboring nations and potential warring rivals.

The Israelites were told to occupy their own territory by genocide (see Chapter 13), but neighboring ("far off") territory was treated somewhat differently. Pacification was achieved when the residents of a town that did not worship the Lord Jealous were either killed or turned into slaves:

> When you draw near to a town to fight against it, offer it **terms of peace**
> [shalom]. If it accepts your terms of peace and surrenders to you, then all
> the people in it shall serve you at forced labor. If it does not submit to you
> peacefully, but makes war against you, then you shall besiege it; And
> when the Lord your God gives it into your hand, you shall put all its

males to the sword. You may, however, take as your booty the women, the children, livestock, and everything else in the town, all its spoil. You may enjoy the spoil of your enemies, which the Lord your God has given you. (DEUTERONOMY 20:10–14)

When the military threat of neighboring people is neutralized by violent force, then you can "be still." In the Old Testament, even "peace" is a form of bullying.

As a bronze-age deity, the God of the Old Testament had his limits. No matter how fiercely he thumped his chest, he couldn't compete against advanced iron-age military technology superior to the swords, clubs, and slingshots of the Israelites:

The Lord was with Judah, and he took possession of the hill country, but could not drive out the inhabitants of the plain, because they had chariots of iron. (JUDGES 1:19)

The Lord Jealous was not so tough after all. He ran away when he met a bigger bully.

PART II

𝔇awkins 𝔚as 𝔗oo 𝔎ind

LIKE KING SAUL, RICHARD DAWKINS FALLS A BIT SHORT. Saul lost his throne because he did not completely follow genocidal orders (see Chapter 8). God declared that he was the one who was evil. If Saul can be called "wicked" for not going far enough in his brutality, I will pronounce Dawkins "too gentle" for not going far enough in his condemnation of the big bully.

Richard's nineteen denunciations are certainly more than enough to demonstrate the downright depravity of the Lord Jealous, but he overlooked a few more. He forgot to mention that the God of the Old Testament is also a pyromaniacal, angry, merciless, curse-hurling, vaccicidal, aborticidal, cannibalistic slavemonger.

20

𝔓𝔶𝔯𝔬𝔪𝔞𝔫𝔦𝔞𝔠𝔞𝔩

"For the Lord your God is a devouring fire, a jealous God."
—DEUTERONOMY 4:24

The God of the Old Testament is described as a "man of war" (EXODUS 15:3, KJV). After fleeing Egypt, making it across the Red Sea before it drowned the Egyptian forces, the Israelites, now free to worship, sang a song of praise to their Lord for his military prowess:

> I will sing to the Lord, for he has triumphed gloriously; horse and rider
> he has thrown into the sea. The Lord is my strength and my might, and he
> has become my salvation; this is my God, and I will praise him, my father's
> God, and I will exalt him. **The Lord is a warrior**; the Lord is his name.
> (EXODUS 15:1–3)

In the Exodus story, the war god's arsenal included death by drowning. Although he killed more people by water, including Noah's flood, his independent acts of drowning were rare. He more often attacked with fire. The pages of the Old Testament are scorched by the flame-throwing blaze of his anger.

The phrase "burnt offering" appears more than 250 times in the Old Testament, too many to list here. Those roasted offerings are often described as a "pleasing odor" to the Lord. Beyond the blazing altars of animal sacrifice, here are more than eighty examples of the flame-happy God of the Old Testament.

Fire came down on the earth

EXODUS 9:22–24 "And the Lord said to Moses, 'Stretch forth your hand toward heaven, that there may be hail in all the land of Egypt, upon man and beast and every plant of the field, throughout the land of Egypt.' Then Moses stretched forth his rod toward heaven; and the Lord sent thunder and hail, and **fire ran down to the earth**. And the Lord rained hail upon the land of Egypt; there was hail, and **fire flashing continually** in the midst of the hail, very heavy hail, such as had never been in all the land of Egypt since it became a nation." RSV

Like a devouring fire

EXODUS 24:17 "And the sight of the glory of the Lord was **like devouring fire** on the top of the mount in the eyes of the children of Israel." KJV

Burnt offering a "sweet savour"

EXODUS 29:18 "And thou shalt **burn the whole ram** upon the altar: it is a burnt offering unto the Lord: it is a sweet savour, **an offering made by fire** unto the Lord." KJV (*See also* EXODUS 29:25, 29:41, 30:20.)

Offering by fire a "pleasing odor"

LEVITICUS 1:9 "But his inwards and his legs shall he wash in water: and the priest shall burn all on the altar, to be a burnt sacrifice, an **offering made by fire, of a sweet savour** [NRSV "pleasing odor"] **unto the Lord**." KJV (*See also* LEVITICUS 1:13, 1:17, 2:2, 2:3, 2:9, 2:10, 2:11, 2:16, 3:3, 3:5, 3:9, 3:11, 3:14, 3:16, 4:35, 5:12, 7:5, 7:30, 7:35, 8:17, 8:21, 8:28, 21:6, 23:18, 23:25, 23:36, 24:9.)

Burnt offering a "sweet savour"

NUMBERS 15:2-3 "When ye be come into the land of your habitations, which I give unto you, And will make an **offering by fire** unto the Lord, a **burnt offering**, or a sacrifice in performing a vow, or in a freewill offering, or in your solemn feasts, to make a **sweet savour** [NRSV "pleasing odor"] **unto the Lord**, of the herd or of the flock." KJV (*See also* NUMBERS 15:10, 15:13, 15:14, 15:25, 18:17, 28:2, 28:6, 28:8, 28:13, 28:24, 29:6, 29:8, 29:13, 29:36.)

Fire came out from the Lord

LEVITICUS 9:23-24 "And the glory of the Lord appeared unto all the people. And there **came a fire out from before the Lord**, and consumed upon the altar the burnt offering and the fat: which when all the people saw, they shouted, and fell on their faces." KJV

Fire from the Lord consumed them

LEVITICUS 10:1-3 "And Nadab and Abihu, the sons of Aaron, took either of them his censer, and put fire therein, and put incense thereon, and offered strange fire before the Lord, which he commanded them not. And there went out **fire from the Lord**, and devoured them, and they died before the Lord. Then Moses said unto Aaron, This is it that the Lord spake, saying, I will be sanctified in them that come nigh me, and before all the people I will be glorified. And Aaron held his peace." KJV (*Of course Aaron was silent. The God he loved had just burned his children for not worshipping him in the right manner.*)

Prostitute burned to death
LEVITICUS 21:9 "And the daughter of any priest, if she profane herself by playing the whore, she profaneth her father: she shall be **burnt with fire**." KJV (*Notice that her "crime" is profaning her father.*)

Grumblers burned by God
NUMBERS 11:1–3 "And when the people complained, it displeased the Lord: and the Lord heard it; and his anger was kindled; and **the fire of the Lord** burnt among them, and consumed them that were in the uttermost parts of the camp. And the people cried unto Moses; and when Moses prayed unto the Lord, the fire was quenched. And he called the name of the place Taberah: because **the fire of the Lord** burnt among them." KJV (*Taberah means "burning."*)

God's great fire will consume us
DEUTERONOMY 5:25 "Now therefore why should we die? for **this great fire will consume us**: if we hear the voice of the Lord our God any more, then we shall die." KJV

Burn the heathen idols
DEUTERONOMY 7:5, 25 "But thus shall ye deal with them; ye shall destroy their altars, and break down their images, and cut down their groves, and **burn their graven images with fire**. . . . The graven images of their gods shall ye **burn with fire**." KJV

Burn their sacred groves
DEUTERONOMY 12:3 "And ye shall overthrow their altars, and break their pillars, and **burn their groves with fire**; and ye shall hew down the graven images of their gods, and destroy the names of them out of that place." KJV

God is like a consuming fire
DEUTERONOMY 9:3 "Understand therefore this day, that the Lord thy God is he which goeth over before thee; as a **consuming fire** he shall destroy them, and he shall bring them down before thy face: so shalt thou drive them out, and destroy them quickly, as the Lord hath said unto thee." KJV

Mountains set on fire

DEUTERONOMY 32:22 **"For a fire is kindled by my anger, and burns to the depths of Sheol;** it devours the earth and its increase, and **sets on fire** the foundations of the mountains."

People who stole sacred objects were burned

JOSHUA 7:15–26 "And it shall be, that he that is taken with the accursed thing shall be **burnt with fire**, he and all that he hath: because he hath transgressed the covenant of the Lord. . . . And all Israel stoned him with stones, and **burned them with fire**, after they had stoned them with stones. And they raised over him a great heap of stones unto this day. So the Lord turned from the fierceness of his anger. Wherefore the name of that place was called, The valley of Achor, unto this day." KJV ("Achor" *means* "trouble.")

David's hymn to a fire-breathing dragon

2 SAMUEL 22:2, 9, 13 "The Lord is my rock, and my fortress, and my deliverer. . . . **There went up a smoke out of his nostrils, and fire out of his mouth devoured: coals were kindled by it**. . . . Through the brightness before him were **coals of fire kindled**." KJV

The godless are consumed with fire

2 SAMUEL 23:6–7 "But godless men are all like thorns that are thrown away; for they cannot be taken with the hand; but the man who touches them arms himself with iron and the shaft of a spear, and they are **utterly consumed with fire**." RSV

God answers by fire

1 KINGS 18:24, 38 "And call ye on the name of your gods, and I will call on the name of the Lord: and the **God that answereth by fire**, let him be God. And all the people answered and said, It is well spoken. . . . **Then the fire of the Lord fell**, and consumed the burnt sacrifice, and the wood, and the stones, and the dust, and licked up the water that was in the trench." KJV

Killing fire came down from heaven (twice)

2 KINGS 1:10–12 "And Elijah answered and said to the captain of fifty, If I be a man of God, then let fire come down from heaven, and consume thee and thy fifty. **And there came down fire from heaven**, and consumed him and his fifty. . . . And Elijah answered and said unto them, If I be a man of God, let fire come down from heaven, and consume thee and thy fifty. **And the fire of God came down from heaven,** and consumed him and his fifty." KJV

Philistines burned at God's command

1 CHRONICLES 14:10–12 "And David enquired of God, saying, Shall I go up against the Philistines? And wilt thou deliver them into mine hand? And the Lord said unto him, Go up; for I will deliver them into thine hand. . . . David gave a commandment, and they were **burned with fire**." KJV

God punishes Job with fire from heaven

JOB 1:16 "While he was yet speaking, there came also another, and said, **The fire of God** is fallen from heaven, and hath burned up the sheep, and the servants, and consumed them; and I only am escaped alone to tell thee." KJV

More fire from heaven

1 CHRONICLES 21:26–27 "And David built there an altar unto the Lord, and offered burnt offerings and peace offerings, and called upon the Lord; and he answered him from heaven by fire upon the altar of burnt offering. And the Lord commanded the angel; and he put up his sword again into the sheath thereof." KJV

Rain of fire

PSALM 11:6 "Upon the wicked he shall rain **snares, fire and brimstone**, and an horrible tempest: this shall be the portion of their cup." KJV

Fire from heaven, glory to God

2 CHRONICLES 7:1–3 "Now when Solomon had made an end of praying, the **fire came down from heaven**, and consumed the burnt offering and the sacrifices; and the glory of the Lord filled the house. . . . And when all the children of Israel saw how **the fire came down**, and the glory of the Lord upon the house, they bowed themselves with their faces to the ground upon the pavement, and worshipped, and praised the Lord." KJV

God's devouring fire

ISAIAH 26:11 "Lord, when thy hand is lifted up, they will not see: but they shall see, and be ashamed for their envy at the people; yea, the **fire of thine enemies shall devour them**." KJV

Fire will devour them

PSALM 21:9 "Thou shalt make them as a **fiery oven** in the time of thine anger: the Lord shall swallow them up in his wrath, and **the fire shall devour them**." KJV

Devoured like burning wood

JEREMIAH 5:14 "Therefore thus says the Lord, the God of hosts: Because they have spoken this word, I am now making my words in your mouth a **fire**, and this people wood, and **the fire shall devour them**."

Hot breath of God

PSALM 29:7 "The voice of the Lord flashes forth **flames of fire**." KJV

A raging fire against nonbelievers

PSALM 78:21 "Therefore, when the Lord heard, he was full of wrath; **a fire was kindled** against Jacob, his anger mounted against Israel; because they had no faith in God." KJV

Fire consumed the young men

PSALM 78:59–63 "When God heard this, he was wroth. . . . **The fire consumed their young men**; and their maidens were not given to marriage." KJV

"Burn up their houses"

EZEKIEL 23:46–47 "For thus saith the Lord God; I will bring up a company upon them, and will give them to be removed and spoiled. And the company shall stone them with stones, and dispatch them with their swords; they shall slay their sons and their daughters, and **burn up their houses with fire**." KJV

The hills melt like wax

PSALM 97:1–5 "The Lord reigneth; let the earth rejoice. . . . **A fire goeth before him**, and **burneth** up his enemies round about. His lightnings enlightened the world: the earth saw, and trembled. The hills **melted like wax** at the presence of the Lord, at the presence of the Lord of the whole earth." KJV

Land burned by God's wrath

ISAIAH 9:19 "Through the wrath of the Lord of hosts **the land is burned**, and the people are like **fuel for the fire**; no man spares his brother." RSV

The Lord's flame of a devouring fire

ISAIAH 29:5–6 "And in an instant, suddenly, you will be visited by the Lord of hosts with thunder and with earthquake and great noise, with whirlwind and tempest, and the flame of a **devouring fire**." RSV

Burning tongue

ISAIAH 30:27 "Behold, the name of the Lord cometh from far, burning with his anger, and the burden thereof is heavy: his lips are full of indignation, and his tongue as a **devouring fire**." KJV

The land shall burn

ISAIAH 34:8–10 "For it is the day of the Lord's vengeance, and the year of recompences for the controversy of Zion. And the streams thereof shall be turned into pitch, and the dust thereof into brimstone, and **the land thereof shall become burning pitch**. It shall not be quenched night nor day; the **smoke** thereof shall go up for ever: from generation to generation it shall lie waste; none shall pass through it for ever and ever." KJV

God is pleased to burn

ISAIAH 42:21, 25 "The Lord was pleased, for his righteousness' sake, to magnify his law and make it glorious. . . . So he poured upon him the **heat** of his anger and the might of battle; it set him on **fire** round about, but he did not understand; it **burned** him, but he did not take it to heart. " RSV

Arm of fire

ISAIAH 30:30 "And the Lord shall cause his glorious voice to be heard, and shall shew the lighting down of his arm, with the indignation of his anger, and with the **flame of a devouring fire**, with scattering, and tempest, and hailstones." KJV

Fire in Zion, furnace in Jerusalem

ISAIAH 31:9 "And he shall pass over to his strong hold for fear, and his princes shall be afraid of the ensign, saith the Lord, whose **fire** is in Zion, and his **furnace** in Jerusalem." KJV

His burning place

ISAIAH 30:33 "For a **burning place** has long been prepared; yea, for the king it is made ready, its pyre made deep and wide, with **fire** and wood in abundance; the breath of the Lord, like a stream of **brimstone**, kindles it." RSV

Fire in his nostrils

ISAIAH 65:5 "Which say, Stand by thyself, come not near to me; for I am holier than thou. These are a **smoke in my nose**, a **fire** that **burneth** all the day." KJV

He rebukes in flames of fire

ISAIAH 66:15–16 "For, behold, the Lord will come with **fire**, and with his chariots like a whirlwind, to render his anger with fury, and his rebuke with **flames of fire**. For by **fire** and by his sword will the Lord plead with all flesh: and the slain of the Lord shall be many." KJV

Circumcision or fire

JEREMIAH 4:4 "Circumcise yourselves to the Lord, and take away the foreskins of your heart, ye men of Judah and inhabitants of Jerusalem: lest my fury come forth like **fire**, and **burn** that none can quench it, because of the evil of your doings." KJV

Jerusalem devoured by fire

JEREMIAH 17:27 "But if ye will not hearken unto me to hallow the sabbath day, and not to bear a burden, even entering in at the gates of Jerusalem on the sabbath day; then will **I kindle a fire in the gates** thereof, and it shall devour the palaces of Jerusalem, and it shall not be quenched." KJV

Cities of Judah set on fire

JEREMIAH 34:22 "Behold, I will command, saith the Lord, and cause them to return to this city; and they shall fight against it, and take it, and **burn it with fire**: and I will make the cities of Judah a desolation without an inhabitant." KJV

Surrender or burn

JEREMIAH 38:17–18, 23 "Thus saith the Lord, the God of hosts, the God of Israel; If thou wilt assuredly go forth unto the king of Babylon's princes, then thy soul shall live, and this city shall not be **burned with fire**; and thou shalt live, and thine house: But if thou wilt not go forth to the king of Babylon's princes, then shall this city be given into the hand of the Chaldeans, and they shall **burn it with fire**, and thou shalt not escape out of their hand. . . . So they shall bring out all thy wives and thy children to the Chaldeans: and thou shalt not escape out of their hand, but shalt be taken by the hand of the king of Babylon: and thou shalt cause this city to be **burned with fire**." KJV

Temples burned

JEREMIAH 43:12–13 "And I will **kindle a fire** in the houses of the gods of Egypt; and he shall **burn** them, and carry them away captives. . . . and the houses of the gods of the Egyptians shall he **burn with fire**." KJV

Villages burned

JEREMIAH 49:2 "Therefore, behold, the days are coming, says the Lord, when I will cause the battle cry to be heard against Rabbah of the Ammonites; it shall become a desolate mound, and its villages shall be **burned with fire**; then Israel shall dispossess those who dispossessed him, says the Lord." KJV

Babylon's homes set on fire

JEREMIAH 51:30 "The mighty men of Babylon have forborn to fight, they have remained in their holds: their might hath failed; they became as women: they have **burned** her dwellingplaces; her bars are broken." KJV

Flaming Fire against Jacob

LAMENTATIONS 2:3 "He hath cut off in his fierce anger all the horn of Israel: he hath drawn back his right hand from before the enemy, and he burned against Jacob like a **flaming fire**, which devoureth round about." KJV

No escape from the fire

EZEKIEL 15:6–8 "Therefore thus saith the Lord God; As the vine tree among the trees of the forest, which I have given to the **fire for fuel**, so will I give the inhabitants of Jerusalem. And I will set my face against them; they shall go out from one **fire**, and another **fire** shall devour them; and ye shall know that I am the Lord, when I set my face against them. And I will make the land desolate, because they have committed a trespass, saith the Lord God." KJV

God threatened a forest fire

EZEKIEL 20:45–48 "Say to the forest of the south, Hear the word of the Lord; Thus saith the Lord God; Behold, I will **kindle a fire** in thee, and it shall devour every green tree in thee, and every dry tree: the **flaming flame** shall not be quenched, and all faces from the south to the north shall be **burned** therein. And all flesh shall see that I the Lord have **kindled** it: it shall not be quenched." KJV

Burn the cedars of Lebanon, oaks of Bashan

ZECHARIAH 11:1–2 "Open thy doors, O Lebanon, that the **fire may devour thy cedars**. Howl, fir tree; for the cedar is fallen; because the mighty are spoiled: howl, O ye oaks of Bashan; for the forest of the vintage is come down." KJV

Survivors devoured by fire

EZEKIEL 23:25 "And I will direct my indignation against you, that they may deal with you in fury. They shall cut off your nose and your ears, and your survivors shall fall by the sword. They shall seize your sons and your daughters, and your survivors shall be **devoured by fire**." RSV

"Burn their houses"

EZEKIEL 23:46–47 "For thus saith the Lord God; I will bring up a company upon them, and will give them to be removed and spoiled. And the company shall stone them with stones, and dispatch them with their swords; they shall slay their sons and their daughters, and **burn up their houses with fire**." KJV

"Burn their bones"

EZEKIEL 24:9–12 "Therefore thus saith the Lord God; Woe to the bloody city! [Tyre] I will even make the pile for **fire** great. Heap on wood, **kindle the fire**, consume the flesh, and spice it well, and **let the bones be burned**. Then set it empty upon the **coals** thereof, that the brass of it may be **hot**, and may **burn**, and that the filthiness of it may be **molten** in it, that the scum of it may be consumed. She hath wearied herself with lies, and her great scum went not forth out of her: her scum shall be in the **fire**." KJV

Hebrew towns set on fire during Jewish civil war

JUDGES 20:23, 48 "And the Lord said, Go up against him. . . . And the men of Israel turned again upon the children of Benjamin, and smote them with the edge of the sword, as well the men of every city, as the beast, and all that came to hand: also **they set on fire all the cities** that they came to." KJV

A heathen city becomes a "burnt offering to the Lord"

DEUTERONOMY 13:12–16 "If you hear in one of your cities . . . 'Let us go and serve other gods,' . . . **burn the city and all its spoil with fire, as a whole burnt offering to the Lord your God**." RSV

Cities burned with fire

ISAIAH 1:7–9 "Your country is desolate, **your cities are burned with fire**. . . . Except the Lord of hosts had left unto us a very small remnant, we should have been as Sodom, and we should have been like unto Gomorrah." KJV

Tyre devoured with fire

ZECHARIAH 9:3–4 "And Tyrus did build herself a strong hold, and heaped up silver as the dust, and fine gold as the mire of the streets. Behold, the Lord will cast her out, and he will smite her power in the sea; and she shall be **devoured with fire**." KJV

Tyre turned to ashes

EZEKIEL 28:18 "Therefore will I bring forth a **fire** from the midst of thee, it shall devour thee, and I will bring thee to **ashes** upon the earth in the sight of all them that behold thee." KJV

Fire on Tyre

AMOS 1:10 "But I will send a **fire** on the wall of Tyrus, which shall devour the palaces thereof." KJV

Fire on Hazor

JOSHUA 11:11 "And they smote all the souls that were therein with the edge of the sword, utterly destroying them: there was not any left to breathe: and **he burnt Hazor with fire**." KJV

Fire on Jerusalem

JUDGES 1:8 "Now the children of Judah had fought against Jerusalem, and had taken it, and smitten it with the edge of the sword, and **set the city on fire**." KJV

Fire on Hazael

AMOS 1:4 "But I will send a **fire** into the house of Hazael, which shall devour the palaces of Benhadad." KJV

Fire on Gaza

AMOS 1:7 "But I will send a **fire** on the wall of Gaza, which shall devour the palaces thereof." KJV

Fire on Teman

AMOS 1:12 "But I will send a **fire** upon Teman, which shall devour the palaces of Bozrah." KJV

Fire on Rabbah

AMOS 1:14 "But I will kindle a **fire** in the wall of Rabbah, and it shall devour the palaces thereof, with shouting in the day of battle, with a tempest in the day of the whirlwind." KJV

Fire on Moab

AMOS 2:2 "But I will send a **fire** upon Moab, and it shall devour the palaces of Kirioth: and Moab shall die with tumult, with shouting, and with the sound of the trumpet." KJV

Fire on Judah

AMOS 2:5 "But I will send a **fire** upon Judah, and it shall devour the palaces of Jerusalem." KJV

Fire on Ai

JOSHUA 8:8–28 "And it shall be, when ye have taken the city, that ye shall **set the city on fire**: according to the commandment of the Lord shall ye do. See, I have commanded you . . . and they entered into the city, and took it, and hasted and **set the city on fire**. . . . **So Joshua burned Ai**, and made it forever a heap of ruins, as it is to this day." KJV

Fire on Zoan

EZEKIEL 30:14 "I will make Pathros a desolation, and will **set fire to Zo'an**, and will execute acts of judgment upon Thebes." RSV

Fire on Sodom and Gomorrah

GENESIS 19:24–28 "Then the Lord rained upon Sodom and upon Gomorrah **brimstone and fire from the Lord** out of heaven. . . . And [Abraham] looked toward Sodom and Gomorrah, and toward all the land of the plain, and beheld, and, lo, the **smoke** of the country went up as **the smoke of a furnace**." KJV

Fire on Israel

EZEKIEL 5:4 "Then take of them again, and cast them into the **midst of the fire**, and **burn** them in the **fire**; for thereof shall a **fire** come forth into all the house of Israel." KJV

Fire on Egypt

EZEKIEL 30:8 "And they shall know that I am the Lord, when I have set a **fire** in Egypt, and when all her helpers shall be destroyed." KJV

Fire on Magog

EZEKIEL 39:6 "And I will send a **fire** on Magog, and among them that dwell carelessly in the isles: and they shall know that I am the Lord." KJV

Fire on Heshbon, Sihon, and Medeba

NUMBERS 21:21–30 "Then Israel sent messengers to King Sihon of the Amorites, saying, 'Let me pass through your land.' . . . But Sihon would not allow Israel to pass through his territory . . . [then] **fire came out from Heshbon, flame from the city of Sihon.** It devoured Ar of Moab, and swallowed up the heights of the Arnon. . . . And we laid waste until **fire spread to Medeba.**"

Fire on the fenced cities

HOSEA 8:14 "For Israel hath forgotten his Maker, and buildeth temples; and Judah hath multiplied fenced cities: but I will send a **fire upon his cities**, and it shall devour the palaces thereof." KJV

God's throne of fire

DANIEL 7:9–10 "I beheld till the thrones were cast down, and the Ancient of days did sit, whose garment was white as snow, and the hair of his head like the pure wool: **his throne was like the fiery flame**, and his wheels as **burning fire**. A fiery stream issued and came forth from before him." KJV

Judgment by fire

AMOS 7:4 "Thus the Lord God showed me: behold, the Lord God was calling for a **judgment by fire**, and it devoured the great deep and was eating up the land." RSV

Samaria's wealth burned with fire

MICAH 1:7 "And all the graven images thereof shall be beaten to pieces, and all the hires thereof shall be **burned with the fire**, and all the idols thereof will I lay desolate: for she gathered it of the hire of an harlot, and they shall return to the hire of an harlot." KJV

Burn them all

OBADIAH 1:18 "And the house of Jacob shall be a **fire**, and the house of Joseph a **flame**, and the house of Esau for stubble, and they shall **kindle** in them, and devour them; and there shall not be any remaining of the house of Esau; for the Lord hath spoken it." KJV

Burn the city with the wrong religion

DEUTERONOMY 13:12–16 "If thou shalt hear say in one of thy cities, which the Lord thy God hath given thee to dwell there, saying, Certain men, the children of Belial, are gone out from among you, and have withdrawn the inhabitants of their city, saying, Let us go and serve other gods, which ye have not known, . . . Thou shalt surely smite the inhabitants of that city with the edge of the sword, destroying it utterly, and all that is therein, and the cattle thereof, with the edge of the sword. And thou shalt gather all the spoil of it into the midst of the street thereof, and shalt **burn with fire the city**, and all the spoil thereof every whit, for the Lord thy God: and it shall be an heap for ever; it shall not be built again." KJV

21

Angry

*"For a fire is kindled by my anger,
and burns to the depths of Sheol."*
—Deuteronomy 32:22

The emotion most often expressed by the God of the Old Testament is not love. Not mercy. Not empathy. Not joy. The Lord Jealous is most often described as a God of anger.

God's anger was not the good kind. Sometimes anger is deserved. Parents occasionally get angry at their children when they do something harmful or risky. Anger can be part of the motivation behind protecting someone you love. But the God of the Old Testament rarely gets angry when he sees his people doing morally harmful things. No, he regularly *orders* them to do morally harmful things, as previous chapters have shown.

God's anger is almost always jealous, not protective. The Lord Jealous becomes enraged when he sees someone loving a god other than himself.

Jealous anger

Deuteronomy 6:14–15 "Ye shall not go after other gods, of the gods of the people which are round about you; (For the Lord thy God is a **jealous** God among you) lest the **anger of the Lord thy God** be kindled against thee, and destroy thee from off the face of the earth." KJV

Deuteronomy 29:18–20 "Lest there should be among you man, or woman, or family, or tribe, whose heart turneth away this day from the Lord our God, to go and serve the gods of these nations. . . . The Lord will not spare him, but then the **anger** of the Lord and his **jealousy** shall smoke against that man, and all the curses that are written in this book shall lie upon him, and the Lord shall blot out his name from under heaven." KJV

DEUTERONOMY 11:16 "Take heed to yourselves, that your heart be not deceived, and ye turn aside, and serve other gods, and worship them; And then the Lord's **wrath** be kindled against you." KJV

JEREMIAH 25:6–7 "And go not after other gods to serve them, and to worship them, and provoke me not to **anger** with the works of your hands; and I will do you no hurt. Yet ye have not hearkened unto me, saith the Lord; that ye might provoke me to **anger** with the works of your hands to your own hurt." KJV (*It's your own fault if I get mad.*)

1 KINGS 14:9–10 "But hast done evil above all that were before thee: for thou hast gone and made thee other gods, and molten images, to provoke me to **anger**, and hast cast me behind thy back: Therefore, behold, I will bring evil upon the house of Jeroboam, and will cut off from Jeroboam him that pisseth against the wall, and him that is shut up and left in Israel, and will take away the remnant of the house of Jeroboam, as a man taketh away dung, till it be all gone." KJV (*Notice that in this verse and the next verse, "evil" and "wickedness" are equated with idolatry, not with moral harm.*)

2 KINGS 17:11 "And there they burnt incense in all the high places, as did the heathen whom the Lord carried away before them; and wrought wicked things to provoke the Lord to **anger**." KJV

JEREMIAH 44:3 "Because of their wickedness which they have committed to provoke me to **anger**, in that they went to burn incense, and to serve other gods, whom they knew not." KJV

JEREMIAH 44:7–8 "Wherefore commit ye this great evil against your souls, to cut off from you man and woman, child and suckling, out of Judah, to leave you none to remain; In that ye provoke me unto **wrath** with the works of your hands, burning incense unto other gods in the land of Egypt, whither ye be gone to dwell?" KJV

1 KINGS 22:53 "For he served Baal, and worshipped him, and provoked to **anger** the Lord God of Israel, according to all that his father had done." KJV

NUMBERS 25:3 "And Israel joined himself unto Baalpeor: and the **anger of the Lord** was kindled against Israel." KJV

2 KINGS 22:17 "Because they have forsaken me, and have burned incense unto other gods, that they might provoke me to **anger** with all the works of their hands; therefore my wrath shall be kindled against this place, and shall not be quenched." KJV

*   *   *

The writers of the Old Testament found many creative ways to portray the anger of God:

God the angry superhero

JEREMIAH 21:5–6 "And I myself will fight against you with an outstretched hand and with a strong arm, even in **anger**, and in **fury**, and in **great wrath**. And I will smite the inhabitants of this city, both man and beast: they shall die of a great pestilence." KJV

God the furious swordfighter

EZEKIEL 21:5–17 "Then all people will know that I the Lord have drawn my sword from its sheath; it will not return again. . . . A sword, a sword, sharpened and polished—sharpened for the slaughter, polished to flash like lightning! . . . Strike your hands together. Let the sword strike twice, even three times. It is a sword for slaughter—a sword for great slaughter, closing in on them from every side. So that hearts may melt with fear and the fallen be many, I have stationed the sword for slaughter at all their gates. Look! It is forged to strike like lightning, it is grasped for slaughter. **Slash to the right, you sword, then to the left**, wherever your blade is turned. I too will strike my hands together, and my **wrath** will subside. I the Lord have spoken." NIV

God the angry archer

LAMENTATIONS 2:1–4 "How hath the Lord covered the daughter of Zion with a cloud in his **anger**, and cast down from heaven unto the earth the beauty of Israel, and remembered not his footstool in the day of his **anger**! The Lord hath swallowed up all the habitations of Jacob, and hath not pitied: he hath thrown down in his **wrath** the strong holds of the daughter of Judah; he hath brought them down to the ground: he hath polluted the kingdom and the princes thereof. He hath cut off in his **fierce anger** all the horn of Israel: he hath drawn back his right hand from before the enemy, and he burned against Jacob like a flaming fire, which devoureth round about. He hath **bent his bow** like an enemy: he stood with his right hand as an adversary, and slew all that were pleasant to the eye in the tabernacle of the daughter of Zion: he poured out his **fury like fire**." KJV

God the furious whirlwind

JEREMIAH 23:19–20 "Behold, a whirlwind of the Lord is gone forth in **fury**, even a grievous whirlwind: it shall fall grievously upon the head of the wicked. The **anger of the Lord** shall not return, until he have executed, and till he have performed the thoughts of his heart." KJV

God the fierce tornado

JEREMIAH 30:23–24 "See, the storm of the Lord will burst out in **wrath**, a driving wind swirling down on the heads of the wicked. The **fierce anger** of the Lord will not turn back until he fully accomplishes the purposes of his heart." NIV

God the angry volcano

2 SAMUEL 22:8–9 "Then the earth shook and trembled; the foundations of heaven moved and shook, because he was **wroth**. There went up a smoke out of his nostrils, and fire out of his mouth devoured: coals were kindled by it." KJV

God the fire-breathing dragon

PSALM 18:7–8 "The earth trembled and quaked, and the foundations of the mountains shook; they trembled because he was **angry**. Smoke rose from his nostrils; consuming fire came from his mouth, burning coals blazed out of it." NIV

God will melt you with his hot angry breath

EZEKIEL 22:20–22 "As they gather silver, and brass, and iron, and lead, and tin, into the midst of the furnace, to blow the fire upon it, to melt it; so will I gather you in mine **anger** and in my **fury**, and I will leave you there, and melt you. Yea, I will gather you, and blow upon you in the **fire of my wrath**, and ye shall be melted in the midst thereof. As silver is melted in the midst of the furnace, so shall ye be melted in the midst thereof; and ye shall know that I the Lord have poured out my **fury** upon you." KJV

God's toxic breath

JOB 4:9 "By the breath of God they perish, and by **the blast of his anger** they are consumed." RSV

Really bad breath

ISAIAH 30:27, 30, 33: "Behold, the name of the Lord comes from far, **burning with his anger,** and in thick rising smoke; his lips are full of **indignation**, and his tongue is like a devouring fire. . . . And the Lord will cause his majestic voice to be heard and the descending blow of his arm to be seen, in **furious anger** and a flame of devouring fire, with a cloudburst and tempest and hailstones. . . . The breath of the Lord, like a stream of brimstone, kindles it." RSV

Tearing, gnashing, biting anger

JOB 16:9 "He teareth me in his **wrath**, who hateth me: he gnasheth upon me with his teeth." KJV

Furious sneeze

EXODUS 15:6–8 "And in the greatness of thine excellency thou hast overthrown them that rose up against thee: thou sentest forth thy **wrath**, which consumed them as stubble. And with the blast of thy nostrils the waters were gathered together, the floods stood upright as an heap, and the depths were congealed in the heart of the sea." KJV

Angry laughter. "Ha, ha, ha!"

PSALM 2:4–6 "The One enthroned in heaven laughs; the Lord scoffs at them. He rebukes them in his **anger** and terrifies them in his **wrath**, saying, 'I have installed my king on Zion, my holy mountain.'" NIV

Wrath in the marketplace

EZEKIEL 7:2 "The time has come! The day has arrived! Let not the buyer rejoice nor the seller grieve, for my **wrath** is on the whole crowd." NIV

God squashes people like grapes, proudly staining his robes red

ISAIAH 63:1–6 "Who is this coming from Edom, from Bozrah, with his garments stained crimson? Who is this, robed in splendor, striding forward in the greatness of his strength? 'It is I, proclaiming victory, mighty to save.' Why are your garments red, like those of one treading the winepress? 'I have trodden the winepress alone; from the nations no one was with me. I trampled them in my **anger** and trod them down in my **wrath**; their blood spattered my garments, and I stained all my clothing. It was for me the day of vengeance; the year for me to redeem had come. I looked, but there was no one to help, I was appalled that no one gave support; so my own arm achieved salvation for me, and my own **wrath** sustained me. I trampled the nations in my **anger**; in my **wrath** I made them drunk and poured their blood on the ground.'" NIV

Grapes of wrath

JEREMIAH 25:15 "Thus the Lord, the God of Israel, said to me: Take from my hand this cup of the **wine of wrath**, and make all the nations to whom I send you drink it." KJV

Drink the wrath

JOB 21:17–20 "How oft is the candle of the wicked put out! and how oft cometh their destruction upon them! God distributeth sorrows in his **anger**. They are as stubble before the wind, and as chaff that the storm carrieth away. God layeth up his iniquity for his children: he rewardeth him, and he shall know it. His eyes shall see his destruction, and he shall **drink of the wrath of the Almighty**." KJV

The cup of his fury

ISAIAH 51:17 "Awake, awake, stand up, O Jerusalem, which hast drunk at the hand of the Lord **the cup of his fury**; thou hast drunken the dregs of the cup of trembling, and wrung them out." KJV

Earthquakes caused by God's anger

JOB 9:4–6 "Who hath hardened himself against him, and hath prospered? Which removeth the mountains, and they know not: which overturneth them in his **anger**. Which shaketh the earth out of her place, and the pillars thereof tremble." KJV

Seismic anger

ISAIAH 5:25 "Therefore is the **anger of the Lord** kindled against his people, and he hath stretched forth his hand against them, and hath smitten them: and the hills did tremble, and their carcases were torn in the midst of the streets. For all this his **anger** is not turned away, but his hand is stretched out still." KJV

Angry earthquakes

JEREMIAH 10:10 "But the Lord is the true God, he is the living God, and an everlasting king: at his **wrath** the earth shall tremble, and the nations shall not be able to abide his **indignation**." KJV

Earth and heaven quake

ISAIAH 13:13 "Therefore I will shake the heavens, and the earth shall remove out of her place, in the **wrath** of the Lord of hosts, and in the day of his **fierce anger**." KJV

Angry drought

DEUTERONOMY 11:16–17 "Take heed to yourselves, that your heart be not deceived, and ye turn aside, and serve other gods, and worship them; And then the Lord's **wrath** be kindled against you, and he shut up the heaven, that there be no rain, and that the land yield not her fruit; and lest ye perish quickly from off the good land which the Lord giveth you." KJV

Scorched earth caused by God's anger

JEREMIAH 4:26–27 "I looked, and lo, the fruitful land was a desert, and all its cities were laid in ruins before the Lord, before his **fierce anger**. For thus says the Lord, 'The whole land shall be a desolation.'" RSV

Scorched-earth policy

JEREMIAH 7:20 "Therefore thus saith the Lord God; Behold, mine **anger** and my **fury** shall be poured out upon this place, upon man, and upon beast, and upon the trees of the field, and upon the fruit of the ground; and it shall burn, and shall not be quenched." KJV

Pestilential anger

EZEKIEL 14:19 "Or if I send a pestilence into that land, and **pour out my wrath** upon it with blood, to cut off from it man and beast." RSV

Cannibalistic fury

LEVITICUS 26:27–29 "And if in spite of this you will not hearken to me, but walk contrary to me, then I will walk contrary to you in **fury**, and chastise you myself sevenfold for your sins. You shall eat the flesh of your sons, and you shall eat the flesh of your daughters." RSV

Weapons of mass indignation

ISAIAH 13:2–6 "I have commanded my sanctified ones, I have also called my mighty ones for mine **anger**, even them that rejoice in my highness. The noise of a multitude in the mountains, like as of a great people; a tumultuous noise of the kingdoms of nations gathered together: the Lord of hosts mustereth the host of the battle. They come from a far country, from the end of heaven, even the Lord, and the **weapons of his indignation**, to destroy the whole land. Howl ye; for the day of the Lord is at hand; it shall come as a destruction from the Almighty." KJV

An armory of indignation

JEREMIAH 50:25 "The Lord hath opened his armoury, and hath brought forth the weapons of his indignation." KJV

Angry arrows of famine

EZEKIEL 5:15–16 "So it shall be a reproach and a taunt, an instruction and an astonishment unto the nations that are round about thee, when I shall execute judgments in thee in **anger** and in **fury** and in **furious rebukes**. I the Lord have spoken it. When I shall send upon them the evil arrows of famine, which shall be for their destruction, and which I will send to destroy you: and I will increase the famine upon you, and will break your staff of bread." KJV

Fist and club of anger

ISAIAH 10:4–6 "But even then **the Lord's anger** will not be satisfied. His **fist** is still poised to strike. What sorrow awaits Assyria, **the rod of my anger. I use it as a club to express my anger**. I am sending Assyria against a godless nation, against a people with whom I am **angry**. Assyria will plunder them, trampling them like dirt beneath its feet." NLT

Armor of fury

ISAIAH 59:17 "He put on righteousness as a breastplate, and a helmet of salvation upon his head; he put on garments of vengeance for clothing, and wrapped himself in **fury** as a mantle." RSV

Whip of anger

ISAIAH 10:24–26 "So this is what the Lord, the Lord of Heaven's Armies, says: 'O my people in Zion, do not be afraid of the Assyrians when they oppress you with rod and club as the Egyptians did long ago. In a little while my **anger** against you will end, and then my **anger** will rise up to destroy them.' The Lord of Heaven's Armies will **lash them with his whip**, as he did when Gideon triumphed over the Midianites at the rock of Oreb, or when the Lord's staff was raised to drown the Egyptian army in the sea." NLT

Rod of wrath

LAMENTATIONS 3:1–3 "I am the man who has seen affliction by **the rod of the Lord's wrath**. He has driven me away and made me walk in darkness rather than light; indeed, he has turned his hand against me again and again, all day long." NIV

God was so angry he made a donkey talk

NUMBERS 22:22–30 "And **God's anger was kindled** because he went: and the angel of the Lord stood in the way for an adversary against him. Now he was riding upon his ass, and his two servants were with him. . . . And the Lord opened the mouth of the ass, and she said unto Balaam, What have I done unto thee, that thou hast smitten me these three times? . . . Am not I thine ass, upon which thou hast ridden ever since I was thine unto this day? was I ever wont to do so unto thee?" KJV

God was angry with a wall!

EZEKIEL 13:12–15 "When the wall collapses, will people not ask you, 'Where is the whitewash you covered it with?' Therefore this is what the Sovereign Lord says: In my **wrath** I will unleash a violent wind, and in my **anger** hailstones and torrents of rain will fall with destructive **fury**. I will tear down the wall you have covered with whitewash and will level it to the ground so that its foundation will be laid bare. When it falls, you will be destroyed in it; and you will know that I am the Lord. So I will pour out my **wrath** against the wall and against those who covered it with whitewash. I will say to you, 'The wall is gone and so are those who whitewashed it.'" NIV

Angry butcher

1 SAMUEL 11:6–7 "And the Spirit of God came upon Saul when he heard those tidings, and his **anger was kindled greatly**. And he took a

yoke of oxen, and hewed them in pieces, and sent them throughout all
the coasts of Israel by the hands of messengers, saying, Whosoever cometh
not forth after Saul and after Samuel, so shall it be done unto his oxen.
And the fear of the Lord fell on the people, and they came out with one
consent." KJV

Angry environmental destruction

DEUTERONOMY 29:22–24 "So that the generation to come of your children
that shall rise up after you, and the stranger that shall come from a far land,
shall say, when they see the plagues of that land, and the sicknesses which
the Lord hath laid upon it; And that the whole land thereof is brimstone,
and salt, and burning, that it is not sown, nor beareth, nor any grass groweth
therein, like the overthrow of Sodom, and Gomorrah, Admah, and Zeboim,
which the Lord overthrew in his **anger**, and in his **wrath**. Even all nations
shall say, Wherefore hath the Lord done thus unto this land? what meaneth
the heat of this **great anger**?" KJV

Make the earth a desolation

ISAIAH 13:9–10 "Behold, the day of the Lord cometh, cruel both with **wrath**
and **fierce anger**, to lay the land desolate: and he shall destroy the sinners
thereof out of it. For the stars of heaven and the constellations thereof
shall not give their light: the sun shall be darkened in his going forth, and
the moon shall not cause her light to shine." KJV (*This looks like nuclear
winter, or air pollution.*)

Harvests ruined by his fierce anger

JEREMIAH 12:13 "They have sown wheat, but shall reap thorns: they have
put themselves to pain, but shall not profit: and they shall be ashamed of
your revenues because of the **fierce anger of the Lord**." KJV

Noses and ears furiously cut off

EZEKIEL 23:25 "I will direct my **jealous anger** against you, and they will
deal with you in **fury**. They will cut off your noses and your ears, and those
of you who are left will fall by the sword." NIV

God makes overeaters vomit?

JOB 20:21–23 "Because his greed knew no rest, he will not save anything
in which he delights. There was nothing left after he had eaten; therefore
his prosperity will not endure. In the fulness of his sufficiency he will be
in straits; all the force of misery will come upon him. To fill his belly to
the full God will send his **fierce anger** into him, and rain it upon him as
his food." RSV

God angrily kicks his victims out of their country

Deuteronomy 29:27–28 "And the **anger of the Lord** was kindled against this land, to bring upon it all the curses that are written in this book: And the Lord rooted them out of their land in **anger**, and in **wrath**, and in **great indignation**, and cast them into another land, as it is this day." KJV

Angry giant

Habakkuk 3:12 "Thou didst bestride the earth in **fury**, thou didst trample the nations in **anger**." RSV

Messenger of death

Proverbs 16:14 "The **wrath of a king** is as messengers of death: but a wise man will pacify it." KJV (*The "king" in this passage is the "Lord."*)

Flirting with other gods was not the only thing that made the Lord Jealous angry.

Don't intermarry

Deuteronomy 7:3–4 "Neither shalt thou make **marriages** with them; thy daughter thou shalt not give unto his son, nor his daughter shalt thou take unto thy son. For they will turn away thy son from following me, that they may serve other gods: so will the **anger of the Lord** be kindled against you, and destroy thee suddenly." KJV

Ezra 9:14 "Shall we then break your commands again and **intermarry** with the peoples who commit such detestable practices? Would you not be **angry** enough with us to destroy us, leaving us no remnant or survivor?" NIV

Ezra 10:14 "Let our officials stand for the whole assembly; let all in our cities who have taken **foreign wives** come at appointed times, and with them the elders and judges of every city, till the **fierce wrath of our God** over this matter be averted from us." RSV

Don't touch that box!

1 Chronicles 13:10 "And the **anger of the Lord** was kindled against Uzza, and he smote him, because he put his hand to the ark: and there he died before God." KJV

2 Samuel 6:6–7 "Uzzah put forth his hand to the ark of God, and took hold of it; for the oxen shook it. And the **anger of the Lord** was kindled against Uzzah; and God smote him there for his error; and there he died by the ark of God." KJV

Don't break the sabbath

Nehemiah 13:18 "Did not your fathers thus, and did not our God bring all this evil upon us, and upon this city? yet ye bring more **wrath** upon Israel by profaning the sabbath." KJV

God is angry with those who do not mutilate their genitals

JEREMIAH 4:4 "Circumcise yourselves to the Lord, and take away the foreskins of your heart, ye men of Judah and inhabitants of Jerusalem: lest my **fury** come forth like fire, and burn that none can quench it, because of the evil of your doings." KJV (*Women can ignore this particular curse.*)

God is angry with any nation that is not his own

ISAIAH 34:2 "For the **indignation** of the Lord is upon all nations, and his **fury** upon all their armies: he hath utterly destroyed them, he hath delivered them to the slaughter." KJV

Kiss God's feet, or else

PSALM 2:11–12 "Serve the Lord with fear, with trembling kiss his feet, lest he be **angry**, and you perish in the way; for his **wrath** is quickly kindled." RSV (*The phrase "kiss his feet" is unclear in the Hebrew. Some translations say "kiss his son." The Orthodox Jewish Bible says "kiss the bar," whatever that means.*)

No fortune-telling

2 KINGS 17:17 "And they caused their sons and their daughters to pass through the fire, and used divination and enchantments, and sold themselves to do evil in the sight of the Lord, to provoke him to **anger**." KJV

No wizardry

2 KINGS 21:6 "And he made his son pass through the fire, and observed times, and used enchantments, and dealt with familiar spirits and wizards: he wrought much wickedness in the sight of the Lord, to provoke him to **anger**." KJV

The God of the Old Testament had a dysfunctional family. His chosen people didn't love him as much as he demanded, so he continually had to punish them in anger.

God is angry with his own people

JUDGES 2:14 "And the **anger of the Lord** was hot against Israel, and he delivered them into the hands of spoilers that spoiled them, and he sold them into the hands of their enemies round about, so that they could not any longer stand before their enemies." KJV

NUMBERS 32:13–14 "And **the Lord's anger** was kindled against Israel, and he made them wander in the wilderness forty years, until all the generation, that had done evil in the sight of the Lord, was consumed. And, behold, ye are risen up in your fathers' stead, an increase of sinful men, to augment yet the **fierce anger of the Lord** toward Israel." KJV

Judges 2:20 "And the **anger of the Lord** was hot against Israel." KJV

Judges 3:8 "Therefore the **anger of the Lord** was hot against Israel, and he sold them into the hand of Chushanrishathaim king of Mesopotamia." KJV (*God sold the Israelites? Who got the money?*)

Judges 10:7 "And the **anger of the Lord** was hot against Israel, and he sold them into the hands of the Philistines, and into the hands of the children of Ammon." KJV

2 Kings 13:3 "And the **anger of the Lord** was kindled against Israel, and he delivered them into the hand of Hazael king of Syria." KJV

Deuteronomy 9:7–8 "Remember, and forget not, how thou [Israel] provokedst the Lord thy God to **wrath** in the wilderness: from the day that thou didst depart out of the land of Egypt, until ye came unto this place, ye have been rebellious against the Lord. Also in Horeb ye provoked the Lord to **wrath**, so that the Lord was **angry** with you to have destroyed you." KJV

2 Kings 17:18 "Therefore the Lord was very **angry** with Israel, and removed them out of his sight: there was none left but the tribe of Judah only." KJV

2 Samuel 24:1 "And again the **anger** of the Lord was kindled against Israel, and he moved David against them to say, Go, number Israel and Judah." KJV (*However*, 1 Chronicles 21:1, *telling the same story, says* "Satan," *not God*, "stood up against Israel, and provoked David to number Israel.")

1 Kings 14:15 "For the Lord shall smite Israel, as a reed is shaken in the water, and he shall root up Israel out of this good land, which he gave to their fathers, and shall scatter them beyond the river, because they have made their groves, provoking the Lord to **anger**." KJV

Jeremiah 11:17 "For the Lord of hosts, that planted thee, hath pronounced evil against thee, for the evil of the house of Israel and of the house of Judah, which they have done against themselves to **provoke me to anger** in offering incense unto Baal." KJV

2 Kings 21:14–15 "And I will forsake the remnant of mine inheritance, and deliver them into the hand of their enemies; and they shall become a prey and a spoil to all their enemies; Because they have done that which was evil in my sight, and have provoked me to **anger**." KJV

Numbers 11:33 "But while the meat was still between their teeth and before it could be consumed, **the anger of the Lord** burned against the people, and he struck them with a severe plague." NIV (*Because they complained about living conditions in the desert.*)

Blame the victim. "You are hurting yourself"

JEREMIAH 44:6–7 "Therefore, my **fierce anger** was poured out; it **raged** against the towns of Judah and the streets of Jerusalem and made them the desolate ruins they are today. Now this is what the Lord God Almighty, the God of Israel, says: **Why bring such great disaster on yourselves** by cutting off from Judah the men and women, the children and infants, and so leave yourselves without a remnant?" NIV

How much emotional control does God have? How long does his fury last?

Will his anger never cease?

PSALM 79:5–6 "How long, O Lord? Wilt thou be **angry for ever**? Will thy **jealous wrath** burn like fire? Pour out thy **anger** on the nations that do not know thee, and on the kingdoms that do not call on thy name." RSV

How long will he be angry?

PSALM 80:4 "O Lord God of hosts, how long wilt thou be **angry** against the prayer of thy people?" KJV

Forever?

PSALM 85:3–5 "Thou hast taken away all thy **wrath**: thou hast turned thyself from the **fierceness of thine anger**. Turn us, O God of our salvation, and cause thine **anger** toward us to cease. Wilt thou be **angry** with us for ever? wilt thou draw out thine **anger** to all generations?" KJV

Please, God, don't be mad forever

ISAIAH 64:9 "Be not **exceedingly angry**, O Lord, and remember not iniquity for ever. Behold, consider, we are all thy people." RSV

Maybe he will let up a little, if we are lucky

JONAH 3:9 "Who knows, God may yet repent and turn from his **fierce anger**, so that we perish not?" RSV

Anger management . . .

PSALM 78:38 "Yet he, being compassionate, forgave their iniquity, and did not destroy them; he restrained his **anger** often, and did not stir up all his **wrath**." RSV

. . . but not for long

PSALM 78:49–50 "He let loose on them his **fierce anger**, **wrath**, **indignation**, and distress, a company of destroying angels. He made a path for his **anger**; he did not spare them from death, but gave their lives over to the plague." RSV

"I'm not finished until I'm finished"

EZEKIEL 24:13 "Because I would have cleansed you and you were not cleansed from your filthiness, you shall not be cleansed any more **till I have satisfied my fury** upon you." RSV

Isn't seventy years long enough to be angry?

ZECHARIAH 1:12 "Then the angel of the Lord answered and said, O Lord of hosts, how long wilt thou not have mercy on Jerusalem and on the cities of Judah, against which thou hast had **indignation** these threescore and ten years?" KJV

"I treated you badly, but I'll make it up to you."

ISAIAH 54:8 "In **overflowing wrath** for a moment I hid my face from you, but with everlasting love I will have compassion on you, says the Lord, your Redeemer." RSV

Eternal anger for a whole group of people

MALACHI 1:2–4 "'I have loved you,' says the Lord. But you say, 'How hast thou loved us?' 'Is not Esau Jacob's brother?' says the Lord. 'Yet I have loved Jacob but I have **hated** Esau; I have laid waste his hill country and left his heritage to jackals of the desert.' If Edom says, 'We are shattered but we will rebuild the ruins,' the Lord of hosts says, 'They may build, but I will tear down, till they are called the wicked country, the people with whom **the Lord is angry for ever**.'" RSV

You will be punished seven times harder than you deserve

LEVITICUS 26:28 "In my **anger** I will be hostile toward you, and I myself will punish you for your sins seven times over." NIV

God does not relent

ZECHARIAH 8:14 "For thus says the Lord of hosts: 'As I purposed to do **evil** to you, when your fathers provoked me to **wrath**, and I did not relent, says the Lord of hosts.'" RSV

God will not give up

JOB 9:13 "God will not turn back his **anger**." RSV

The Lord did not turn from his wrath

2 KINGS 23:26 "Notwithstanding the Lord turned not from the **fierceness of his great wrath**, wherewith **his anger was kindled** against Judah, because of all the provocations that Manasseh had provoked him withal." KJV

Many believers consider the Psalms to be comforting, spiritually uplifting poetry. "The Lord is my shepherd, I shall not want" conjures images of soothing harps and restful pastures. Good Christians and Jews don't want to focus on the wrath of God. It embarrasses them to think the plan of salvation reduces to appeasing the demanding anger of a hot-tempered father. The Presbyterian Church in the United States came under criticism in 2013 when it dropped the song "In Christ Alone" from its hymnbook because it contains the line "Till on that cross as Jesus died / The wrath of God was satisfied." It bothers these kind and peaceful people to think they might be worshipping a god of wrath. They would certainly be uncomfortable with the line in the "Battle Hymn of the Republic" that says "Mine eyes have seen the glory of the coming of the Lord / He is trampling out the vintage where the grapes of wrath are stored." (See Isaiah 63:1–6 and Jeremiah 25:15, above.)

But look closely, and you will see that those lyrical verses in the Psalms, meant to be sung during worship, are shotgunned full of indignant fury. In addition to the passages above, here are twenty more from the Psalms that describe God's anger.

Sing a song of anger

Psalm 6:1 "O Lord, rebuke me not in thine **anger**, neither chasten me in thy **hot displeasure**." KJV

Psalm 7:6 "Arise, O Lord, in thine **anger**, lift up thyself because of the rage of mine enemies: and awake for me to the judgment that thou hast commanded." KJV

Psalm 7:11 "God is a righteous judge, and a God who has **indignation** every day. If a man does not repent, God will whet his sword; he has bent and strung his bow." RSV

Psalm 38:1 "Lord, do not rebuke me in your **anger** or discipline me in your **wrath**. Your arrows have pierced me, and your hand has come down on me. Because of your **wrath** there is no health in my body." NIV

Psalm 59:13 "Consume them in **wrath**, consume them till they are no more, that men may know that God rules over Jacob to the ends of the earth." RSV

Psalm 60:1 "You have rejected us, God, and burst upon us; you have been **angry**—now restore us! You have shaken the land and torn it open; mend its fractures, for it is quaking." NIV

Psalm 74:1 "O God, why hast thou cast us off for ever? why doth thine **anger** smoke against the sheep of thy pasture?" KJV

Psalm 76:7–8 "Thou, even thou, art to be feared: and who may stand in thy sight when once thou art **angry**? Thou didst cause judgment to be heard from heaven; the earth feared, and was still." KJV

Psalm 78:21–22 "When the Lord heard them, he was **furious**; his fire broke out against Jacob, and his **wrath** rose against Israel, for they did not believe in God." NIV

PSALM 78:62 "He gave his people over to the sword, and vented his **wrath** on his heritage." RSV

PSALM 88:6–7 "Thou hast laid me in the lowest pit, in darkness, in the deeps. Thy **wrath** lieth hard upon me, and thou hast afflicted me with all thy waves." KJV

PSALM 88:16 "Thy fierce **wrath** goeth over me; thy **terrors** have cut me off." KJV

PSALM 90:7 "For we are consumed by thine **anger**, and by thy **wrath** are we troubled." KJV

PSALM 90:11 "Who knoweth the power of thine **anger**? even according to thy fear, so is thy **wrath**." KJV

PSALM 102:9–10 "For I have eaten ashes like bread, and mingled my drink with weeping. Because of thine **indignation** and thy **wrath**: for thou hast lifted me up, and cast me down." KJV

PSALM 106:29 "Thus they provoked him to **anger** with their inventions: and the plague brake in upon them." KJV

PSALM 106:40–41 "Therefore was the **wrath** of the Lord kindled against his people, insomuch that he abhorred his own inheritance. And he gave them into the hand of the heathen; and they that hated them ruled over them." KJV

PSALM 110:5 "The Lord at thy right hand shall strike through kings in the day of his **wrath**." KJV

When I was a child, my mother told me that nobody can make you angry. If you are angry, it is because you choose to be. That may not be true for everyone. Some individuals may be naturally more tightly wired to blow up at the slightest provocation. God is like that. The authors of the Old Testament usually say "his anger was provoked" rather than "he was provoked." His anger appears to respond to its own inner indignant impulses, sitting on a hair trigger. It is "provoked," "roused," and "kindled," as if it had a mind of its own.

Perhaps this was idiomatic language, a literary way to say "God was upset." Metaphorical or not, God is not a happy fellow, and he can blame it on his uncontrollable urges. Many of the passages quoted above portray God's anger as an object that can be prompted to response by an outside stimulus. Here are a few more examples.

Irascible temper

DEUTERONOMY 31:17 "Then my **anger will be kindled** against them in that day, and I will forsake them and hide my face from them, and they will be devoured; and many evils and troubles will come upon them, so that they will say in that day, 'Have not these evils come upon us because our God is not among us?'" RSV

NUMBERS 11:10 "Then Moses heard the people weep throughout their families, every man in the door of his tent: and **the anger of the Lord was kindled greatly**; Moses also was displeased." KJV

EZEKIEL 38:18 "When Gog attacks the land of Israel, my **hot anger will be aroused**, declares the Sovereign Lord [KJV: "fury shall come up in my face"]." NIV

JEREMIAH 7:29 "Shave your head in mourning, and weep alone on the mountains. For the Lord has rejected and forsaken this generation that has **provoked his fury**." NLT

JEREMIAH 32:29–32 "And the Chaldeans, that fight against this city, shall come and set fire on this city, and burn it with the houses, upon whose roofs they have offered incense unto Baal, and poured out drink offerings unto other gods, to **provoke me to anger**. . . . For the children of Israel have only **provoked me to anger** with the work of their hands, saith the Lord. For this city hath been to me as a **provocation of mine anger** and of my **fury** from the day that they built it even unto this day; that I should remove it from before my face, because of all the evil of the children of Israel and of the children of Judah, which they have done to **provoke me to anger**." KJV

1 KINGS 16:1–3 "Then the word of the Lord came to Jehu the son of Hanani against Baasha, saying, Forasmuch as I exalted thee out of the dust, and made thee prince over my people Israel; and thou hast walked in the way of Jeroboam, and hast made my people Israel to sin, to **provoke me to anger** with their sins; behold, I will take away the posterity of Baasha." KJV

1 KINGS 16:7 "And also by the hand of the prophet Jehu the son of Hanani came the word of the Lord against Baasha, and against his house, even for all the evil that he did in the sight of the Lord, in **provoking him to anger** with the work of his hands, in being like the house of Jeroboam; and because he killed him." KJV

1 KINGS 16:33 "And Ahab did more to **provoke the Lord God of Israel to anger** than all the kings of Israel that were before him." KJV

1 KINGS 21:22 "And will make thine house like the house of Jeroboam the son of Nebat . . . for the **provocation** wherewith thou hast **provoked me to anger,** and made Israel to sin." KJV

2 KINGS 21:14–15 "They shall become a prey and a spoil to all their enemies; because they have done that which was evil in my sight, and have **provoked me to anger**, since the day their fathers came forth out of Egypt." KJV

2 Kings 22:13 "Go ye, enquire of the Lord for me, and for the people, and for all Judah, concerning the words of this book that is found: for great is the **wrath of the Lord that is kindled** against us, because our fathers have not hearkened unto the words of this book." KJV

Numbers 12:9 "And the **anger of the Lord was kindled** against them; and he departed." KJV

Exodus 4:14 "And the **anger of the Lord was kindled** against Moses." KJV

Job 42:7 "And it was so, that after the Lord had spoken these words unto Job, the Lord said to Eliphaz the Temanite, **My wrath is kindled** against thee, and against thy two friends: for ye have not spoken of me the thing that is right, as my servant Job hath." KJV

Ezekiel 24:8 "**To rouse my wrath**, to take vengeance, I have set on the bare rock the blood she has shed, that it may not be covered." RSV

*   *   *

The anger of the God of the Old Testament is often portrayed as a substance that can be dispensed, "poured out," "come upon," "spent," "vented," or "turned toward" people like a firehose or flamethrower. This is certainly also idiomatic, perhaps similar to how we might say "spread the cheer." Figurative or not, the authors of the Old Testament fiction wanted to "spread the fear."

Anger let loose

Hosea 5:10 "The princes of Judah were like them that remove the bound: therefore I will **pour out my wrath upon them like water**." KJV

Nahum 1:6 "Who can stand before his **fierce anger**? Who can survive his burning fury? His **rage blazes forth like fire**, and the mountains crumble to dust in his presence." NLT

Isaiah 1:24 "Therefore the Lord says, the Lord of hosts, the Mighty One of Israel: 'Ah, I will **vent my wrath** on my enemies, and avenge myself on my foes.'" RSV

Jeremiah 10:25 "**Pour out your wrath** on the nations that do not acknowledge you, on the peoples who do not call on your name." NIV

Ezekiel 22:22 "As silver is melted in the midst of the furnace, so shall ye be melted in the midst thereof; and ye shall know that I the Lord have **poured out my fury** upon you." KJV

Ezekiel 30:15 "And I will **pour my fury** upon Sin, the strength of Egypt; and I will cut off the multitude of No." KJV (*"Sin" is Pelusium and "No" is Thebes.*)

EZEKIEL 36:18 "Wherefore I **poured my fury** upon them for the blood that they had shed upon the land, and for their idols wherewith they had polluted it." KJV

JEREMIAH 6:11 "Therefore I am **full of the fury of the Lord**; I am weary with holding in: **I will pour it out** upon the children abroad, and upon the assembly of young men together: for even the husband with the wife shall be taken, the aged with him that is full of days." KJV

JEREMIAH 42:18 "For thus saith the Lord of hosts, the God of Israel; As **mine anger and my fury hath been poured forth** upon the inhabitants of Jerusalem; so shall **my fury be poured forth** upon you, when ye shall enter into Egypt: and ye shall be an execration, and an astonishment, and a curse, and a reproach." KJV

EZEKIEL 20:33–35 "As I live, saith the Lord God, surely with a mighty hand, and with a stretched out arm, and **with fury poured out**, will I rule over you: And I will bring you out from the people, and will gather you out of the countries wherein ye are scattered, with a mighty hand, and with a stretched out arm, and **with fury poured out**." KJV

2 CHRONICLES 34:21 "For great is the **wrath of the Lord that is poured out** upon us, because our fathers have not kept the word of the Lord." KJV

EZEKIEL 6:12–13 "One who is far away will die of the plague, and one who is near will fall by the sword, and anyone who survives and is spared will die of famine. So will I **pour out my wrath** on them. And they will know that I am the Lord, when their people lie slain among their idols around their altars." NIV

EZEKIEL 7:3 "Now the end is upon you, and **I will let loose my anger** upon you, and will judge you according to your ways; and I will punish you for all your abominations." RSV

NUMBERS 16:46 "And Moses said unto Aaron, Take a censer, and put fire therein from off the altar, and put on incense, and go quickly unto the congregation, and make an atonement for them: for **there is wrath gone out from the Lord**; the plague is begun." KJV

2 CHRONICLES 19:2 "Should you help the wicked and love those who hate the Lord? Because of this, **wrath has gone out** against you from the Lord." RSV

2 CHRONICLES 29:8–10 "Therefore the **wrath of the Lord came on Judah** and Jerusalem, and he has made them an object of horror, of astonishment, and of hissing, as you see with your own eyes. For lo, our fathers have fallen by the sword and our sons and our daughters and our wives are in captivity for this. Now it is in my heart to make a covenant with the Lord, the God of Israel, that **his fierce anger may turn away** from us." RSV

2 Chronicles 19:10 "Ye shall even warn them that they trespass not against the Lord, and so **wrath come upon you**, and upon your brethren." KJV

2 Chronicles 32:26 "Notwithstanding Hezekiah humbled himself for the pride of his heart, both he and the inhabitants of Jerusalem, so that **the wrath of the Lord came not upon them** in the days of Hezekiah." KJV

Ezra 7:23 "Whatever the God of heaven has prescribed, let it be done with diligence for the temple of the God of heaven. Why should his **wrath fall** on the realm of the king and of his sons?" NIV

Numbers 25:4 "And the Lord said unto Moses, Take all the heads of the people, and hang them up before the Lord against the sun, that the **fierce anger of the Lord may be turned away** from Israel." KJV

2 Chronicles 12:12 "And when he humbled himself, **the wrath of the Lord turned** from him, that he would not destroy him altogether: and also in Judah things went well." KJV

2 Chronicles 30:8 "Yield yourselves unto the Lord, and enter into his sanctuary, which he hath sanctified for ever: and serve the Lord your God, that **the fierceness of his wrath may turn away** from you." KJV

Proverbs 24:17–18 "Rejoice not when thine enemy falleth, and let not thine heart be glad when he stumbleth: lest the Lord see it, and it displease him, and he **turn away his wrath** from him." KJV

Isaiah 9:12 "They shall devour Israel with open mouth. For all this **his anger is not turned away**, but his hand is stretched out still." KJV

Isaiah 9:21 "For all this **his anger is not turned away**, but his hand is stretched out still." KJV

Jeremiah 4:8 "For this gird you with sackcloth, lament and howl: for **the fierce anger of the Lord is not turned back** from us." KJV

I think most believers are good and happy people. They are nicer than God. To many of them, Jonathan Edwards's 18th-century sermon "Sinners in the Hands of an Angry God" appears overly harsh and puritanical.

> *The God that holds you over the pit of hell, much as one holds a spider, or some loathsome insect over the fire, abhors you, and is dreadfully provoked: his wrath towards you burns like fire; he looks upon you as worthy of nothing else, but to be cast into the fire; he is of purer eyes than to bear to have you in his sight; you are ten thousand times more abominable in his eyes, than the most hateful venomous serpent is in ours. (July 8, 1741)*

Most believers, I think, want to focus on a God of love and mercy rather than an infuriated punitive parent. Horror stories can have literary merit, and Edwards deserves some credit as a skilled orator, if not a kind person, striving to put the "fear of God" into his congregation. Although his descriptions of hell were imaginative, his basic point was dead on: the deity depicted in the Old Testament is indeed an "Angry God."

The Angry God

NUMBERS 11:10 "Because thou [Saul] obeyedst not the voice of the Lord, nor executedst his **fierce wrath** upon Amalek, therefore hath the Lord done this thing unto thee this day." KJV

DEUTERONOMY 1:34–37 "And the Lord heard the voice of your words, and was **wroth**, and sware, saying, Surely there shall not one of these men of this evil generation see that good land, which I sware to give unto your fathers. . . . Also **the Lord was angry** with me for your sakes, saying, Thou also shalt not go in thither." KJV

DEUTERONOMY 3:26 "But because of you **the Lord was angry** with me and would not listen to me. 'That is enough,' the Lord said. 'Do not speak to me anymore about this matter.'" NIV

DEUTERONOMY 4:21 "Furthermore **the Lord was angry** with me for your sakes, and sware that I should not go over Jordan, and that I should not go in unto that good land, which the Lord thy God giveth thee for an inheritance." KJV

2 KINGS 24:20 "For through **the anger of the Lord** it came to pass in Jerusalem and Judah, until he had cast them out from his presence." KJV

EZRA 5:12 "But after that our fathers had provoked the God of heaven unto **wrath**, he gave them into the hand of Nebuchadnezzar the king of Babylon." KJV

EZRA 8:22 "His power and his **wrath** is against all them that forsake him." KJV

JOB 19:11 "He hath also **kindled his wrath** against me, and he counteth me unto him as one of his enemies." KJV

ECCLESIASTES 5:6 "Suffer not thy mouth to cause thy flesh to sin; neither say thou before the angel, that it was an error: wherefore **should God be angry** at thy voice, and destroy the work of thine hands?" KJV

ISAIAH 47:6 "I was **angry** with my people, I profaned my heritage; I gave them into your [Babylonia] hand, you showed them no mercy; on the aged you made your yoke exceedingly heavy." RSV

ISAIAH 51:20 "Thy sons have fainted, they lie at the head of all the streets, as a wild bull in a net: they are full of the **fury of the Lord**, the **rebuke of thy God**." KJV

ISAIAH 57:17 "Because of the iniquity of his covetousness I was **angry**, I smote him, I hid my face and was **angry**." RSV

JEREMIAH 33:5 "They come to fight with the Chaldeans, but it is to fill them with the dead bodies of men, whom I have slain in mine **anger** and in my **fury**, and for all whose wickedness I have hid my face from this city." KJV

JEREMIAH 36:7 "For great is the **anger** and the **fury** that the Lord hath pronounced against this people." KJV

JEREMIAH 49:37 "For I will cause Elam to be dismayed before their enemies, and before them that seek their life: and I will bring evil upon them, even **my fierce anger**, saith the Lord; and I will send the sword after them, till I have consumed them." KJV

JEREMIAH 50:13 "Because of the **wrath of the Lord** it shall not be inhabited, but it shall be wholly desolate: every one that goeth by Babylon shall be astonished, and hiss at all her plagues." KJV

LAMENTATIONS 2:6 "And he hath violently taken away his tabernacle, as if it were of a garden: he hath destroyed his places of the assembly: the Lord hath caused the solemn feasts and sabbaths to be forgotten in Zion, and hath despised in the **indignation of his anger** the king and the priest." KJV

LAMENTATIONS 3:42–44 "We have transgressed and have rebelled: thou hast not pardoned. Thou hast **covered with anger**, and persecuted us: thou hast slain, thou hast not pitied. Thou hast covered thyself with a cloud, that our prayer should not pass through." KJV

EZEKIEL 25:14 "And I will lay my vengeance upon Edom by the hand of my people Israel: and they shall do in Edom according to mine **anger** and according to my **fury**; and they shall know my vengeance, saith the Lord God." KJV

EZEKIEL 25:17 "And I will execute great vengeance upon them with **furious rebukes**; and they shall know that I am the Lord, when I shall lay my vengeance upon them." KJV

EZEKIEL 43:8 "They have even defiled my holy name by their abominations that they have committed: wherefore I have consumed them in mine **anger**." KJV

DANIEL 9:16 "O Lord, according to all thy righteousness, I beseech thee, let thine **anger** and thy **fury** be turned away from thy city Jerusalem." KJV

HOSEA 13:11 "I gave thee a king in mine **anger**, and took him away in my **wrath**." KJV

HABAKKUK 3:8 "Were you **angry** with the rivers, Lord? Was your **wrath** against the streams? Did you **rage** against the sea when you rode your horses and your chariots to victory?" NIV

ZECHARIAH 7:12 "They made their hearts like adamant lest they should hear the law and the words which the Lord of hosts had sent by his Spirit through the former prophets. Therefore **great wrath** came from the Lord of hosts." RSV

ZEPHANIAH 2:1–3 "Gather yourselves together, yea, gather together, O nation not desired; Before the decree bring forth, before the day pass as the chaff, before the **fierce anger of the Lord** come upon you, before the day of the **Lord's anger** come upon you. Seek ye the Lord, all ye meek of the earth, which have wrought his judgment; seek righteousness, seek meekness: it may be ye shall be hid in **the day of the Lord's anger**." KJV

22

𝕸𝖊𝖗𝖈𝖎𝖑𝖊𝖘𝖘

"I will not pity, nor spare, nor have mercy,
but destroy them."
—JEREMIAH 13:14

ike a nervous wife trying to calm an abusive husband, the ingratiating Psalmist often told the Lord Jealous what he wanted to hear:

The Lord is gracious, and full of compassion; slow to anger, and of great
mercy. The Lord is good to all: and his tender mercies are over all his works.
*(*PSALM 145:8–9*)*

Not only do those wishful thoughts fail to describe the impetuous and violent actions of the Lord Jealous as displayed through the Old Testament, but they contradict the Psalmist's own words:

For as the heaven is high above the earth, so great is his mercy toward them
*that fear him. (*PSALM 103:11*)*

He professes that God is "good to all," but then admits that his mercy applies only to those who fear him. In other words, the God of the Old Testament will be gracious if you will cower before him in humble obedience. The mercy of the Lord Jealous was conditional and selfish, based not his love for the people, but on the people's love for *him*.

The psalmist was right about one thing: God's mercy is indeed "high above the earth." It is nothing we would recognize in human terms. I don't think "mercy" meant to the Israelites what we take it to mean today. Believers will *say* the Lord is merciful, but actions speak louder than words.

Show no mercy to those you invade and slaughter

DEUTERONOMY 7:1–2 "When the Lord your God brings you into the land which you are entering to take possession of it, and clears away many nations before you . . . then you must utterly destroy them; you shall make no covenant with them, and **show no mercy to them**." RSV

Show no pity to those you destroy

DEUTERONOMY 7:16 "And you shall destroy all the peoples that the Lord your God will give over to you, **your eye shall not pity them**; neither shall you serve their gods, for that would be a snare to you." RSV

God overthrew cities without pity

ISAIAH 20:16 "Let that man be like the cities which the Lord overthrew **without pity**; let him hear a cry in the morning and an alarm at noon." RSV

"I will have no pity"

EZEKIEL 5:11 "Wherefore, as I live, says the Lord God, surely, because you have defiled my sanctuary with all your detestable things and with all your abominations, therefore I will cut you down; my eye will not spare, and **I will have no pity**." RSV

Eye for an eye with no pity

DEUTERONOMY 19:21 "**Your eye shall not pity**; it shall be life for life, eye for eye, tooth for tooth, hand for hand, foot for foot." RSV

No pity for helpful wife

DEUTERONOMY 25:11–12 "When men fight with one another, and the wife of the one draws near to rescue her husband from the hand of him who is beating him, and puts out her hand and seizes him by the private parts, then you shall cut off her hand; **your eye shall have no pity**." RSV

God showed his "mercy" to David by killing 70,000 people

1 CHRONICLES 21:13–14 "David said to Gad, 'I am in deep distress. Let me fall into the hands of the Lord, for **his mercy is very great**; but do not let me fall into human hands.' So the Lord sent a plague on Israel, and **seventy thousand men of Israel fell dead**." NIV

There was no remedy

2 CHRONICLES 36:16 "But they mocked the messengers of God, and despised his words, and misused his prophets, until the wrath of the Lord arose against his people, till **there was no remedy**." KJV

"They shall not enter into my rest"

PSALM 95:11 "Unto whom I sware in my wrath that they should not enter into my rest." KJV (*This verse is quoted in the New Testament:* HEBREWS 3:11, HEBREWS 4:3.)

Excessive pitiless punishment for defamation

PSALM 109:1–12 "My God, whom I praise, do not remain silent, for people who are wicked and deceitful have opened their mouths against me; they have spoken against me with lying tongues. . . . When he is tried, let him be found guilty. . . . May his children be wandering beggars; may they be driven from their ruined homes. May a creditor seize all he has; may strangers plunder the fruits of his labor. **May no one extend kindness to him or take pity on his fatherless children**." NIV

Deaf to the pleas for mercy

JEREMIAH 11:11 "Therefore, thus says the Lord, Behold, I am bringing evil upon them which they cannot escape; **though they cry to me, I will not listen to them**." RSV

"I smite without pity"

EZEKIEL 7:9 "And my eye will not spare, **nor will I have pity**; I will punish you according to your ways, while your abominations are in your midst. Then you will know that I am the Lord, who smite." RSV (*Similarly, see also* EZEKIEL 7:4; 8:18; 9:5; 9:10.)

God delivered people to a merciless killer

JEREMIAH 21:7 "And afterward, saith the Lord, I will deliver Zedekiah king of Judah, and his servants, and the people . . . into the hand of Nebuchadrezzar king of Babylon, and into the hand of their enemies, and into the hand of those that seek their life: and he shall smite them with the edge of the sword; he shall not spare them, neither have pity, **nor have mercy**." KJV

He destroyed without mercy

LAMENTATIONS 2:17–22 "But it is the Lord who did just as he planned. He has fulfilled the promises of disaster he made long ago. He has destroyed Jerusalem **without mercy**. . . . You have invited terrors from all around, as though you were calling them to a day of feasting. In the day of the Lord's anger, no one has escaped or survived." NLT

"I hate them. I love them no more."

HOSEA 9:15 "Every evil of theirs is in Gilgal; there I began to hate them. Because of the wickedness of their deeds I will drive them out of my house. **I will love them no more**; all their princes are rebels." RSV

Callous and pitiless

EZEKIEL 8:18 "Therefore will I also deal in fury: **mine eye shall not spare, neither will I have pity**: and though they cry in mine ears with a loud voice, **yet will I not hear them.**" KJV

"I will not repent"

EZEKIEL 24:13–14 "In thy filthiness is lewdness: because I have purged thee, and thou wast not purged, thou shalt not be purged from thy filthiness any more, till I have caused my fury to rest upon thee. I the Lord have spoken it: it shall come to pass, and I will do it; **I will not go back, neither will I spare, neither will I repent**; according to thy ways, and according to thy doings, shall they judge thee, saith the Lord God." KJV

Mercy no more

HOSEA 1:6 "She conceived again and bore a daughter. And the Lord said to him, 'Call her name **Not pitied**, for I will **no more have pity** on the house of Israel, to forgive them at all.'" RSV

No mercy to doomed children

HOSEA 2:4 "And **I will not have mercy upon her children**; for they be the children of whoredoms." KJV (*Why are the children blamed?*)

No mercy to murdered children

ISAIAH 13:11–18 "I will punish the world for its evil. . . . Whoever is found will be thrust through, and whoever is caught will fall by the sword. Their infants will be dashed in pieces before their eyes; their houses will be plundered and their wives ravished. . . . Their bows will slaughter the young men; they will have **no mercy** on the fruit of the womb; their eyes will not pity children." RSV

No mercy to orphans or widows

ISAIAH 9:17 "Therefore the Lord shall have no joy in their young men, **neither shall have mercy** on their fatherless and widows. . . . For all this his anger is not turned away, but his hand is stretched out still." KJV

No mercy to those who do not understand

ISAIAH 27:11 "When the boughs thereof are withered, they shall be broken off: the women come, and set them on fire: for it is a people of no understanding: therefore he that made them **will not have mercy** on them, and he that formed them will shew them no favor." KJV

"I will destroy without mercy"

JEREMIAH 13:14 "And I will dash them one against another, even the fathers and the sons together, saith the Lord: **I will not pity, nor spare, nor have mercy**, but destroy them." KJV

Exterminated without mercy

JOSHUA 11:20 "For it was the Lord's doing to harden their hearts that they should come against Israel in battle, in order that they should be utterly destroyed, and should **receive no mercy** but be exterminated, as the Lord commanded Moses." RSV

Punishment not mitigated

AMOS 1:11 "Thus says the Lord: 'For three transgressions of Edom, and for four, **I will not revoke the punishment**; because he pursued his brother with the sword, and cast off all pity, and his anger tore perpetually, and he kept his wrath for ever.'" RSV

"I will deliver none"

ZECHARIAH 11:6 "For I will **no longer have pity** on the inhabitants of this land, says the Lord. Lo, I will cause men to fall each into the hand of his shepherd, and each into the hand of his king; and they shall crush the earth, and I will deliver none from their hand." RSV

Merciless wrath

LAMENTATIONS 2:2 "The Lord has destroyed **without mercy** all the habitations of Jacob; in his wrath he has broken down the strongholds of the daughter of Judah." RSV

23

Curse Hurling

*"All the curses written in this book will descend on them,
and the Lord will blot out their names from under heaven."*
—Deuteronomy 29:20

The God of the Old Testament was unpleasant not only in his actions and emotions; his unmannerly verbal abuse could also reach holy heights of horridness. In Chapter 15, we saw his drawn-out diatribe of 82 curses packed into the 54 verses of Deuteronomy 28:15–68, including the threat of fever, inflammation, heat, drought, blight, mildew, dust, boils, ulcers, scurvy, itch, madness, blindness, disaster, panic, frustration, pestilence, consumption, confusion of mind, abuse, robbery, butchery, worms, cicadas, locusts, aliens, nakedness, cannibalism, diseases, dread, trembling heart, and languishing spirit. That passage begins with curses:

> But if you will not obey the Lord your God by diligently observing all his
> commandments and decrees, which I am commanding you today, then all
> these **curses** shall come upon you and overtake you: **Cursed** shall you be in
> the city, and **cursed** shall you be in the field. **Cursed** shall be your basket and
> your kneading bowl. **Cursed** shall be the fruit of your womb, the fruit of your
> ground, the increase of your cattle and the issue of your flock. **Cursed** shall
> you be when you come in, and **cursed** shall you be when you go out. The Lord
> will send upon you disaster, panic, and frustration in everything you attempt
> to do, until you are destroyed and perish quickly. (Deuteronomy 28:15–20)

To be thorough, he inserts an "including but not limited to" clause into the contract, reserving the right to carry out *any* threat conceivable under heaven:

Every other malady and affliction, even though not recorded in the book of this law, the Lord will inflict on you until you are destroyed. (DEUTERONOMY 28:61)

That should pretty much cover it.

The Old Testament begins with curses:

Cursed be the serpent

GENESIS 3:14 "And the Lord God said unto the serpent, Because thou hast done this, thou art **cursed** above all cattle, and above every beast of the field; upon thy belly shalt thou go, and dust shalt thou eat all the days of thy life." KJV

Woman is cursed

GENESIS 3:16 "Unto the woman he said, I will greatly multiply thy sorrow and thy conception; in sorrow thou shalt bring forth children; and thy desire shall be to thy husband, and he shall rule over thee." KJV

Man is cursed

GENESIS 3:17 "And unto Adam he said, Because thou hast hearkened unto the voice of thy wife, and hast eaten of the tree, of which I commanded thee, saying, Thou shalt not eat of it: **cursed** is the ground for thy sake; in sorrow shalt thou eat of it all the days of thy life." KJV

Cursed be Cain

GENESIS 4:9–11 "And the Lord said unto Cain, Where is Abel thy brother? And he said, I know not: Am I my brother's keeper? And he said, What hast thou done? the voice of thy brother's blood crieth unto me from the ground. And now art thou **cursed** from the earth, which hath opened her mouth to receive thy brother's blood from thy hand." KJV

Cursed be anyone who threatens his chosen people

GENESIS 12:3 "And I will bless them that bless thee, and **curse** him that curseth thee: and in thee shall all families of the earth be blessed." KJV

And the Old Testament ends with the word "curse."

He will turn the hearts of parents to their children and the hearts of children to their parents, so that I will not come and strike the land with a **curse**. (MALACHI 4:6)

God's curses, like his actions, stem mainly from his jealousy. If you are faithful to him, he will be nice to you. If you have a wandering eye, watch out.

Jealous curse

DEUTERONOMY 11:26–28 "Behold, I set before you this day a blessing and a **curse**; A blessing, if ye obey the commandments of the Lord your God, which I command you this day: And a **curse**, if ye will not obey the commandments of the Lord your God, but turn aside out of the way which I command you this day, to go after other gods, which ye have not known." KJV

Evil curses

2 CHRONICLES 34:24–25 "Thus saith the Lord, Behold, I will bring evil upon this place, and upon the inhabitants thereof, even all the **curses** that are written in the book which they have read before the king of Judah: Because they have forsaken me, and have burned incense unto other gods." KJV

Jealous curse fulfilled

DEUTERONOMY 29:26–27 "For they went and served other gods, and worshipped them, gods whom they knew not, and whom he had not given unto them: And the anger of the Lord was kindled against this land, to bring upon it all the **curses** that are written in this book." KJV

The kings knew God's jealousy led to curses

1 SAMUEL 26:19 "Now therefore, I pray thee, let my lord the king hear the words of his servant. If the Lord have stirred thee up against me, let him accept an offering: but if they be the children of men, **cursed** be they before the Lord; for they have driven me out this day from abiding in the inheritance of the Lord, saying, Go, serve other gods." KJV (*This is King Saul pleading with King David for his life.*)

In a normal wedding ceremony, public vows are pronounced affirming love and fidelity. The words spoken before a gathered assembly are overwhelmingly positive and uplifting. Even the passing references to negative possibilities—"for better or for worse"—are couched in terms of respect and commitment. A wedding is a happy event.

God's wedding vows are not happy at all. In the 29th chapter of Deuteronomy, as the Israelites were being shepherded from Egypt toward the Promised Land, we read the curse-hurling "covenant" (marriage oath) that the Lord Jealous made with his chosen people:

All of you are standing today in the presence of the Lord your God . . . to enter into a covenant with the Lord your God, a covenant the Lord is making with you this day and sealing with an oath, to confirm you this day as his people,

that he may be your God. . . . Make sure there is no man or woman, clan or
tribe among you today whose heart turns away from the Lord our God to go
and worship the gods of those nations. . . . The Lord will never be willing
to forgive them; his **wrath** *and zeal will burn against them. All the* **curses**
written in this book will fall on them, and the Lord will blot out their names
from under heaven. The Lord will single them out from all the tribes of Israel
for disaster, according to all the **curses of the covenant** *written in this Book*
of the Law. . . . It is because this people abandoned the covenant of the Lord,
the God of their ancestors, the covenant he made with them when he brought
them out of Egypt. They went off and worshiped other gods and bowed down
to them, gods they did not know, gods he had not given them. Therefore the
Lord's anger burned against this land, so that he brought on it all the **curses**
*written in this book." NIV (*Deuteronomy 29:10–27*)*

God's covenant with his people was not sealed with a kiss: it was clinched with
a curse. The prophet Jeremiah later reaffirmed those vile vows:

Thus says the Lord, the God of Israel: **Cursed** *be anyone who does not heed*
the words of this covenant, which I commanded your ancestors when I
brought them out of the land of Egypt, from the iron-smelter, saying, Listen
to my voice, and do all that I command you. So shall you be my people, and
*I will be your God. (*Jeremiah 11:3–4*)*

Daniel said the same thing:

All Israel has transgressed your law and turned aside, refusing to obey your
voice. So **the curse and the oath written in the law of Moses**, *the servant of*
God, have been poured out upon us, because we have sinned against you.
*(*Daniel 9:11*)*

Imagine if the groom in a 21st-century wedding, after being asked "Do you take
this woman to be your lawfully wedded wife?" answered: "I do. And if she cheats on
me I will beat her bloody. If she even glances sideways at another man, I will starve
her and make her eat our children and pull out her hair and spread dog poop on her
face and burn her possessions and. . . ."

"Enough!" says the officiant, realizing that the man is a maniac.

After the wedding, the curses continue.

I will spread dung on your face

Malachi 2:2–3 "If ye will not hear, and if ye will not lay it to heart, to give
glory unto my name, saith the Lord of hosts, I will even send a **curse** upon
you, and I will **curse** your blessings: yea, I have **cursed** them already, because

ye do not lay it to heart. Behold, I will corrupt your seed, and spread dung upon your faces, even the dung of your solemn feasts; and one shall take you away with it." KJV

I'll pull your hair out

NEHEMIAH 13:25 "And I contended with them and **cursed** them and beat some of them and pulled out their hair; and I made them take oath in the name of God, saying, 'You shall not give your daughters to their sons, or take their daughters for your sons or for yourselves.'" RSV (*The prophet Nehemiah did this in the name of God.*)

Do you want to live?

DEUTERONOMY 30:19 "I call heaven and earth to record this day against you, that I have set before you life and death, blessing and **cursing**: therefore choose life, that both thou and thy seed may live." KJV

Do you want to die of thirst?

JEREMIAH 17:5–6 "Thus saith the Lord; **cursed** be the man that trusteth in man, and maketh flesh his arm, and whose heart departeth from the Lord. For he shall be like the heath in the desert, and shall not see when good cometh; but shall inhabit the parched places in the wilderness, in a salt land and not inhabited." KJV

Do you want to lose your inheritance?

PSALM 37:22 "For such as be blessed of him shall inherit the earth; and they that be **cursed** of him shall be cut off." KJV

I'll destroy the ground you walk on

ISAIAH 24:1, 6 "Behold, the Lord maketh the earth empty, and maketh it waste, and turneth it upside down, and scattereth abroad the inhabitants thereof. . . . Therefore hath the **curse** devoured the earth, and they that dwell therein are desolate: therefore the inhabitants of the earth are burned, and few men left." KJV

Say "Amen" to my curses

DEUTERONOMY 27:15–26 "**Cursed** be the man that maketh any graven or molten image, an abomination unto the Lord, the work of the hands of the craftsman, and putteth it in a secret place. And all the people shall answer and say, Amen. **Cursed** be he that setteth light by his father or his mother. . . . **Cursed** be he that removeth his neighbor's landmark. . . . **Cursed** be he that maketh the blind to wander out of the way. . . . **Cursed** be he that perverteth the judgment of the stranger, fatherless, and widow. . . . **Cursed** be he that lieth with his father's wife; because he uncovereth his father's skirt. . . . **Cursed** be he that lieth with any manner of beast. . . . **Cursed** be he that lieth with his sister, the daughter of his father, or the daughter of his mother. . . . **Cursed** be he that lieth with his mother in law. . . . **Cursed** be he that smiteth his neighbor secretly. . . . **Cursed** be he that confirmeth not all the words of this law to do them. And all the people shall say, Amen." KJV

That passage, by the way, is one of the few places in the Old Testament where God's curses are prompted in part by actions (some of them) that might be considered naturally immoral: moving a property line, committing incest, adultery, bestiality, manslaughter, bribery, and mistreating the blind, orphans, and widows. None of these prohibitions is anything surprising that societies have not figured out on their own for purely natural reasons. However, notice that this passage, like the Ten Commandments, begins with anti-idol jealousy, which is not an ethical motivation. It contains no moral reasoning, only curses.

Despite a few exceptions which prove the rule, most of God's curses have nothing to do with immorality. The words "evil," "wickedness," "crime," and "abomination" are terms of jealousy, not ethics, as in this curse-hurling passage by Jeremiah:

> *Thus saith the Lord of hosts, the God of Israel; Ye have seen all the* **evil** *that I have brought upon Jerusalem, and upon all the cities of Judah; and, behold, this day they are a desolation, and no man dwelleth therein, Because of their* **wickedness** *which they have committed to provoke me to anger, in that they went to burn incense, and* **to serve other gods**, *whom they knew not, neither they, ye, nor your fathers. . . . Have ye forgotten the* **wickedness** *of your fathers, and the* **wickedness** *of the kings of Judah, and the* **wickedness** *of their wives, and your own* **wickedness**, *and the* **wickedness** *of your wives, which they have committed in the land of Judah, and in the streets of Jerusalem? . . . So that the Lord could no longer bear, because of the* **evil** *of your doings, and because of the* **abominations** *which ye have committed; therefore is your land a desolation, and an astonishment, and a* **curse**, *without an inhabitant, as at this day. NIV (*Jeremiah 44:2–9,22*)*

Cursing is a part of God's regular vocabulary.

A city is bitterly cursed for minding its own business
Judges 5:23 "**Curse** ye Meroz, said the angel of the Lord, **curse** ye bitterly the inhabitants thereof; because they came not to the help of the Lord, to the help of the Lord against the mighty." KJV

A house is cursed
Proverbs 3:33 "The **curse** of the Lord is in the house of the wicked: but he blesseth the habitation of the just." KJV

A curse as payback

LAMENTATIONS 3:64–66 "Pay them back what they deserve, Lord, for what their hands have done. Put a veil over their hearts, and may your **curse be on them**! Pursue them in anger and destroy them from under the heavens of the Lord." NIV

Curse God's enemies

DEUTERONOMY 30:7–8 "And the Lord thy God will put all these **curses** upon thine enemies, and on them that hate thee, which persecuted thee. And thou shalt return and obey the voice of the Lord, and do all his commandments which I command thee this day." KJV

A passage does not have to contain the word "curse" to be a curse. Here is the Lord Jealous threatening Egypt:

*I will therefore spread out my **net** over thee with a company of many people; and they shall bring thee up in my **net**. Then will I leave thee upon the land, I will **cast thee forth** upon the open field, and will cause all the fowls of the heaven to remain upon thee, and I will fill the **beasts** of the whole earth with thee. And I will lay thy **flesh upon the mountains**, and fill the valleys with thy height. I will also water with thy **blood** the land wherein thou swimmest, even to the mountains; and the rivers shall be full of thee. And . . . I will cover the heaven, and make the stars thereof **dark**; I will cover the sun with a **cloud**, and the moon shall not give her light. All the bright lights of heaven will I make **dark** over thee. . . . I will also **vex** the hearts of many people, when I shall bring thy **destruction** among the nations, into the countries which thou hast not known. Yea, I will make many people amazed at thee, and their kings shall be **horribly afraid** for thee, when I shall **brandish my sword** before them; and they shall tremble at every moment, every man for his own life, in the day of thy fall. . . . The **sword** of the king of Babylon shall come upon thee. By the **swords** of the mighty will I cause thy multitude to fall, the **terrible** of the nations, all of them: and they shall **spoil** the pomp of Egypt, and all the multitude thereof shall be **destroyed**. I will **destroy** also all the beasts thereof from beside the great waters; neither shall the foot of man trouble them any more, nor the hoofs of beasts trouble them. Then will I make their waters deep, and cause their rivers to run like oil. . . . When I shall make the land of Egypt **desolate**, and the country shall be **destitute** of that whereof it was full, when I shall **smite** all them that dwell therein, then shall they know that I am the Lord. (EZEKIEL 32:3–15, KJV)*

Incredible. When everything gets completely destroyed, then the world will know who God is. If such a God actually existed, he might be worthy of our fear, but certainly not our love or respect.

24

Vaccicidal

"I will destroy all its livestock from beside abundant waters."
—EZEKIEL 32:13

All animals on the earth, except those lucky enough to be on the Ark, were drowned in Noah's flood. The fifth plague that God inflicted on the Egyptians was a disease that killed all of their livestock. Livestock at that time would include domesticated cattle, oxen, sheep, goats, and other animals meant for food and clothing. Vaccicide technically applies only to cows, but since there doesn't seem to be a word for the general killing of non-human animals, let's let it refer to all livestock.

There was no concept of animal rights in the time of the Old Testament. Life was cheap all around. Since the Lord Jealous was reckless with human life, it is not surprising that he would treat the "lesser" animals with even lower regard. Like today, the slaying of animals was not equivalent to murder: "One who kills an animal shall make restitution for it; but one who kills a human being shall be put to death" (LEVITICUS 24:21, NIV). Livestock, like women, were property, a measure of patriarchal wealth.

In the fifth plague, livestock included horses, donkeys, and camels:

Then the Lord said to Moses, "Go to Pharaoh, and say to him, 'Thus says the Lord, the God of the Hebrews: Let my people go, so that they may worship me. For if you refuse to let them go and still hold them, the hand of the Lord will strike with a deadly pestilence **your livestock in the field***: the horses, the donkeys, the camels, the herds, and the flocks.'". . . And on the next day the Lord did so;* **all the livestock of the Egyptians died***. (EXODUS 9:1–3, 6, NIV)*

There is a glaring anachronism in that passage. There were no domesticated camels at that time in the Middle East. The exodus was not a historical event, but the authors, writing in the fifth or sixth century B.C.E., wanted us to think it had occurred way back in *their* ancient history, at least a thousand years earlier in the second or third millennium B.C.E. They didn't know that domesticated camels had been introduced into the area no earlier than the tenth century B.C.E.—archaeologists and scholars have pinpointed it to almost exactly 930 B.C.E.—so including them in the patriarchal stories was a mistake that betrays the fiction. Camels or not, the writers tell us that all the livestock of the Egyptians was destroyed by God.

The prophet Ezekiel affirmed that plague:

> **I will destroy all her cattle** *from beside abundant waters no longer to be stirred by the foot of man or muddied by the hooves of cattle. Then I will let her waters settle and make her streams flow like oil, declares the Sovereign Lord. When I make Egypt desolate and strip the land of everything in it,* **when I strike down all who live there,** *then they will know that I am the Lord.* (EZEKIEL 32:13–15, NIV)

Forgetting that they were already dead, God ordered the livestock killed again in the tenth plague, where he murdered all the first-born children:

> *At midnight the Lord struck down all the firstborn in Egypt, from the firstborn of Pharaoh, who sat on the throne, to the firstborn of the prisoner, who was in the dungeon, and the* **firstborn of all the livestock** *as well.* (EXODUS 12:29, NIV)

The only time animals get a break in the Old Testament is when they are counted as war booty remaining after the humans were slaughtered:

> *We completely destroyed them, as we had done with Sihon king of Heshbon, destroying every city—men, women and children. But all the livestock and the plunder from their cities we carried off for ourselves.* (DEUTERONOMY 3:6–7, NIV)

> *For Joshua did not draw back the hand that held out his javelin until he had destroyed all who lived in Ai. But Israel did carry off for themselves the livestock and plunder of this city, as the Lord had instructed Joshua.* (JOSHUA 8:26–27, NIV)

> *The Israelites carried off for themselves all the plunder and livestock of these cities, but all the people they put to the sword until they completely destroyed them, not sparing anyone that breathed.* (JOSHUA 11:14, NIV)

Sometimes they weren't so lucky. King Saul was deposed because he kept a few animals alive (see Chapter 8). The numerous genocides that the Lord Jealous commanded often included the animals:

You must certainly put to the sword all who live in that town. You must destroy it completely, both its people and its livestock. (DEUTERONOMY 13:15, NIV)

Now go, attack the Amalekites and totally destroy all that belongs to them. Do not spare them; put to death men and women, children and infants, **cattle and sheep, camels and donkeys**. (1 SAMUEL 15:3, NIV)

From God's point of view, it seems the main value of animals was to produce a supply of burnt offerings to be slaughtered for the worship of his glory. To dedicate the altar in the tabernacle, he demanded:

The total number of **animals** *for the burnt offering came to twelve young* **bulls**, *twelve rams and twelve male* **lambs** *a year old, together with their grain offering. Twelve male* **goats** *were used for the sin offering. The total number of* **animals** *for the sacrifice of the fellowship offering came to twenty-four* **oxen**, *sixty* **rams**, *sixty male* **goats** *and sixty male* **lambs** *a year old. These were the offerings for the dedication of the altar after it was anointed.* (NUMBERS 7:87–88, NIV)

Although he liked the smell of roasting flesh, God obviously did not eat those animals—the people had to share the meat with the priests, a nice arrangement for the clergy. (Since God is fictional but the authors were not, I wonder who enjoyed the smell of cooking meat.) The Old Testament is stuffed with examples of animals being killed as an act of devotion to God. (See Chapter 7.)

Immediately after the Ten Commandments were pronounced in EXODUS 20, the next commandment the Lord Jealous gave his people was to slaughter animals for his glory:

Do not make any gods to be alongside me; do not make for yourselves gods of silver or gods of gold. Make an altar of earth for me and sacrifice on it your burnt offerings and fellowship offerings, **your sheep and goats and your cattle**. *Wherever I cause my name to be honored, I will come to you and bless you.* (EXODUS 20:23–24, NIV)

25

Aborticidal

"Their little ones shall be dashed in pieces,
and their pregnant women ripped open."
—Hosea 13:16

Noah's flood would have drowned hundreds of thousands of pregnant women. All of the Lord's massacres in Chapter 13 dispatched fetuses along with children and their parents. This can be called feticide or aborticide: the killing or expulsion of a fetus. Sometimes the aborticide was explicit:

You shall acknowledge no God but me. . . . You are destroyed, Israel. . . .
The people of Samaria must bear their guilt, because they have
rebelled against their God. They will fall by the sword; their little ones
will be dashed to the ground, their **pregnant women ripped open**.
(Hosea 13:4, 9, 16, NIV)

The God of the Old Testament used feticide as a punishment for infidelity:

Then the Lord said to Moses . . . "If a man's wife goes astray and is unfaith-
ful to him . . . the priest shall bring her and have her stand before the Lord.
Then he shall take some holy water in a clay jar and put some dust from
the tabernacle floor into the water. . . . Then the priest shall put the woman
under oath and say to her, 'If no other man has had sexual relations with
you and you have not gone astray and become impure while married to your
husband . . . may the Lord cause you to become a curse among your people

*when he makes your womb miscarry and your abdomen swell. May this
water that brings a curse enter your body so that your abdomen swells or
your womb miscarries.' Then the woman is to say, 'Amen. So be it.' . . . This,
then, is the law of jealousy when a woman goes astray and makes herself
impure while married to her husband, or when feelings of jealousy come
over a man because he suspects his wife. The priest is to have her stand
before the Lord and is to apply this entire law to her. The husband will be
innocent of any wrongdoing, but the woman will bear the consequences of
her sin.*" (Numbers 5:11–31, NIV)

It is true that the men punishing her may not have known she was pregnant.
But they also would not have known she wasn't. When God ordered his righteous
warriors to kill all the nonvirgin women ("Kill every woman who has known a man
by sleeping with him," Numbers 31:17; "Kill every male and every woman who is
not a virgin," Judges 21:11, NIV), he must have known that many of those women
would have been pregnant. Any woman who commits adultery or who is not a virgin on her wedding night, pregnant or not, should be put to death (Leviticus 20:10;
Deuteronomy 22:20–21).The God of the Old Testament was clearly not "pro-life."

Ephraim's glory will fly away like a bird—**no birth, no pregnancy, no
conception**. *Even if they rear children, I will bereave them of every one. . . .
But Ephraim will bring out their children to the slayer. Give them, Lord—
what will you give them? Give them* **wombs that miscarry and breasts that
are dry**. . . . *"I will no longer love them. . . . Even if they bear children,* **I will
slay their cherished offsprin**g." (Hosea 9:11–16, NIV)

Biblical passages that show God-ordained genocide and aborticide have understandably created ethical distress among theologians and defenders of the faith.
Even the steely determinist John Calvin wrestled with the moral implications of the
aborticide of Hosea 13:16:

*But if any one objects and says, that infants, and babes as yet concealed
in the wombs of their mothers, deserve not such a grievous punishment,
as they have not hitherto merited such a thing; it may be answered, that
the whole human race are guilty before God, so that* **infants though not yet
come forth to the light, are yet included as being under guilt; so that God
cannot be charged with cruelty**, *though he may use his own right towards
them. And further, we hear what he declares in many places, that he will
devolve the sins of parents on their children. Since it is so, let us learn to
acquiesce in these awful judgments of God, though very repugnant to
our feelings; for we know that we must not contend with God, and that*

it would be extreme presumption to do so; nay, it would be impious
audacity. Though then the reason for this punishment may not appear
to us, we ought yet reverently to regard this judgment of God.
(John Calvin's Commentaries)

It was their own fault! The babies and fetuses deserved to die. Calvin does not explain where he got the rule that "God cannot be charged with cruelty." Doesn't it follow that if his actions were cruel, then he was cruel?

26

Cannibalistic

"You shall eat the flesh of your sons,
and you shall eat the flesh of your daughters."
—LEVITICUS 26:28–29

Be sure you are not eating as you read these words from the Good Book:

Because you did not serve the Lord your God with joyfulness and gladness of heart . . . **you shall eat the offspring of your own body, the flesh of your sons and daughters,** *whom the Lord your God has given you. . . . The man who is the most tender and delicately bred among you will grudge food to his brother, to the wife of his bosom, and to the last of the children who remain to him; so that he will not give to any of them any of* **the flesh of his children whom he is eating**. *. . . The most tender and delicately bred woman among you, who would not venture to set the sole of her foot upon the ground because she is so delicate and tender, will grudge to the* **husband** *of her bosom, to* **her son and to her daughter, her afterbirth** *that comes out from between her feet and her* **children** *whom she bears, because* **she will eat them secretly,** *for want of all things, in the siege and in the distress with which your enemy shall distress you in your towns.* (DEUTERONOMY 28:47–57, RSV)

Those ghastly threats were spoken by the God we are supposed to love and praise. If you don't "serve the Lord your God joyfully and with gladness of heart," you will be forced to eat your children.

It is not just children who are victims of the Lord Ravenous:

By the wrath of the Lord Almighty the land will be scorched and the people will be fuel for the fire; they will not spare one another. On the right they will devour, but still be hungry; on the left they will eat, but not be satisfied. Each will **feed on the flesh of their own offspring**. (Isaiah 9:19–20, NIV)

But this is what the Lord says . . . I will make your oppressors **eat their own flesh**; *they will be* **drunk on their own blood,** *as with wine. Then all mankind will know that I, the Lord, am your Savior, your Redeemer, the Mighty One of Jacob.* (Isaiah 49:25–26, NIV)

Notice that God is not simply reporting what desperate people might do. He takes full responsibility: "I will make your oppressors eat their own flesh."

Here are some verses that should be posted in the windows of "family bookstores."

Eat Your Kids

Leviticus 26:27–29 "And if ye will not for all this hearken unto me, but walk contrary unto me; Then I will walk contrary unto you also in fury; and I, even I, will chastise you seven times for your sins. And **ye shall eat the flesh of your sons, and the flesh of your daughters shall ye eat**." KJV

Deuteronomy 28:53 "And thou shalt eat the fruit of thine own body, **the flesh of thy sons and of thy daughters**, which the Lord thy God hath given thee." KJV

Jeremiah 19:7–9 "And their carcasses will I give to be meat for the fowls of the heaven, and for the beasts of the earth. . . . And I will cause them to **eat the flesh of their sons** and the **flesh of their daughters**, and they shall eat every one the **flesh of his friend** in the siege." KJV

Ezekiel 5:8–10 "Therefore this is what the Sovereign Lord says: I myself am against you, Jerusalem, and I will inflict punishment on you in the sight of the nations. Because of all your detestable idols, I will do to you what I have never done before and will never do again. Therefore in your midst **parents will eat their children, and children will eat their parents**." NIV

Lamentations 2:20 "Look, O Lord, and see! With whom hast thou dealt thus? **Should women eat their offspring**, the children of their tender care? Should priest and prophet be slain in the sanctuary of the Lord?" RSV

Lamentations 4:9–11 "Happier were the victims of the sword than the victims of hunger, who pined away, stricken by want of the fruits of the field. The hands of compassionate **women have boiled their own children;**

they became their food in the destruction of the daughter of my people. The Lord gave full vent to his wrath, he poured out his hot anger." RSV

Some compassionate defenders of the faith claim that the cannibalism in the Old Testament was merely an indirect consequence of apostasy, not a direct order from God. The actual text says otherwise. When the Lord says "I will make them eat the flesh of their sons and the flesh of their daughters," it is impossible not to see this as a direct aim of God's punishment.

Nor is this in conflict with Christian theology. Metaphorical cannibalism is practiced every Sunday morning around the globe as Christians eat the body and drink the blood of their Lord—the son of the God of the Old Testament—during Holy Communion. According to the Catholic doctrine of transubstantiation, the consecrated wine and wafer actually *become* the blood and body of Christ. True believers actually think they are eating God.

27

Slavemonger

"They are not to be punished if the slave recovers after a day or two, since the slave is their property."
—Exodus 21:21

If the God of the Old Testament were more than a fictional character, he might have been free to rise above the culture of his authors to denounce slavery. Instead, we had to wait millennia to abolish the biblically approved practice on our own, a progress that was hampered by faith in an ancient slavemonger deity. Like the writers who invented him, God had no choice but to endorse and encourage the cruel and inhumane customs of their primitive age.

The Ten Commandments, the allegedly supreme moral law of the world, acknowledge the Lord's approval of slavery. The fourth commandment says:

Six days you shall labor and do all your work. But the seventh day is a sabbath to the Lord your God; you shall not do any work—you, your son or your daughter, your male or female **slave***, your livestock, or the alien resident in your towns. (*Exodus 20:9–10*)*

The tenth commandment says:

You shall not covet your neighbor's house; you shall not covet your neighbor's wife, or male or female **slave***, or ox, or donkey, or anything that belongs to your neighbor. (*Exodus 20:17*)*

It's a sin to covet slaves. It is not a sin to own them.

The treatment of slaves by the Israelites varied from harsh to moderately lenient, depending on whether the subjugated human being was one of their own people or a foreigner. They were most cruel when they captured non-Hebrew people.

*When Israel became strong, they pressed the Canaanites into **forced labor** but never drove them out completely. . . . Neither did Zebulun drive out the Canaanites living in Kitron or Nahalol, so these Canaanites lived among them, but Zebulun did subject them to **forced labor**. . . . And the Amorites were determined also to hold out in Mount Heres, Aijalon and Shaalbim, but when the power of the tribes of Joseph increased, they too were pressed into **forced labor**.* (Judges 1:28, 30, 35, NIV)

*Your male and female **slaves** are to come from the nations around you; **from them you may buy slaves**. You may also buy some of the temporary residents living among you and members of their clans born in your country, and **they will become your property**. You can bequeath them to your children as inherited property and can make them **slaves for life**, but you must not rule over your fellow Israelites ruthlessly.* (Leviticus 25:44–46, NIV)

So they were less cruel when they purchased their own people as slaves, and if the purpose was to pay off a debt, it sometimes slightly resembled indentured servitude. Hebrew slaves were treated less severely, but hardly humanely. Right after the Ten Commandments were spoken in Exodus 20, God continues with more laws in Exodus 21, beginning with ordinances on how to treat Hebrew slaves:

*When you buy a Hebrew **slave**, he shall serve six years, and in the seventh he shall go out free, for nothing. If he comes in single, he shall go out single; if he comes in married, then his wife shall go out with him. If his master gives him a wife and she bears him sons or daughters, the wife and her children shall be her **master's** and he shall go out alone. But if the slave plainly says, "I love my **master**, my wife, and my children; I will not go out free," then his **master** shall bring him to God, and he shall bring him to the door or the doorpost; and his **master** shall bore his ear through with an awl; and he shall **serve him for life**. When a man **sells his daughter as a slave**, she shall not go out as the male **slaves** do. If she does not please her **master**, who has designated her for himself, then he shall let her be redeemed; he shall have no right to sell her to a foreign people, since he has dealt faithlessly with her. If he designates her for his son, he shall deal with her as with a daughter. If he takes another wife to himself, he shall not diminish her food, her clothing, or her marital rights. And if he does not do these three things for her, she shall go out for nothing, without payment of money.* (Exodus 21:2–11, RSV)

The first sentence might resemble a six-year work contract, but what employer gets to keep the wife and children when the job is over? The slave held on to his wife only if they were married before purchase. If the man wanted to stay with his family, he became the master's branded property for life. A girl slave could never leave, unless she did not please the master sexually, in which case he could sell her to another Hebrew, or give her to one of his sons. Notice that wives were equated with slaves. The bible truly has an odd concern for "family values."

A few verses later, we find a perverse token of fairness regarding Hebrew slaves:

> An owner who hits a male or female slave in the eye and destroys it must let
> the slave go free to compensate for the eye. And an owner who knocks out the
> tooth of a male or female slave must let the slave go free to compensate for
> the tooth. (EXODUS 21:26–27, NIV)

According to the God of the Old Testament, there is nothing wrong with owning or beating slaves. Just don't hit them so hard they lose body parts. Bruises and broken bones were tolerable violence. Slaves were treated not as human beings, but as commodity subject to ancient laws of financial recompense. They could be pummeled almost to death as long as the property value was not lost:

> Anyone who beats their male or female slave with a rod must be punished
> if the slave dies as a direct result, but they are not to be punished if the
> slave recovers after a day or two, since **the slave is their property**.
> (EXODUS 21:20–21, NIV)

The cruel slave owner Simon Legree in *Uncle Tom's Cabin* appears to be modeled on those ancient Israelite practices, but Harriet Beecher Stowe reversed one of the causes of his anger toward his slaves: while Simon Legree beat Tom for believing in God, the Lord Jealous walloped people for not believing in him.

The God of the Old Testament approved of the master-slave relationship, and not just for labor:

> If a man has sexual relations with a woman who is a slave, designated for
> another man but not ransomed or given her freedom, an inquiry shall be
> held. They shall not be put to death, since she has not been freed; but he shall
> bring a guilt offering for himself to the Lord, at the entrance of the tent of
> meeting, a ram as guilt offering. And the priest shall make atonement for him
> with the ram of guilt offering before the Lord for his sin that he committed;
> and the sin he committed shall be forgiven him. (LEVITICUS 19:20–22)

So it's not a capital crime to have sex with a female slave belonging to another man. You can pay for it with a ram. The slave woman is lucky in that she cannot be put to death for the act because that would lower the value of her master's estate.

Nothing in that passage prohibits the slave owner himself from having sex with the woman he possesses.

The story of the slave Hagar has made one of the greatest impacts on human history. We saw in Chapter 14 how Abraham and Sarah took matters into their own hands after God had predicted that they would become parents of a great nation:

> Now Sarai, Abram's wife, bore him no children. She had an Egyptian
> slave-girl whose name was Hagar, and Sarai said to Abram, "You see that
> the Lord has prevented me from bearing children; go in to my slave-girl;
> it may be that I shall obtain children by her." ... Sarai, Abram's wife, took
> Hagar the Egyptian, her slave-girl, and gave her to her husband Abram as a
> wife. He went in to Hagar, and she conceived. (GENESIS 16:1–4)

The slave was property, to be given away, even to one's husband for sexual purposes. However, after Hagar got pregnant, she became haughty with her master. Sarah complained to her husband about the change in attitude:

> But Abram said to Sarai, "Your slave-girl is in your power; do to her as
> you please." Then Sarai dealt harshly with her, and she ran away from her.
> (GENESIS 16:6)

Slaves were not allowed to run away, so God sent out a bounty hunter. His angel found her in the wilderness:

> The angel of the Lord said to her, "Return to your mistress, and submit to
> her." (GENESIS 16:9)

The pregnant slave had no choice but to return. But worse than that, her offspring would be cursed:

> The angel of the Lord also said to her, "I will so greatly multiply your
> offspring that they cannot be counted for multitude. ... Now you have
> conceived and shall bear a son; you shall call him Ishmael, for the Lord has
> given heed to your affliction. He shall be a wild ass of a man, with his hand
> against everyone, and everyone's hand against him; and he shall live at odds
> with all his kin." (GENESIS 16:10–12)

Abraham later banished Hagar and her son to the wilderness. Ishmael is the purported father of the Arabs, hence of the Muslims. That horrible slur against a whole group of people ("a wild ass of a man") is still fueling hatred in the Middle East. The Christian writers perpetuated the curse of Ishmael:

> But what does the scripture say? "Drive out the slave and her child; for the
> child of the slave will not share the inheritance with the child of the free

*woman." So then, friends, we are children, not of the slave but of the free woman. (*GALATIANS 4:30–31*)*

King David, "a man after God's own heart," turned captive enemies into hard-labor slaves:

> *So David gathered all the people together and went to Rabbah, and fought against it and took it. . . . He also brought forth the spoil of the city, a very great amount. He brought out the people who were in it, and set them to work with saws and iron picks and iron axes, or sent them to the brickworks. Thus he did to all the cities of the Ammonites. (*2 SAMUEL 12:29–31*)*

Translators disagree about whether David tortured and butchered the people or whether he merely captured them for forced labor. Where the NRSV above has "set them to work with saws and iron picks and iron axes, or sent them to the brickworks," the KJV has the torturous "put them under saws, and under harrows of iron, and under axes of iron, and made them pass through the brick-kiln." In the same story repeated in 1 CHRONICLES 20:3, the New Revised Standard Version has "he brought out the people who were in it, and set them to work with saws and iron picks and axes," while the King James Version has "he brought out the people that were in it, and cut them with saws, and with harrows of iron, and with axes."

If you like the King James Version, you have a God who baked and hacked people to death. If you don't like the more literal translations, then you can go with the nicer God who merely turned human beings into slaves.

28

What About Jesus?

"Whoever has seen me has seen the Father."
—John 14:9

Christians believe God should not be judged by the Old Testament alone. The New Testament changed everything, they say. Perhaps the Lord Jealous of the Israelites was fierce and angry, but gentle Jesus, the humble and loving son of God, fulfilled the old law and made everything new.

Why do they think that? According to the New Testament, Jesus *was* the God of the Old Testament. He was not just a chip off the old block: he was the block itself.

When the Jews asked Jesus if he was their Messiah, he replied: "The Father and I are one" (John 10:30), and said, "the Father is in me and I am in the Father" (John 10:38). Asking for proof, one of his disciples said, "Lord, show us the Father, and we will be satisfied." Jesus replied:

> Have I been with you all this time, Philip, and you still do not know me?
> **Whoever has seen me has seen the Father.** How can you say, "Show us the
> Father"? Do you not believe that I am in the Father and the Father is in
> me? The words that I say to you I do not speak on my own; but the Father
> who dwells in me does his works. Believe me that I am in the Father and
> the Father is in me; but if you do not, then believe me because of the works
> themselves. (John 14:9–11)

"If you've seen me, you've seen God," Jesus insisted. The Gospel of John opens with an unambiguous statement that Jesus was identical with the God of the Old Testament. John starts with "In the beginning," exactly like Genesis 1:1:

In the beginning was the Word, and the Word was with God, and **the Word was God.** *He was in the beginning with God. All things came into being through him, and without him not one thing came into being.* (JOHN 1:1–3)

Who was "in the beginning"? Of which creator god can it be said that "all things came into being through him"? John tells us that "the Word became flesh" (JOHN 1:14), and he identified that incarnation with Jesus: "For God so loved the world that he gave his only Son" (JOHN 3:16). God became a "son" of himself when he obtained a human mother. According to the New Testament, Jesus was the Lord Jealous himself.

Those who disagree are calling Jesus a liar when he claimed "The Father and I are one." He said as much to the Jews: "If I would say that I do not know him, I would be a liar like you" (JOHN 8:55).

How do we know Jesus was identifying himself with the God of the Old Testament? He told the Jews: "It is my Father who glorifies me, he of whom you say, 'He is our God,' though you do not know him. But I know him" (JOHN 8:54–55). He told them he was talking about *their* God. The Jews were confused, because they used the word "father" to refer to Abraham, not to Yahweh. "Abraham is our father," they said to him (JOHN 8:39). Jesus replied: "Very truly, I tell you, before Abraham was, I am" (JOHN 8:58). At that remark, the Jews picked up stones to throw at him.

Why were they so angry? It wasn't simply because Jesus was claiming to be a son or prophet of their God. The Jews attacked him because they knew exactly who he was referring to when he said "I am." Jesus was directly equating himself with Yahweh, quoting the Old Testament. When Moses talked to the burning bush, he asked God for his name:

> "If I come to the Israelites and say to them, 'The God of your ancestors has sent me to you,' and they ask me, 'What is his name?' what shall I say to them?" God said to Moses, "**I am who I am**." He said further, "Thus you shall say to the Israelites, '**I am** has sent me to you.'" God also said to Moses, "Thus you shall say to the Israelites, 'The Lord, the God of your ancestors, the God of Abraham, the God of Isaac, and the God of Jacob, has sent me to you.' This is my name forever, and this my title for all generations."
> (EXODUS 3:13–15)

When Jesus told the Jews, "Before Abraham was, I am," he knew that they would understand he was calling himself what their God called himself: "I am."

It follows that every single attribute Richard Dawkins used to describe the fictional God of the Old Testament applies equally to Jesus, because he claimed he *was* the God of the Old Testament. We can therefore say: the Jesus of the New Testament is arguably the most unpleasant character in all fiction: jealous and proud of it; a petty, unjust, unforgiving control freak; a vindictive, bloodthirsty ethnic cleanser;

a misogynistic, homophobic, racist, infanticidal, genocidal, filicidal, pestilential, megalomaniacal, sadomasochistic, capriciously malevolent bully; a pyromaniacal, angry, merciless, curse-hurling, vaccicidal, aborticidal, cannibalistic slavemonger.

If you think that sentence is unwarranted, then you believe Jesus was somebody other than who he claimed to be. You may be right. There may have been a "Jesus of history," a simple man who was humbler than the "Jesus of the New Testament" character. If you hold that view, then you agree that the New Testament Jesus was fictional, a legendary caricature exaggerated from one of the many self-proclaimed messiahs in that time of history.

In any event, the Jesus of the New Testament thought and taught that he was the God of the Old Testament.

Another reason we know this is because whenever Jesus quoted his Father, he pulled directly from the Old Testament scriptures. He told his disciples that "everything written about me in the law of Moses, the prophets, and the psalms must be fulfilled" (LUKE 24:44). When a lawyer asked Jesus what was God's greatest commandment, his reply contained a quote from the Old Testament:

> *"You shall love the Lord your God with all your heart, and with all your soul, and with all your mind." This is the greatest and first commandment.* (MATTHEW 22:37–38)

That sounds very lofty and loving, but if we look at the actual source of Jesus's quote, we realize that those are genocidal words of the Old Testament war god! They are part of the angry, curse-hurling commandments of the "jealous God" delivered by Moses in the 6th chapter of Deuteronomy:

> *Hear, O Israel: The Lord is our God, the Lord alone.* **You shall love the Lord your God with all your heart, and with all your soul, and with all your might**. *Keep these words that I am commanding you today in your heart. . . . When the Lord your God has brought you into the land that he swore to your ancestors, to Abraham, to Isaac, and to Jacob, to give you—a land with fine, large cities that you did not build, houses filled with all sorts of goods that you did not fill, hewn cisterns that you did not hew, vineyards and olive groves that you did not plant—and when you have eaten your fill, take care that you do not forget the Lord, who brought you out of the land of Egypt, out of the house of slavery.* **The Lord your God you shall fear;** *him you shall serve, and by his name alone you shall swear.* **Do not follow other gods, any of the gods of the peoples who are all around you,** *because the Lord your God, who is present with you, is* **a jealous God.** *The* **anger of the Lord your God** *would*

be kindled against you and he would destroy you from the face of the earth.
(Deuteronomy 6:4–15)

Those "loving" words that Jesus quoted were spoken to the Israelites during a pep rally as they were looking forward to their bloody invasion of the Promised Land. The Lord Jealous was essentially telling his people: "After you steal their land, don't be tempted by their gods. Love me, and me alone." If the Jesus of the New Testament was the God of the Old Testament, then he was indeed jealous, angry, and genocidal.

When Jesus was being tempted by the Devil and replied, "Again it is written, 'Do not put the Lord your God to the test'" (more famously known from the KJV: "Thou shalt not tempt the Lord thy God," Matthew 4:7), applying the word "Lord" to himself, he was quoting the Old Testament incompletely and out of context. If we look at the actual source of the quotation, a continuation of that Promised Land pep rally above, we see that Jesus was again calling himself the jealous, angry, destructive, and genocidal God of the Old Testament:

The Lord your God, who is present with you, is a jealous God. The anger of
the Lord your God would be kindled against you and he would destroy you
from the face of the earth. **Do not put the Lord your God to the test**, *as you*
tested him at Massah. You must diligently keep the commandments of the
Lord your God, and his decrees, and his statutes that he has commanded you.
Do what is right and good in the sight of the Lord, so that it may go well with
you, and so that you may go in and occupy the good land that the Lord swore
to your ancestors to give you, thrusting out all your enemies from before you,
as the Lord has promised. (Deuteronomy 6:15–19)

There you have it. Jesus endorsed invasion and bloodshed.

Many of the verses in Jesus's Sermon on the Mount, which include the Beatitudes, were taken from the Old Testament. His comments about murder, adultery, and swearing falsely are direct quotes from the Ten Commandments of the jealous God. His endorsement of divorce in Matthew 5:31 is pulled from Deuteronomy 24:1. His "eye for an eye" comment is from Exodus 21:23–25. "One does not live by bread alone" comes from Deuteronomy 8:3. And so on, in many other verses throughout the Gospels. Jesus never quoted any other god but the God of the Old Testament.

Some modern Christians will cherry-pick a "proof text" from the bible to support a tenuous argument, and Jesus did the same thing. In one case, it was to justify his sloppy sanitary habits. If Jesus were truly the son of an omniscient God, he would have known to tell people to wash their hands before they eat. He could have informed them about germs millennia before science figured it out. The Jewish elders, at least, had enough sense to wash their hands, and they asked why Jesus and his disciples were not following that tradition. Rather than reply with a reasonable defense of his actions, Jesus brushed off their good question with an irrelevant vituperous attack lifted out of context from the Old Testament:

> Then Pharisees and scribes came to Jesus from Jerusalem and said, "Why do your disciples break the tradition of the elders? For they do not wash their hands before they eat." He answered them, "And why do you break the commandment of God for the sake of your tradition? For God said, 'Honor your father and your mother,' and, 'Whoever speaks evil of father or mother must surely die.' But you say that whoever tells father or mother, 'Whatever support you might have had from me is given to God,' then that person need not honor the father. So, for the sake of your tradition, you make void the word of God. You hypocrites! Isaiah prophesied rightly about you when he said: 'This people honors me with their lips, but their hearts are far from me; in vain do they worship me, teaching human precepts as doctrines.'" (MATTHEW 15:1–9)

Those testy beside-the-point remarks contain three quotes from the Old Testament. "This people honors me with their lips" comes from ISAIAH 29. Jesus was telling the Pharisees of the first century that the Old Testament contained a prophecy about *them*, but that is quite a stretch. He was Sermonizing. The passage he quoted is actually a violent threat from the angry pyromaniacal Lord Jealous against the Israelites of the past. Here is the context:

> Yet I will distress Ariel, and there shall be moaning and lamentation, and Jerusalem shall be to me like an Ariel. And like David I will encamp against you; I will besiege you with towers and raise siegeworks against you. . . . And in an instant, suddenly, you will be visited by the Lord of hosts with thunder and earthquake and great noise, with whirlwind and tempest, and the flame of a devouring fire. . . . The Lord said: **Because these people draw near with their mouths and honor me with their lips**, while their hearts are far from me, and their worship of me is a human commandment learned by rote; so I will again do amazing things with this people, shocking and amazing. (ISAIAH 29:2–14)

Notice the moaning, thunder, earthquake, whirlwind, tempest, and "flame of a devouring fire." The "prophecy" to which Jesus angrily referred promised to repeat those "shocking and amazing" punishments by the God of the Old Testament. Jesus equated himself with that curse-hurling God, and he knew the Jewish elders would understand the threat.

When a parent reminds a child to wash his hands before he eats, it would be a comic overreaction for the brat to respond with violent threats of biblical proportions. But Jesus had no choice. He proudly claimed he and the fearful God of the Old Testament were one and the same person.

After the Last Supper on the night before he died, when Jesus predicted the betrayal of Peter and the cowardliness of the disciples before and after the crucifixion, he quoted again from the Old Testament:

> Then Jesus said to them, You will all become deserters because of me this night; for it is written, "I will strike the shepherd, and the sheep of the flock will be scattered." But after I am raised up, I will go ahead of you to Galilee. (MATTHEW 26:31–32)

Again, Jesus is sermonizing from scripture out of context, sanitizing the violence, making it look like the Old Testament was talking about *him*. He cherry-picks from an irrelevant passage and turns it into a forced prophecy about his own life, trimming the words about killing thousands of people (including "the little ones") that immediately follow what he quoted:

> Awake, O sword, against my shepherd, against the man who is my associate, says the Lord of hosts. **Strike the shepherd, that the sheep may be scattered;** I will turn my hand against the little ones. In the whole land, says the Lord, two-thirds shall be cut off and perish, and one-third shall be left alive. And I will put this third into the fire, refine them as one refines silver, and test them as gold is tested. They will call on my name, and I will answer them. I will say, "They are my people"; and they will say, "The Lord is our God." (ZECHARIAH 13:7–9)

The Lord predicted that two thirds of the people "in the whole land" would be killed, but Jesus pulled it out of context and pretended that "the shepherd" was himself and the sheep were his twelve followers. The disciples did cower for a day, but they didn't scatter. Three days later eleven of them traveled together to meet Jesus up in Galilee. Notice also that in Zechariah, God is speaking to a sword! He commanded the sword to kill the shepherd. Jesus was quoting with approval the swashbuckling words of an angry and bloodthirsty God, a God who he claimed to be. At the same meal, he told his disciples: "The one who has no sword must sell his cloak and buy one" (LUKE 22:36).

Most Christians think Jesus was a man of peace, but quoting the Old Testament, he said the opposite:

> Do not think that I have come to bring peace to the earth; **I have not come to bring peace, but a sword**. For I have come to set a man against his father, and

a daughter against her mother, and a daughter-in-law against her mother-in-law; and one's foes will be members of one's own household. Whoever loves father or mother more than me is not worthy of me; and whoever loves son or daughter more than me is not worthy of me. (MATTHEW 10:34–37)

Jesus, claiming to be the war god of the Old Testament, believed the violence of the sword was more important than family values. He was referring to the prophet Micah:

For the son treats the father with contempt, the daughter rises up against her mother, the daughter-in-law against her mother-in-law; your enemies are members of your own household. (MICAH 7:6)

So much for family values.

The New Testament is one colossal missed opportunity. This would have been the perfect place for the Word of God to mature into a real moral tale: the old model replaced by the new, anger and jealousy replaced by kindness and understanding. The God of the Old Testament had blown his chance to turn the stories of Adam and Eve, Noah, Korah, Jephthah, Sodom, Saul, Pinehas, Samson, Beth Shemesh, and Job into teachable moments of mercy, love and human value, and it appears that his son inherited his moral myopia. Instead of reforming the cruel policies of the past, Jesus reconfirmed them:

Do not think that I have come to abolish the law or the prophets; I have come not to abolish but to fulfill. For truly I tell you, until heaven and earth pass away, not one letter, not one stroke of a letter, will pass from the law until all is accomplished. Therefore, whoever breaks one of the least of these commandments, and teaches others to do the same, will be called least in the kingdom of heaven; but whoever does them and teaches them will be called great in the kingdom of heaven. (MATTHEW 5:17–19)

That is disappointing. Instead of a newer, kinder, more loving testament, we get the same taxi with a different driver. Jesus was like a politician who gets elected, promising sweeping reforms, but immediately takes up with the same old corruption. In that passage, he paints a picture of paradise as a perpetual pecking order of political favoritism.

Why didn't Jesus denounce the practices of the previous administration and proclaim that ethnic cleansing and wholesale bloodshed are wrong? He could have said, "I apologize for the crimes of my Father. He should not have exterminated entire towns or drowned twenty million people, including innocent infants and fetuses." But no, he quoted his murderous father with glowing approval. Instead of saying,

"Despotic violence is morally abhorrent," he tells a parable in which he approves of a thieving king who says "But as for these enemies of mine who did not want me to be king over them—bring them here and slaughter them in my presence." (Luke 19:27)

Why didn't Jesus point out that vindictive pestilential genocide is criminal? Why didn't he apologize for his father being a petty control freak? Wasn't he supposed to be better than that? Aren't we? He should have felt horrible about his father's inhumane treatment of animals (see Chapter 24), but had no qualms about causing a herd of swine to drown in the sea (Matthew 8:30–32).

Why didn't Jesus condemn his father's flame-happy pyromania? Instead, he tells us that nonbelievers should be incinerated: "Whoever does not abide in me is thrown away like a branch and withers; such branches are gathered, thrown into the fire, and burned." (John 15:6) The burning of witches, heretics, and atheists throughout the shameful history of Christianity was based on that one cruel verse spoken by the loving Jesus.

Jesus seemed obsessed with fire, just like his father. One of the actually new teachings in the New Testament was his promotion of scorching torment in the afterlife.

> The Son of Man [Jesus himself] will send his angels, and they will collect out of his kingdom all causes of sin and all evildoers, and they will throw them into the **furnace of fire**, where there will be weeping and gnashing of teeth. (Matthew 13:41–42)

> Then he will say to those at his left hand, "Depart from me, you cursed, into the **eternal fire** prepared for the devil and his angels." (Matthew 25:41)

Instead of putting out the fire, he threw gasoline on it.

Like the angry Old Testament God, Jesus threatened punishment with drowning, but preferred the torment of fire:

> If any of you put a stumbling block before one of these little ones who believe in me, it would be better for you if a great millstone were hung around your neck and you were thrown into the sea. If your hand causes you to stumble, cut it off; it is better for you to enter life maimed than to have two hands and to go to hell, to **the unquenchable fire**. And if your foot causes you to stumble, cut it off; it is better for you to enter life lame than to have two feet and to be **thrown into hell**. And if your eye causes you to stumble, tear it out; it is better for you to enter the kingdom of God with one eye than to have two eyes and to be **thrown into hell**, where their worm never dies, and **the fire is never quenched**. (Mark 9:42–48)

Thanks to Jesus, the world is now blessed with the threat of hell.

Instead of saying "I'm sorry my father was so angry," Jesus looked at his critics "with anger" (MARK 3:5), and attacked merchants with a whip (JOHN 2:15). He indignantly and irrationally cursed a fig tree for being fruitless out of season when he was hungry (MATTHEW 21:18–19 and MARK 11:13–14). He was his father's son.

Instead of wincing at the overweening megalomania of the Lord Jealous, the humble Jesus said he himself was "greater than the temple" (MATTHEW 12:6), "greater than Jonah" (MATTHEW 12:41), and "greater than Solomon" (MATTHEW 12:42). He appeared to suffer from a warlord paranoia when he said, "Whoever is not with me is against me" (MATTHEW 12:30).

Jesus failed to say "It was horribly sexist and cruel for my father to threaten to rape nonbelieving women" (see Chapter 17). He could have made great strides in women's equality by condemning his father's macho misogynistic mindset, but chose to maintain the status quo. His inner circle of twelve disciples were all male. No women were invited to the Last Supper. Women were present on the sidelines of the New Testament story, but never in positions of leadership. The women who discovered the empty tomb on Easter were instructed to tell the male disciples to meet Jesus in Galilee. Women were not invited.

Perhaps the greatest missed opportunity of the New Testament was the chance to decry the capture and ownership of human beings. Why didn't Jesus simply say slavery is wrong? We know it is wrong. Why didn't he? He could have said "I humbly apologize. My father—I mean I myself—was stuck in a primitive patriarchal mindset where the possession and abuse of human beings was perceived as economically prudent, but I have come to abolish that cruel institution and emancipate all captive people." God changed his mind on other matters (see Chapter 18), so why not here? He could have eliminated slavery more than 1,800 years before the American Civil War, saving rivers of blood and oppression. Instead, he talks about human bondage as if it were the most natural order, incorporating it into his parables as if he or his writers were simply reflecting their own culture at the time.

I suppose we should award Jesus a few points of compassion for pointing out that some slaves should not be beaten as hard as others:

> That slave who knew what his master wanted, but did not prepare himself
> or do what was wanted, will receive a severe beating. But the one who did
> not know and did what deserved a beating will receive a light beating.
> (LUKE 12:47–48)

Jesus understood that punishment should match the offense, but he didn't see the larger offense, the bigger picture. (Those words, by the way, are not part of a parable—they are the direct thoughts immediately following a parable.) Jesus accepted the institution of bondage and encouraged the beating of slaves. He blew his chance to become a true moral leader.

* * *

I used to preach that Jesus was a man of family values. But he never used the word "family." He never got married or had any children. Like a cult leader, he preached family hatred:

> Whoever comes to me and does not hate father and mother, wife and children, brothers and sisters, yes, and even life itself, cannot be my disciple. (LUKE 14:26)

When one of his disciples requested time off for his father's funeral, Jesus coldly rebuked him: "Follow me, and let the dead bury their own dead" (MATTHEW 8:22). He encouraged castration—or at least austere celibacy, depending on your interpretation:

> For there are eunuchs who have been so from birth, and there are eunuchs who have been made eunuchs by others, and there are eunuchs who have made themselves eunuchs for the sake of the kingdom of heaven. Let anyone accept this who can. (MATTHEW 19:12)

Some believers, including the early church father Origen, have interpreted this gruesome verse literally and castrated themselves. They imagined that when Jesus said "Let anyone accept this who can," he was talking about them. But even interpreting it metaphorically, that advice is in appalling taste. Jesus clearly held the family and love-making in the lowest regard.

He could have taken the opportunity to establish programs to help the poor, but was more interested in attracting attention to himself. Rather than sell expensive ointment to feed the needy, Jesus lavished it on his own feet, saying:

> You always have the poor with you, and you can show kindness to them whenever you wish; but you will not always have me. (MARK 14:7)

"You always have the poor" is not the most empathetic or socially conscious remark. It is a defeatist attitude admitting a lack of vision for attacking world hunger: "I may as well spend it on myself." Sounds more like a greedy TV evangelist or a comfortable cardinal in the luxurious Vatican than a compassionate ethical leader.

In some ways the New Testament is better than the Old. God's chosen people were no longer fighting genocidal wars—they had become pacified under the Pax Romana. The death of Jesus ended the practice of burning animals during worship, for Christians at least. Jesus and his disciples talked a little less about violence and a little more about love. That shows some improvement over the Old Testament God.

The New Testament Jesus healed people, and that is not bad. But he was performing those acts as a sign of his deity and power, not out of true compassion. In one case, he refused to heal a sick child until he was pressured by the mother (MATTHEW 15:22–28). The tiny handful of people he healed ended up dying, sooner or later. He could have helped millions more if he had bothered to tell us about microbes, parasites, water-borne diseases like cholera, the benefits of boiling water, lead poisoning, mosquito nets, skin cancer, tsunami awareness, earthquake preparedness, and so on. Jesus cared more about "spiritual" health than medical health, which means he didn't care at all.

It might seem like a positive development that the New Testament introduced the idea of eternal life, but that is cancelled out by eternal punishment. The happiness of heaven is balanced by the horror of hell. Heaven sounds like a nice idea, but it is nothing more than a carrot-and-stick, bliss-or-misery mentality. Jesus could have said we should be kind to others because human beings deserve to be treated with fairness and equality. Instead he said turn, or burn.

What superior moral advice did Jesus actually bequeath to us? Here are some examples:

> Don't have sexual urges. (MATTHEW 5:28)
>
> If you do something wrong with your eye or hand, cut/pluck it off.
>   (MATTHEW 5:29 spoken in a sexual context)
>
> Marrying a divorced woman is committing adultery. (MATTHEW 5:32)
>
> Don't save money. (MATTHEW 6:19–20)
>
> Don't plan for the future. (MATTHEW 6:34)
>
> Don't become wealthy. (MARK 10:21–25)
>
> Sell everything you have and give it to the poor. (LUKE 12:33)
>
> Don't work to obtain food. (JOHN 6:27)
>
> Make people want to persecute you. (MATTHEW 5:11)
>
> Let everyone know you are better than the rest. (MATTHEW 5:13–16)
>
> Take money from those who have no savings and give it to rich investors.
>   (LUKE 19:23–26)
>
> If someone steals from you, don't try to get it back. (LUKE 6:30)
>
> If someone hits you, invite them to do it again. "Turn the other cheek"
>   (MATTHEW 5:39)
>
> If you lose a lawsuit, give more than the judgment. (MATTHEW 5:40)
>
> If someone forces you to walk a mile, walk two miles. (MATTHEW 5:41)
>
> If anyone asks you for anything, give it to them without question.
>   (MATTHEW 5:42)

Is this good advice? How many Christians teach these lessons to their children?

Jesus did occasionally give some good advice, but it is unremarkable, nothing we would not expect from any other religious leader or moral philosopher. The so-called Golden Rule had been said many times by earlier religious leaders. (Five hundred years earlier, Confucius said it better: "Do not unto others that you would not have them do unto you.")

When Jesus said that the second commandment was to "love your neighbor as yourself" (MARK 12:31, MATTHEW 22:39), that sounds like a compassionate and forgiving attitude, and indeed it is if you happen to be a neighbor. Looking at the Old Testament source of his quote, we learn what "neighbor" actually meant:

> You shall not hate in your heart anyone of your kin; you shall reprove your neighbor, or you will incur guilt yourself. You shall not take vengeance or bear a grudge against any of your people, but **you shall love your neighbor as yourself**: I am the Lord. (LEVITICUS 19:17–18)

"Neighbor" meant "your kin" and "any of your people." The Israelites were commanded merely to love their fellow Israelites. This love did not extend to anyone who worshipped another god, and certainly not to any neighboring tribes or nations. In Jesus's day, the phrase would have meant "fellow believer." Neither the Israelites nor Jesus showed much love to nonbelievers. This is not a novel moral principle. All groups of people have a tendency to "love" those of their own kind.

The Beatitudes spoken by Jesus in MATTHEW 5 do acknowledge some useful ethical principles, such as "blessed are the peacemakers." No surprise there. All religions promote peace, or claim to. The Sermon on the Mount points to a less violent God with comments such as "resist not evil" and "turn the other cheek." It is to their credit that most modern Christians have risen above the monstrous character of the God of the Old Testament by focusing on some of the relatively less violent verses in the New Testament. We applaud gentle and kind Christians who use these passages to argue for a more pacific faith than we find in the Old Testament.

Christ's teachings also include the morally dubious endorsements of meekness, righteousness, and the welcoming of persecution. But notice that the Beatitudes are all conditioned on some kind of reward and punishment, such as "they will inherit the earth," not on moral principles. None of the Beatitudes say "you should act kindly toward others because human beings have an inherent right to be treated with fairness and dignity, regardless of whether you get anything out of it." The Beatitudes are aimed at being good believers, not good human beings. When being a good believer coincides with being a good person, that is admirable because of the consequences, if not the motivation.

*   *   *

Why does anyone believe Christ introduced a new and wonderful philosophy to the world? The name "Jesus" has attained an idealized status as a mythic symbol of love, gentleness, sacrifice and goodness. I know some nonbelievers who think he was a great ethical thinker, but where do they find that in the bible? Reading the New Testament itself, we see that a few of his teachings were passable, some were ambiguous, and many were appalling. Any one of us could have come up with a better system of human conduct. Jesus, after all, was identical with the Lord Jealous. Morally, the Christian faith rests on sinking sand.

Afterword

"A Terrible End"

"A terrible end he will make of all the inhabitants of the earth."
—Zephaniah 1:18

God is planning a "great day" for us. The prophet Zephaniah, claiming the ability to predict the future, assures us that the God of the Old Testament will stay in character forever:

> The great day of the Lord is near, near and hastening fast; the sound of the day of the Lord is bitter, the warrior cries aloud there. That day will be **a day of wrath, a day of distress and anguish, a day of ruin and devastation, a day of darkness and gloom**, a day of clouds and thick darkness, a day of trumpet blast and battle cry against the fortified cities and against the lofty battlements. I will bring such distress upon people that they shall walk like the blind; because they have sinned against the Lord, their blood shall be poured out like dust, and their flesh like dung. Neither their silver nor their gold will be able to save them on the **day of the Lord's wrath**; in the **fire of his passion** the whole earth shall be consumed; for **a full, a terrible end he will make of all the inhabitants of the earth**. (Zephaniah 1:14–18)

Richard Dawkins was right: God is a big bully. If you are a faithful follower of that vindictive Lord Jealous, you believe that everything you know and love will come to "a full and terrible end."

I am nicer than God, and so are you. I used to preach:

> Choose this day whom you will serve. . . . But as for me and my household, we will serve the Lord. (Joshua 24:15)

We indeed have a choice. We can choose reason and human kindness, or we can serve the most unpleasant character in all fiction.

ACKNOWLEDGMENTS

I ESPECIALLY WANT TO THANK MY SON, DAN T. BARKER, FOR TEDIOUSLY CHECKING every single biblical reference in this book, a true labor of love. I also appreciate the astute proofing and helpful comments by Hector Avalos, John Compere, Richard Dawkins, Annie Laurie Gaylor, Glen (Sabrina) Gaylor, Don Gregg, Andrew Seidel, and Michael Thomas Tower. The book has been greatly improved by their feedback and suggestions.

I also owe a huge debt to the people who put together the very useful Bible Gateway website at biblegateway.com, currently owned by the Christian publisher Zondervan. In the old days, when I wanted to look up the occurrences of a biblical word or phrase, I had to consult *Young's Concordance* or *Strong's Concordance*—and I did use those references for this book, especially when looking up some Hebrew words—but they are limited to the King James Version. Zondervan is committed to truth, so I am sure they will be pleased to know that their searchable database of dozens of translations has made it easier to learn the facts about the God of the Old Testament.

CREDITS

BIBLIOGRAPHY

Avalos, Hector. *The Bad Jesus: The Ethics of New Testament Ethics*. Sheffield Phoenix Press Ltd., 2015.

———. *Abolitionism, and the Ethics of Biblical Scholarship*. Sheffield Phoenix Press Ltd, 2013.

———. "Creationists for Genocide." Accessed at talkreason.org/articles/Genocide.cfm, 2007.

———. *Fighting Words: The Origins of Religious Violence*. Prometheus Books, 2005.

Barker, Dan. *Why Jesus? (nontract)*. Freedom From Religion Foundation, 1993.

Boswell, John. *Christianity, Social Tolerance, and Homosexuality*. University of Chicago Press, 2005.

Coogan, Michael, Marc Brettler, and Carol Newsom (eds.), and Pheme Perkins. *The New Oxford Annotated Bible with Apocrypha: New Revised Standard Version*. 4th ed. Oxford University Press, 2010.

Dawkins, Richard. *The God Delusion*. Houghton Mifflin Company, 2006.

———. *The Selfish Gene*. 2nd ed. Oxford University Press, 1990.

Daylight Atheism. "Little-Known Bible Verses." Accessed at patheos.com/blogs/daylightatheism/series/little-known-bible-verses/.

Garcia, Hector. *Alpha God: The Psychology of Religious Violence and Oppression*. Prometheus Books, 2015.

Gaylor, Annie Laurie. *Woe To The Women: The Bible Tells Me So*. Freedom From Religion Foundation, 2004.

Goldberg, Stuart C. *God on Trial 2000: Indictment of God for Crimes Against Job*. Proscop Press, 1999.

Green, Ruth Hurmence. *The Born Again Skeptic's Guide to the Bible*. 4th ed. Freedom From Religion Foundation, 1999.

Helminiak, Daniel A. *What the Bible Really Says About Homosexuality*. Millennium Edition. Alamo Square Press, 2000.

McKenzie, Margaret E. "Filicide in Medieval Narrative," PhD dissertation, Catholic University of America, 2012. Accessed at http://aladinrc.wrlc.org/bitstream/handle/1961/10140/McKenzie_cua_0043A_10265display.pdf?sequence=1.

Pinker, Steven. *The Better Angels of Our Nature: Why Violence Has Declined.* Viking Adult, 2011.

Sapir-Hen, Lidor, and Lidar Ben-Yosef. "The Introduction of Domestic Camels to the Southern Levant: Evidence from the Aravah Valley." *TEL AVIV*, Vol. 40, 2013, 277–285. Tel Aviv University, 2013.

Shermer, Michael. *The Moral Arc: How Science and Reason Lead Humanity Toward Truth, Justice, and Freedom.* (In particular, Chapter 4: "Why Religion Is Not the Source of Moral Progress.") Henry Holt and Company, 2015.

Silberman, Neil Asher, and Israel Finkelstein. *The Bible Unearthed: Archaeology's New Vision of Ancient Israel and the Origin of Its Sacred Texts.* Reprint. Touchstone, 2002.

Stanton, Elizabeth Cady. *The Woman's Bible.* CreateSpace Independent Publishing Platform, 2010.

Strong, James. *The New Strong's Concordance of the Bible: Popular Edition.* Revised ed. Thomas Nelson Inc, 1985.

Sweeney, Julia. *Letting Go of God.* DVD movie. Indefatigable, Inc., 2008.

Tubb, Jonathan N. *Canaanites.* University of Oklahoma Press, 1999.

Wells, Steve. *Drunk With Blood: God's Killings in the Bible.* 2nd ed. SAB Books, 2013.

———. *The Skeptic's Annotated Bible.* SAB Books, 2011.

Wood, Forrest G. *The Arrogance of Faith: Christianity and Race in America.* Knopf, 1990.

Young, Robert. *Young's Analytical Concordance to the Bible.* Hendrickson Publishers, 1984.

Zonszein, Mairav. "Domesticated Camels Came to Israel in 930 B.C., Centuries Later Than Bible Says." *National Geographic*, February 4, 2014.

AB = Amplified Bible	LB = Living Bible (a paraphrase)
CEB = Common English Bible	NIV = New International Version
CEV = Common English Version	NLT = New Living Translation
CJB = Complete Jewish Bible	NRSV = New Revised Standard Version
GNT = Good News Translation	NWT = New World Translation
JUB = Jubilee Bible 2000	OJB = Orthodox Jewish Bible
KJV = King James Version	

INDEX